The Tree of Tradition

The traditions and influences that have shaped
the works of writers and thinkers in all
civilisations, including Nicholas Hagger's
60 Universalist works

CollectiveInk

First published by Liberalis Books, 2024
Liberalis Books is an imprint of Collective Ink Ltd.,
Unit 11, Shepperton House, 89 Shepperton Road, London, N1 3DF
office@collectiveinkbooks.com
www.collectiveinkbooks.com
www.liberalisbooks.com

For distributor details and how to order please visit the 'Ordering' section on our website.

Text copyright: Nicholas Hagger 2023

ISBN: 978 1 80341 426 3
978 1 80341 427 0 (ebook)
Library of Congress Control Number: 2023912869

A CIP catalogue record for this book is available from the British Library.

Design: Lapiz Digital Services

Printed and bound by CPI Group (UK) Ltd, Croydon, CR0 4YY, UK

We operate a distinctive and ethical publishing philosophy in all areas of our business, from our global network of authors to production and worldwide distribution.

The Tree of Tradition

The traditions and influences that have shaped
the works of writers and thinkers in all
civilisations, including Nicholas Hagger's
60 Universalist works

Nicholas Hagger

London, UK
Washington, DC, USA

Also by Nicholas Hagger

The Fire and the Stones
Selected Poems
The Universe and the Light
A White Radiance
A Mystic Way
Awakening to the Light
A Spade Fresh with Mud
Overlord, books 1–2
The Warlords
Overlord
A Smell of Leaves and Summer
Overlord, books 3–6
Overlord, books 7–9
Overlord, books 10–12
The Tragedy of Prince Tudor
The One and the Many
Wheeling Bats and a Harvest Moon
The Warm Glow of the Monastery Courtyard
The Syndicate
The Secret History of the West
The Light of Civilization
Classical Odes
Overlord, one-volume edition
Collected Poems 1958–2005
Collected Verse Plays
Collected Stories
The Secret Founding of America
The Last Tourist in Iran
The Rise and Fall of Civilizations
The New Philosophy of Universalism
The Libyan Revolution
Armageddon
The World Government
The Secret American Dream

A New Philosophy of Literature
A View of Epping Forest
My Double Life 1: This Dark Wood
My Double Life 2: A Rainbow over the Hills
Selected Stories: Follies and Vices of the Modern
Elizabethan Age
Selected Poems: Quest for the One
The Dream of Europa
The First Dazzling Chill of Winter
Life Cycle and Other New Poems 2006–2016
The Secret American Destiny
Peace for our Time
World State
World Constitution
King Charles the Wise
Visions of England
Fools' Paradise
Selected Letters
The Coronation of King Charles
Collected Prefaces
Fools' Gold
The Fall of the West
The Promised Land
The Algorithm of Creation
The Building of the Great Pyramid
The Golden Phoenix
A Baroque Vision
The Essentials of Universalism

"O chestnut tree, great rooted blossomer,
Are you the leaf, the blossom or the bole?
O body swayed to music, O brightening glance,
How can we know the dancer from the dance?"

W.B. Yeats, 'Among School Children'

February 1926

"The Tree of Tradition merely reflects
A more unseen one which hangs from the sky:
The Tree of Imagination projects
All things, and then reclaims them when they die....
An inverted Tree with roots in the sky
Pours the invisible into what is seen...."

Nicholas Hagger, 'The Tree of Imagination'

24, 31 December 1979; revised 26–27 April 1980

"There are many traditions."

Christopher Ricks in conversation with
Nicholas Hagger while walking round
the city of Oxford on 21 June 1993

"I am not an Athenian or a Greek but a citizen of the world."

Socrates, according to Plutarch in
De Exilio (*On Exile*)

"Tradition is a matter of much wider significance. It cannot be inherited, and if you want it you must obtain it by great labour. It involves, in the first place, the historical sense, which we may call nearly indispensable to anyone who would continue to be a poet beyond his twenty-fifth year; and the historical sense involves a perception, not only of the pastness of the past, but of its presence; the historical sense compels a man to write not merely with his own generation in his bones, but with a feeling that the whole of the literature of Europe from Homer and within it the whole of the literature of his own country has a simultaneous existence and composes a simultaneous order. This historical sense, which is a sense of the timeless as well as of the temporal and of the timeless and of the temporal together, is what makes a writer traditional. And it is at the same time what makes a writer most acutely conscious of his place in time, of his own contemporaneity."

T.S. Eliot, 'Tradition and the Individual Talent'

The front cover shows an oak tree on Johns Island (or John's Island) in South Carolina estimated to be at least 400–500 and perhaps 1,400–1,500 years old, whose 25 branches and offshoots symbolise the 25 civilisations, nation-states, disciplines, traditions and influences in all civilisations behind the works of (1) an individual writer, (2) a civilisation's regions, or states (as in the United States) and nation-states (in the case of the European civilisations), and (3) all civilisations that have ever been. In this book the Tree of Tradition is seen as a Tree of Traditions and Influences that have shaped writers and thinkers in 25 civilisations.

Acknowledgments

I am grateful to my PA Ingrid Kirk for her invaluable help. Without her I could not have completed this work.

Contents

Contents

showing section headings and structure

Contents

Contents

Preface

The Tree of Tradition as World Tree in all Civilisations, and a Universalist World State

Traditions and Influences

The Tree of Tradition came to me as *Traditions and Influences* when I was on a two-week cruise round Ireland, after two intense days in the company of Shelley, Swift and Yeats.

On 12 August 2022 I went from Belfast to Mount Stewart at Strangford Lough, sat in the sunken garden in warm sunshine with a view of the 18th-century house, and then entered in search of Lord Castlereagh, Foreign Secretary at the time of the Battle of Waterloo in 1815. I saw the silverware pen-holder, ink-holder and sand-holder, chairs in the dining-room, and desk and three chairs in the drawing-room, all used at the Congress of Vienna.

I visited an exhibition on Castlereagh to be opened that afternoon, and learned that he killed himself at his country retreat at Cray Farm, Kent (today named Loring Hall) on 12 August 1822, exactly 200 years previously to the day. He had opposed the Peterloo Massacre of 20–30 protesters and though he denied responsibility the radical Shelley wrote in *The Masque of Anarchy*, "I met Murder along the way,/ He wore a mask like Castlereagh." This was not published until 1832, and Castlereagh could not have known of these lines when, still Foreign Secretary and about to leave for Greece, depressed at his bad publicity following Peterloo, he slit his own throat.

On 13 August 2022, in Dublin, I stopped at St Patrick's Cathedral where the satirical Jonathan Swift was Dean from 1713 to 1745. I immediately went to Swift's pulpit, where he preached lengthy sermons, some lasting for several hours. It was nearby the communion table where he served the sacrament. In a glass were his two death masks and a model of his skull, and his sermon on sleeping in church. On a nearby wall was his bust and the Latin epitaph Swift wrote for himself (which includes the words, "*saeva indignatio*", "savage indignation"). In the floor and roped off was his grave. He lay buried with his best friend

Esther Johnson (Stella in his poem 'Stella's Birth-day'). He may have had a stroke in 1740 as he could not remember talking to Handel when he visited and played the cathedral's organ in a rehearsal for a coming performance of his *Messiah*.

I was put off our coach in Kildare Street and advised to have coffee for half an hour. Instead I walked to the permanent Yeats exhibition at the nearby National Library and saw manuscripts of many of Yeats' lyrical poems in glass cases, and his wife George's (Georgia's) automatic writing. I saw the manuscript of his 'Innisfree' (beginning "I will arise and go now,/And go to Innisfree"). I had found Innisfree, a place he often visited as a child, during my visit to Sligo in 1966 and stood in "the bee-loud glade", and I saw the manuscript of his epitaph on his grave in Drumcliffe churchyard: "Cast a cold eye/On life and death./ Horse man passed by." It dawned on me that he should have written "Horseman" as one word, which is now the spelling for this last line in all printed books. I walked back, had a quick coffee and caught the coach. I felt I had got closer to Shelley, Swift and Yeats.

I woke on the ship at 5.45am next morning. I lay in bed and could not get back to sleep. Then I realised a new book was being poured into me from my deep source, with a Preface drawing on Shelley's Castlereagh, Swift's grave and the Yeats exhibition. The title was clear in my mind: *Traditions and Influences*. I wrote in my diary: "*Traditions and Influences*. In this short book I present the traditions in which I have written and my influences." The influences would include Shelley, Swift and Yeats.

I returned home on 15 August, and on 17 August I emailed my publisher with the idea for the book. He replied asking me to submit a proposal, which I put in on 31 August. In due course I received a contract for *Traditions and Influences*.

As the days passed I became more and more aware that the title *Traditions and Influences* was a bit of a mouthful for people to remember on their way to a bookshop, but I stuck with it as my deep source is never wrong and has fed me titles of most of my works since my Mystic Way left me with new inner powers. I had unitive vision that instinctively saw the unity of the universe and humankind, and I was habitually fed the title of my next work in my sleep, and regularly told to look at specific page numbers in my current manuscript as there was a mistake – as there always was when I looked.

I also became aware that the book would be about traditions and influences that would shape the works of all writers and thinkers, not just my works.

The Tree of Tradition

As the days went by the idea of *The Tree of Tradition* as the book's title lodged in my mind, with 'Traditions and Influences' being put in the subtitle. I recalled how I had written of "The Tree of Tradition" in my 1979/1980 poem 'The Tree of Imagination' (see Appendix 1), and how I had used "the oak tree of tradition" as the title of an email to Eleanor Laing, Deputy Speaker in the House of Commons, dated 6 September 2019, when reporting a discussion I had had the previous evening with Charles Walker MP, Chairman of the influential Conservative 1922 Committee until earlier that week (see *Selected Letters*, pp.841–843), see pp.9–11.

In this email I showed that in 2019 I was seeing English Literature as a Tree of Tradition, and also the Conservative Party, whose past branches should not be lopped. The same perspective can be applied to all disciplines, and to all political parties, all of which have their own oak tree of tradition.

Oak trees had always been important to me. The oldest oak tree in the UK is in the grounds of Blenheim Palace. It is 1,046 years old and began its growth from an acorn before the Norman Conquest of 1066. There was an oak tree in the field at the school I went to before the end of the war, Oaklands School, Loughton, Essex, that is reputed to be 800 years old. It was and still is on the school badge. As a boy I sat among the buttercups beneath it and picked up acorns. In 1988 I founded a school in Epping, Essex, Coopersale Hall School, that had a holm-oak on its lawn. According to tradition, it was planted by Elizabeth I when she visited nearby Copped Hall in 1562. She set up a Commission to plant trees in "our park" there, planted two holm-oaks at Copped Hall and another one at Coopersale Hall, which is now the second most famous tree in Essex and appears on the school badge. I have four oaks on my lawn where I am now living.

On 11 October 2022 I wrote to my contact at O Books saying the title should be changed to *The Tree of Tradition*. On 14 October I knew I preferred this as a title and uploaded the image now on the front cover which I had found, of an oak tree at least 400–500 years old and considered by some to be 1,500 years old, with 25 branches suggesting the 25 civilisations. Almost immediately that oak tree appeared on a draft front cover.

There was a momentum, and I dictated an outline on 14 October and wrote the book in longhand in Cornwall, in my window overlooking St Austell Bay in stormy weather, from 18 to 25 October, with rolling breakers surging forward beneath my window and rain lashing my window-panes. Because I was dealing with the proofs of *The Promised Land*, *The Algorithm of Creation* and *The Golden Phoenix*, one after the other, it took me until 1 March 2023 to do further work on the detail of the text.

The World Tree

The Tree of Tradition is actually the World Tree (also 'The Tree of Imagination' in the poem in Appendix 1 on pp.187–195), whose forms include the Tree of Knowledge with roots in the Underworld and Heaven, and the Tree of Life, which connects all living things. It is a cosmic tree in which all living things in the cosmos are linked. I set out the forms the Tree of Tradition takes.

The traditions and influences in the Tree of Tradition are behind the works of all writers and thinkers, as I show by giving examples of my own 60 works. There are 84 influences in my 60 works, and these are all listed in the Index of Influences on p.245.

The Tree of Tradition is also the World Tree of all civilisations (see pp.228–229), whose branch-like traditions include the stages living civilisations have passed through, and it is therefore also a tree of the future organisation of the world. As I showed in *The Secret American Destiny*, the US within the North-American civilisation is the youngest and best-placed of the 14 living civilisations to create a future World State that can solve the world's problems.

A Universalist World State

Above all, the Tree of Tradition as World Tree is a Universalist tree. We are living in a Universalist time when both North America and the other 13 living civilisations are in Universalist stages (five living civilisations in stage 43 and eight living civilisations in stage 46, see pp.157–158 and 167–170), and are ripe for Universalist world federation. It is for the next two generations to identify and follow this federal tradition, for which my works are one of the influences, and bring in a Universalist World State that will be a time of peace and prosperity for all humankind.

25 October 2022; 28 February, 1 March 2023

Overview: The Tree of Tradition with some of its traditions and influences

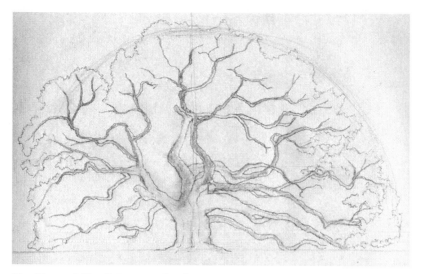

The Tree of Tradition on the front cover with some of its millions of traditions and influences that relate to writers and thinkers, including those represented in the groupings listed in A–R below.

A. 25 civilisations (see p.35)
B. 93 gods of religions (see p.36)
C. 9 medieval and 9 Renaissance academic disciplines (see pp.20–21)
D. 50 'isms' (see pp.17–18)
E. 112 main academic disciplines (see pp.195–198)
F. 1,000 Dewey Decimal classifications, 1876 (see pp.198–217)
G. 228 Library of Congress classifications, 1897 (see pp.218–223)
H. over 1,986 academic disciplines (see p.198)
I. over 2,428 academic fields (see p.198)
J. 7 disciplines (p.148)
K. 7 genres of literature (p.148)
L. 39 literary genres (see pp.28–29)
M. 109 traditions in 7 disciplines of NH's works (pp.148–153)

N. 84 main influences in 7 disciplines of NH's works
    (pp.153–154)
O. 63 Universalist writers and thinkers (see pp.22–25)
P. millions of works
Q. millions of traditions
R. millions of influences

The Tree whose Traditions and Influences Have Shaped the Works of Writers and Thinkers in all Civilisations

The Tree of Tradition as a symbol

The Tree of Tradition represents the traditions and influences that have an impact on the works of writers and thinkers. Writers and thinkers can see in an ancient oak the trunk, branches, offshoots, twigs, leaves, flowers and acorn fruit that represent the traditions and influences that have shaped them and their works. The Tree of Tradition is therefore personal to each writer and thinker. To an English man of letters it may represent the history of English Literature, with branches of narrative, epic and lyrical poetry, and the works of past poets. To a philosopher it may represent the philosophical tradition. To a historian it may represent the strands of history and the past historians who have been an inspiration. To a religious person it may represent the works of past mystics and the sermons of past clerics. To a politician its branches may represent the factions within international politics. In all cases it suggests writers and thinkers who have been past influences.

As well as being personal to each individual writer and thinker, the Tree of Tradition also represents the civilisation in which they live. The trunk represents the religion of the civilisation, the branches represent all the states (in the case of the North-American civilisation) or nation-states (in the case of the European civilisation) or regions of their civilisation, and its offshoots and twigs, flowers and fruit may represent key works and aspects of each writer's and thinker's civilisation.

The Tree also represents the Tree of *all* civilisations (see pp.228–229). Its trunk represents the religions of all civilisations, both living and dead, and the branches represent civilisations that have had an impact on, and influenced, a writer's or thinker's works, perhaps the Indian or Chinese civilisation's literary and philosophical works for one writer or thinker, or perhaps the North-American or European civilisation's literary and philosophical works for another.

As we shall see in greater detail, the Tree of Tradition changes its significance from presenting the works of an individual to bearing the works of the individual's civilisation, and to bearing the works of all civilisations during the last 5,000 years. The Tree of Tradition may be symbolised by an ancient oak as on the front cover, but it is largely a Tree in the mind that embodies all the traditions and influences that have shaped a particular writer and thinker, and each writer or thinker that has ever been.

It is a universal Tree, and for a Universalist who instinctively sees the unity of the universe and humankind it is very much a World Tree. It applies to all civilisations and individuals and so, chameleon-like, it changes its shape and meaning as it adapts from the view of one individual writer or thinker to the view of another writer or thinker. Historically the universal Tree of Tradition has different forms.

The Tree of Tradition of English Literature in 'The Tree of Imagination'

In my writings I have seen this Tree of Tradition in different forms. In 1979 I wrote a poem, 'The Tree of Imagination' (see Appendix 1), in which I actually saw the Tree of Tradition as the Tree of the Tradition of English Literature in the physical world, bearing all the physical works of the writers and thinkers within English Literature from *Beowulf* to my own recent works, with all its traditions and influences. As the notes for 'The Tree of Imagination'[1] say (see Appendix 1, p.191), the Tree of Tradition stands in the physical world, and the Tree of Imagination is in the metaphysical world, bearing symbols and images in the mind that become physical works.

In the poem, which was first written on 24 and 31 December 1979 and subsequently revised, I describe a visit to arguably the Western world's foremost literary critic, Professor Christopher Ricks, at Christ's College, Cambridge. I pass a mulberry tree grown from a root planted in 1609, which was known to Milton (a pupil there from 1625); talk with Ricks and hear my poems being viewed within the tradition of the Metaphysical poets in the Buttery (lines 7–8, see p.187); and see Ricks (in line 9, see p.187) as keeping "the Tree of Tradition" (the traditions and influences of English Literature on writers and thinkers).

The Tree of Imagination

I say this Tree reflects "a more unseen one which hangs from the sky" (line 42), i.e. the Tree of Imagination. The Tree of Imagination ripens symbols which burst like windfalls:

> So images burst round a poet's head,
> Windfalls from a leafy beyond....
> (lines 69–70)

I describe how I dined with the dons and had coffee in the Common Room, and conclude that the actual Tree of Tradition's physical works (line 111) can blot out the invisible, mental Tree of Imagination and its "high symbols on a trunk of air" (line 112). The Tree of Tradition in English Literature shows visual images, whereas symbols have a spiritual layer (see note to line 111 on p.195) and come from the invisible Tree of Imagination.

These two Trees, the physical Tree of Tradition and the invisible, mental Tree of Imagination, are the two oak trees on the coat of arms (an innovation to identify knights in armour at the battle of Agincourt in 1415) that I was awarded by the College of Arms in 2019 on the site of the College of Heralds Shakespeare visited to collect the coat of arms awarded to his father in 1597. (See p.22.) The two oak trees on my coat of arms also suggest time and the finite, and eternity and the infinite, which are united by Universalism's infinity sign – the union between the finite and the infinite, between time and eternity.

The Tree of Imagination and the Tree of Life

'The Tree of Imagination' refers to the Tree of Life (line 55), which, as the note to line 55 says, is a cosmic tree with inverted roots in the sky, suggesting its spiritual origin. The Tree of Imagination itself is a form of the Tree of Life, which is in *Genesis* 2 (6th–5th century BC) as standing in the Garden of Eden, but is earlier as a banyan tree in the *Upanishads* (700–500BC) and later in the *Bhagavad Gita* (400BC–400AD, perhaps

1st–2nd century AD) in the Indian civilisation, where it is presented as being inverted with roots in the sky. As 'The Tree of Imagination' puts it in lines 55–56:

> An inverted Tree with roots in the sky
> Pours the invisible into what is seen.

The Tree of Life also predates *Genesis* in the Kabbalah. It originated in Assyria in the 9th century BC, long before it was a diagram in the Kabbalah, which emerged in the 12th century AD and where the inverted tree of life with spiritual roots is in the Tree-of-Life pattern with 10 or 11 nodes and 22 lines connecting them. In Kabbalistic schools seekers are taught the Kabbalah's Tree of Life, as I was in March 1979 in Ammerdown, Somerset, by being shown eleven chairs arranged in the traditional hopscotch pattern to reflect the *sefirot* (emanations) in the Kabbalistic Tree of Life.

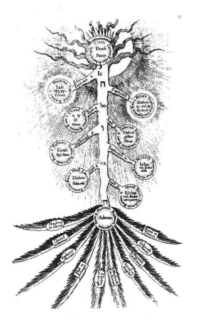

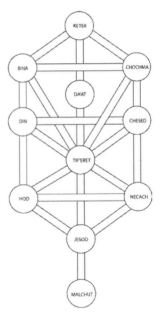

The Tree of Life with inverted roots in the sky based on the 1617 drawing by Robert Fludd in the Deutsche Fotothek.

A version of the Kabbalistic Tree of Life on which the exercise of 11 chairs is based.

4

I had already undergone a centre-shift in 1965, but the seeker is encouraged to sit in chair 2 (counting from the bottom, Yesod, which corresponds to the physical, rational social ego) and then go and sit in chair 5 (counting from the bottom, Tiferet, which corresponds to the psychological soul into which the spiritual and divine worlds flow). The seeker is encouraged to look at the arrangement of the chairs above number 5 and contemplate how there could be a permanent centre-shift from Yesod (Foundation) to Tiferet (Beauty) to open permanently to the higher spiritual and divine worlds. All four worlds of the Kabbalah (the physical, psychological, spiritual and divine) can be contacted all the time if one lives with one's centre in Tiferet. The exercise graphically illuminates the relationship between reason and ego (both in chair 2) and soul (in chair 5).

The Tree of Knowledge of Good and Evil

I have said that the Tree of Life is mentioned in *Genesis* 2. So is the Tree of Knowledge of Good and Evil, which was also in the Garden of Eden. The Lord God planted a garden eastward in Eden and "put the man whom he had formed" there, Adam, and told Adam he could eat from any tree but not the Tree of Knowledge of Good and Evil. While Adam slept God took one of his ribs and created Eve, who was tempted to eat from the Tree of Knowledge of Good and Evil. Adam also ate. Both were told that as a result they would die. This Tree was a moral Tree of Tradition that set the boundary between good and evil.

There were four rivers in the Garden of Eden, according to *Genesis*: the Pishon, Gihon, Tigris and Euphrates rivers. When I was in Iraq, in January 1962 I was taken to Gourna, between the Tigris and the Euphrates and where the two rivers join, and saw the site of the Tree of Knowledge of Good and Evil, and the tree allegedly descended from it. (I dwelt in Baghdad between the Tigris and Euphrates, and between the east of Eden and the land of Nod.)

A jujube tree said to be on the site of the Tree of Knowledge of Good and Evil, where Eve ate the forbidden fruit, at Gourna, Iraq.

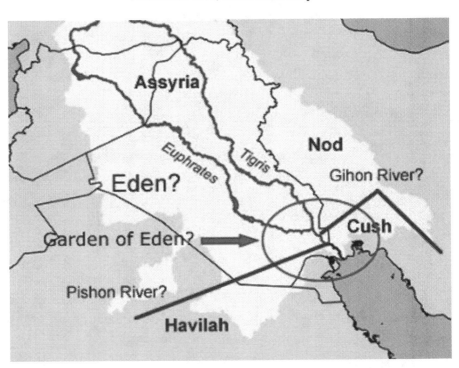

A map of the Garden of Eden showing the four rivers: the Pishon, Gihon, Tigris and Euphrates rivers. Gourna is where the Tigris and Euphrates join.

The Tree of Philosophy and Universalism

While I was writing *The New Philosophy of Universalism* (2009) I came across Descartes' view of philosophy as a tree. I wrote:[2]

> In his *Principia Philosophiae* Descartes referred to philosophy as a tree whose roots are metaphysics, whose trunk is natural philosophy (physics) and whose branches are medicine, mechanics and morals. Descartes was most concerned with the trunk (physics) and he was only concerned with metaphysics to provide a firm foundation for the trunk. The metaphysical was already being weakened in philosophy.

Later on in that book I took up Descartes' view of philosophy as a tree and applied it to my Universalism:[3]

> In a celebrated image Descartes saw philosophy in terms of a tree. In one of his last writings, the Preface to the French edition of the *Principles of Philosophy*, Descartes wrote that "all philosophy is like a tree, whose roots are metaphysics, whose trunk is physics, and whose branches, which grow from this trunk, are all of the other sciences, which reduce to three principal sciences, namely medicine, mechanics and morals". Descartes was re-establishing the Aristotelian-Christian synthesis of metaphysics, physics and the sciences. Universalism, to adapt Descartes' metaphor, is a tree whose roots are in the infinite and metaphysical, whose trunk is the finite universe and whose branches are the sciences which express the infinite and the finite. In this emphasis on the infinite context of the finite, Universalists differ from Aristotle and Whitehead.

The Tree of Civilisation and its metaphysical trunk and sap

In my Universalist history I have seen 25 civilisations going through 61 parallel stages.[4] Each civilisation begins when a mystic has a vision of the Fire or Light, the One (as happened in the case of Mohammed, whose vision of the Fire in a cave is on the first page of the *Koran*), and as word spreads villagers gather together and move to be near him and a town forms. This gathers momentum and a new civilisation grows and expands with the mystic's Fire or Light as its central idea.

Civilisations rise with a metaphysical vision, just as the European civilisation rose round the Light of the World, Christ, and when they turn secular they lose their impelling central idea and begin to decline. Civilisations rise round a metaphysical vision and decline when they turn secular.

In *The New Philosophy of Universalism* I saw a civilisation as a tree, whose trunk is its metaphysical vision, and whose sap is metaphysical:[5]

> In each civilisation, during the growth phase when its vision of Reality or metaphysical Light is strong, its culture is unified round the central metaphysical idea like branches (to adapt Descartes' image) growing from a central trunk, which is the civilisation's religion – in the European civilisation, Christianity. During this early stage the trunk of the religion is fed with metaphysical sap and its branches – art, sculpture, music, literature and philosophy – all express the metaphysical vision of Being that is found in religion. Its leaves, individual works, express sap. There is unity of culture and "unity of Being"....
>
> When the metaphysical sap stops, the branches grow brittle and the culture is fractured and fragmented. Art, religion and philosophy cease to be filled with metaphysical sap and, deprived of natural vigour, start falling apart. When the sap fails, the branches turn dry, sere leaves fall and the civilisation and its culture decline....
>
> When civilisations rise and are healthy, they embody the One, Being, which is reflected first in the mystical vision and later in rational philosophy, as was the case with the Ionian Presocratics like Anaximander and Parmenides, whose works were on one of the branches from the Iranian tradition of the religion of Ahura Mazda. When civilisations lose contact with the One, with the metaphysical Light, there is cultural decline, and art, religion and philosophy turn secular, deal with surfaces and no longer embody the sap in the civilisation's religious trunk. The culture becomes shallow and unhealthy, and declines.

The process of secularisation has taken place in European civilisation today. The metaphysical sap of Christianity began to fail with the Renaissance and was drying up at the end of the 17th century.

The Tree of Tradition and Political Parties

The Tree of Tradition can change its form and, within a civilisation, become the Tree of a political party. A political party is a broad church uniting many different views and branches of thought, ranging from left- to right-wing contributions and factions with different views. And the tradition respects all its forerunners: all past contributions to traditions are respected.

In the UK, the opposite happened in 2019. Prime Minister Johnson expelled 21 senior Conservatives from the Conservative Party for not supporting the Government on a Brexit vote that would result (via a pandemic) in the chaos of a cost-of-living crisis and in massive inflation via the short-lived Truss premiership. On 5 September 2019 I talked with Charles Walker MP on a balcony in the week when he ceased to be Acting Chairman of the 1922 Committee, a very influential Conservative position behind the scenes. To impress on him the need to accept all branches of the tradition including the ones he might disagree with, I pointed to an oak tree at the end of the large lawn in front of us and told him that expelling these pro-EU Conservatives, who included a former Chancellor Ken Clarke and Churchill's grandson Nicholas Soames, was like cutting a branch from the Tree of Tradition of his party.

I wrote to Eleanor Laing, the Deputy Speaker in the House of Commons, who was present that evening. Below is an extract from an email I sent her on 6 September 2019 (see my *Selected Letters*, pp.841–843), which has editing asterisks that are explained in notes at the end:[6]

Subject: The oak tree of tradition*

Dear Eleanor,

It was good to see you yesterday. You did well to leave the Speaker's chair in the Commons and be with us ninety minutes later.

9

Before you came I had quite a long chat with Charles Walker** on the terrace, looking down the slope from the knoll, the hilltop, to the trees. I said the tradition of English Literature is like an oak tree and all the writers since 1350 are its branches, twigs and leaves. T.S. Eliot wrote an essay 'Tradition and the Individual Talent', and the leafy individual writers, who can still be read today, contributed to shaping the tradition, the oak tree. They dealt with issues in their time that were important to them, and our time has different issues, but we don't lop those we are out of sympathy with even though we prefer others.

I said a political party is also like an oak tree. The Conservative tradition grew from the 1760s and Burke's principles, through the Tory party of 1812 and the Conservatives of the 1830s, and through the Conservatives and Unionists of 1909 and of the 1930s and those whose speeches in the 1940s and 1950s can be found in *The New Conservatism* (1955) with Eden and Churchill on its cover, which I acquired in 1956 at the time of Suez and still have. All these individual thinkers and many others since the 1950s contributed to shaping the party's tradition, its oak tree. They dealt with issues in their time and made contributions in times of national crisis, and our time has different issues, and until now we haven't lopped those we are out of sympathy with even though we prefer others.

I said that to follow Beria and lop or "purge" 20 ex-ministers for staying within their time is to miss the point of the tradition, which includes diverse contributions from all branches of Conservatism over many years. We should not lop Churchill, who signed my autograph album at Loughton High School (as Roding Valley High School was then called) in 1951, because his 1946 Zurich speech called for a United States of Europe; or Heath, whose unofficial Ambassador I was, for taking the UK into the European Community. They were of their time, they made contributions to peace in Europe and prosperity, and should be honoured. Churchill's grandson Nicholas Soames, who I met when he came to Epping (to John Padfield's house) a few years ago, reflected his grandfather's position in 37 years of service and was of his time and should not be lopped or purged. It could be argued that promising a non-existent paradise over the horizon and lopping or purging those who question it is failing to see and understand the tradition.

I asked Charles Walker to ask Sir Graham Brady, who took back the Chairmanship of the 1922 Committee from him on Tuesday and is now working closely with him, to reconsider what has happened to the 21 who have been expelled from the party. I said their past contributions to the tree of tradition should be recognised. Returning to acknowledging the tree of tradition may be a way of reuniting the party and dispelling the "toxic atmosphere" you described as pervading Parliament this week. I thought you would want to be aware of my conversation with Charles Walker before you arrived....

With best wishes, Nicholas

*NH founded The Oak-Tree Group of Schools on the edge of Epping Forest. The European civilisation is also an oak tree with many branches (its member nations).

**Charles Walker was Chairman of the 1922 Committee until the previous day, and NH was speaking up for the 21 Conservative MPs who had been expelled for voting for a Bill to stop the Government from forcing through a 'no-deal' Brexit.

NH's works referred to: *Fools' Paradise*; *World State*; *World Constitution*; *The Oak Tree and the Branch*

In this letter I was calling for the oak-tree-like Tree of Tradition to be acknowledged with all its branches, rather than have a branch arbitrarily lopped.

Brexit, the severing of the UK from the EU, was the lopping of a branch of the European civilisation, and the secondary branch containing 21 MPs was lopped because they were all opposed to Brexit and did not believe the promises of "fools' gold" (see my *Fools' Gold*).

The Tree of Tradition and the Universalist World Tree

To move away from the Tree of Tradition's form as a civilisation or a party within a civilisation, the Tree of Tradition is, above all, the World Tree which is found in a number of civilisations' cultures.

In the Greek civilisation it was the oak tree, the sacred tree of Zeus, whose roots reached Tartarus and branches reached the sky, and connected the underworld, the terrestrial earth and the celestial heavens. It is found in the Roman, Judeo-Christian, Sumerian, Armenian, pre-Colombian American, Baltic, Siberian and North-Asian cultures. In Scandinavia the Old Norse Yggdrasil was a giant ash which symbolised the universe. It had three roots that extended into the underworld (Niflheim), into the land of the giants (Jötunheim) and into the home of the gods (Asgard). It connected the Nine Worlds, and Odin sacrificed himself on this Tree.

A painting by Oluf Olufsen Bagge in 1847 of the Norse Yggdrasil described in the Icelandic *Prose Edda*, with roots in the Underworld, land of the giants, and the home of the gods, a form of the World Tree.

Universalism sees the unity of the universe and all humankind, and so adopts this Tree along with Descartes' Tree of Philosophy whose roots are in the infinite and metaphysical, whose trunk is in the finite universe and whose branches are in the sciences; uniting the infinite and the finite. Universalism sees the whole universe, humankind, all civilisations and religions, all disciplines, and all traditions and influences as being united by a World Tree that is also a Tree of Humanity that sees humankind as a unity originating in the emerging *Homo sapiens sapiens*. (See the World Tree on p.xxv.)

The Tree of Tradition in all its forms and emanations, as World Tree

The Tree of Tradition, then, is fundamentally the World Tree that assumes different forms or emanations, all of which are variations of the same Tree: traditions and influences that appear to be on different trees but are in outline the same Tree, the World Tree, the One, whose many variations differ in details.

These emanations or variations include: the Tree of Traditions and Influences of a writer's works; a Tree of Traditions in separate disciplines such as English Literature (see pp.2–3); the Tree of Life that has spiritual origins; the Tree of Knowledge of Good and Evil that offers moral choices; the Tree of Civilisation that shows one civilisation with a metaphysical trunk and branches of different states or nation-states; the Tree of Political Parties that shows all branches of thinking – but above all in its complete form the Tree of Tradition as World Tree, that includes the traditions and influences of all forms of life in the universe, and the works and thoughts of all writers and thinkers.

Centre-shift and instinctively seeing the World Tree

I have already said (on p.5) that I underwent a centre-shift in 1965. In my works I still refer to this centre-shift.[7]

As a young Professor of English Literature in Japan, aged 26, I began having visions and successions of images that at first I thought were connected to my poems. These resulted in my first experience of illumination, the Light, and it slowly became clear that without realising it I was already on a Mystic Way that would last nearly 30 years.

The centre-shift I underwent in 1965 was from my rational, social ego to my psychological soul, which eventually resulted in my instinctively seeing the universe as a unity in spite of all its apparent contradictions: seeing the One behind its many forms, instinctively seeing unity. And with my centre-shift came new powers. I was fed knowledge from a deep source that led to my Theory of Everything in *The Algorithm of Creation*, as its Appendix 1 makes clear.

It is very important to distinguish two ways of perceiving in the Western world. Those who have not been through a centre-shift, and are living in Yesod, chair 2 in the Kabbalah's arrangement of chairs that reveals the Tree of Life, perceive through their physical, rational social ego, which perceives differences and makes distinctions. Those who have undergone a centre-shift see through their psychological soul which opens to the higher worlds, the spiritual and divine worlds, as happens when at the end of the Mystic Way a seeker permanently occupies chair 5, Tiferet. Those who have undergone a centre-shift and have journeyed to the end of the nearly-30-year-long Mystic Way instinctively perceive unity.

The mystic who has been to the end of the Mystic Way, and has gone through a Dark Night of the Soul and Dark Night of the Spirit to emerge with permanent, instinctive unitive vision, Universalist vision, instinctively sees the Tree of Tradition as World Tree that includes everything in the one universe, including a Theory of Everything. Academics who have not undergone a centre-shift naturally see the partial Trees of Tradition such as the Tree of one civilisation or the Tree of Political Parties instead of the universal Tree of Tradition as World Tree.

Coleridge's "esemplastic power of the imagination" and the Tree of Imagination

In *Biographia Literaria* Coleridge refers to the "esemplastic power of the imagination".[8] His word 'esemplastic' comes from the Greek *"eis en plattein"*, meaning "shaping into one". Coleridge wrote in *Biographia Literaria* ch.X, "I constructed it [the word 'esemplastic'] myself from the Greek words *eis en plattein*, to shape into one," whereas the *Shorter Oxford English Dictionary* derives the word from *eis en plassein*, "moulding into unity, unifying".

It was my esemplastic vision that saw the Tree of Imagination in my poem 'The Tree of Imagination', and this Tree of Imagination is a form of the fundamental World Tree with roots in the sky – in the metaphysical. Coleridge's awareness of the "esemplastic power" indicates that he was certainly a Universalist, a perception that is borne out by his study of German Idealism in philosophy which contributed to his arriving at instinctive unitive vision.

Definition of 'traditions' and 'influences'

What are the many traditions that are within the Tree of Tradition? The *Concise Oxford Dictionary* defines 'tradition' as "a custom, opinion or belief handed down to posterity, especially orally and in practice", "the process of handing down, an established practice or custom", "principles based on experienced practice". An influence is "the effect a person or thing has on another", "moral ascendancy or power".

At the level of the rational, social ego's analytical perception of differences, the Tree of Tradition includes the traditions of all practices that we follow that are rooted in the past: in the UK, democratic government based on free speech and Parliamentary debates, polite ways of behaving including queuing, cultural traditions such as putting up Christmas trees, and so on. Some of the traditions have become laws, such as driving on the left-hand side of the road in the UK. There are thousands of traditions of this kind, and they have varying degrees of influence over others.

The Tree of Imagination as a Tree of Universal Knowledge or Universal Mind

The Tree of Imagination also acts as a Tree of Universal Knowledge or Universal Mind: the compendium of all universal events, thoughts, words and emotions in anthroposophy, the Akashic records (access to which was claimed by Rudolf Steiner and Edgar Cayce). Within its branches it contains records of everything that has happened to the universe and humankind.

From September 1980 to July 1981 I knew Tom Dyer, who came as a supply teacher to the school I then worked in. He was seeing if he wanted to become a mature student and train as a teacher, and when I encountered him he had already concluded he was not suited to the teaching profession. It was announced in the staff room he had just become Brain of Britain in the BBC's knock-out radio programme that year, and he then took to asking me to test him. I asked him to tell me the names of the family and children of Amenhotep IV, Pharaoh of Egypt, and he rattled them off. I checked with him in the *Encyclopaedia Britannica*, and he was completely right. I asked, "How do you know that?" He said, "I don't know, I've never read it, the answers float through the air and lodge in my brain. My brain's a receiver for retrieving knowledge." He came round on a starry evening and asked me to look up at the universe and dodge him on the names of particular stars, and again he was completely right on the same basis.

I found I was receiving similar information lodging in my brain when I wrote my Theory of Everything in *The Algorithm of Creation*. The knowledge Tom and I received seems to have come from a Tree of Knowledge, a Tree of Universal Knowledge or Universal Mind that can be instinctively known along with the unity of the universe, and this Tree of Universal Knowledge or Universal Mind seems to be another form of the Tree of Tradition. Hence I declared my deep source as a source for *The Algorithm of Creation* in addition to the many sources in the Notes and References. Besides containing all the traditions and influences writers and thinkers need for their works, the Tree of Tradition contains all knowledge about the universe that has ever existed. It is truly a Universalist World Tree, whose branches contain the entire history of knowledge and memory connected with all stages of the universe and humankind.

The Tree of Tradition as World Tree perceived with esemplastic, instinctive unitive vision

However, the Tree of Tradition I am interested in is the World Tree that is perceived with instinctively unitive vision, the Tree of all civilisations and religions whose roots are in the infinite, whose trunk is filled with the sap of all religions, and whose branches include all nation-states and disciplines, indeed all humankind at all times, but especially in the past. It is this Universalist Tree whose traditions and influences of writing and thinking have influenced writers and thinkers.

Secularisation has fragmented European civilisation's unity into 50 'isms'

Earlier (on pp.7–9) I said that I had written that European civilisation has been secularised, that the metaphysical sap of Christianity began to fade with the Renaissance and was drying up by the end of the 17th century. I went on to say:[9]

Since that time 50 'isms' or doctrinal movements have arisen, representing secular, philosophical and political traditions that demonstrate fragmentation, loss of contact with the One and disunity within the declining European civilisation. They are:

humanism	historicism
scientific revolution/ reductionism	nationalism
	socialism
mechanism	Marxism
Rosicrucianism	anarchism/syndicalism
Rationalism	Darwinism
Empiricism	accidentalism
scepticism	nihilism
atomism/materialism	communism
Enlightenment/deism	conservatism
Idealism	imperialism
Realism	totalitarianism
liberalism	Nazism
capitalism	fascism
individualism	Stalinism
egoism	pragmatism
atheism	progressivism
radicalism	Phenomenology/ Existentialism
utilitarianism	
determinism	stoicism

vitalism

intuitionism

modernism/post-modernism

secularism

objectivism

positivism

analytic and linguistic
  philosophy/logical
  empiricism

ethical relativism

republicanism

hedonism/Epicureanism

structuralism/post-
  structuralism

holism

These 'isms' or doctrinal movements were unthinkable before the Renaissance because Christendom was unified as the medieval philosophy curriculum demonstrated. The diversity of the 'isms' or doctrines reveals the multiplicity within which humans now live.

The multiplicity we now live in reflects the distinctions made by the rational, social ego which sees differences, at the expense of the Oneness of the Middle Ages when the psychological soul saw unity.

T.S. Eliot's 'Tradition and the Individual Talent' and the World Tree

T.S. Eliot's essay 'Tradition and the Individual Talent' (1919) examines the impact of the literary tradition on poets. He writes:[10]

No poet, no artist of any art, has his complete meaning alone. His significance, his appreciation is the appreciation of his relation to the dead poets and artists.

Poets and artists must be compared to and contrasted with the dead, and so must be judged by the standards of the past, how they appear to conform and how individual they are. Eliot writes:[11]

He must be aware that the mind of Europe – the mind of his own country – a mind that he learns in time to be much more important than his own private mind – is a mind which changes.

Two pictures of T.S. Eliot taken by Lady Ottoline Morrell (left) in 1923, four years after 'Tradition and the Individual Talent'; and (right) in 1934, ten years before 'The Man of Letters and the Future of Europe'.

Eliot revisited this idea in 1944 in his essay 'The Man of Letters and the Future of Europe':[12]

> The man of letters as such, is not concerned with the political or economic map of Europe; but he should be very much concerned with its cultural map.... The man of letters... should be able to take a longer view than either the politician or the local patriot.... The cultural health of Europe, including the cultural health of its component parts, is incompatible with extreme forms of both nationalism and internationalism.... The responsibility of the man of letters at the present time... should be vigilantly watching the conduct of politicians and economists, for the purpose of criticizing and warning, when the decisions and actions of the politicians and economists are likely to have cultural consequences. Of these consequences the man of letters should qualify himself to judge. Of the possible cultural consequences of their activities, politicians and economists are usually oblivious; the man of letters is better qualified to foresee them, and to perceive their seriousness.
>
> T.S. Eliot, 'The Man of Letters and
> the Future of Europe' (1944)

Eliot is saying that the man of letters must hold the European politicians to account for what they do to the cultural health of Europe – which means comparing them to and contrasting them with the dead and judging them by the standards of the past.

Eliot sees poetry as being ultimately impersonal:[13]

> The more perfect the artist, the more completely separate in him
> will be the man who suffers and the mind which creates.

We now know that Eliot's own apparently impersonal poetry is full of personal references, that Emily Hale, who he left behind in the US and to whom he wrote more than a thousand letters over 27 years, was "the hyacinth girl" in 'The Waste Land' (1922) and the lady with whom he visited Burnt Norton in 1935 in *Four Quartets*. In 'Tradition and the Individual Talent' (1919) he claims that a poet is not remarkable or interesting because of emotions evoked by particular events in his life but in the way he uses ordinary emotions to express feelings. He says that poetry is an escape from emotion and from personality, and that a poet reaches impersonality by surrendering himself to the work to be done.

What Eliot says about the individual talent being judged in relation to the tradition, which in the case of the European poet is "the mind of Europe", is true. Regardless of how personal or impersonal a poet's works are, there are traditions and influences within the Tree of Tradition as World Tree that illuminate and help all to judge a poet's work.

This work, *The Tree of Tradition*, is within one of those traditions and influences: Eliot's 'Tradition and the Individual Talent'. I seek to carry forward Eliot's thinking by throwing light on the traditions and influences within the Tree of Tradition, by which all poets are ultimately judged.

Nine medieval and nine Renaissance disciplines

The medieval disciplines can be seen in Latin lettering over doors in the Schools Quadrangle at the Bodleian Library, Oxford. There were seven main medieval disciplines: a *trivium* of Logic, Grammar and Rhetoric; and a *quadrivium* of Arithmetic, Geometry, Music and

Astronomy. These were the seven liberal arts and can be seen as *scolae* (schools) over the stone Quadrangle doorways at the Bodleian Library, which was built between 1613 and 1619 as an extension of Thomas Bodley's 1602 Library.

The Renaissance had flourished by 1613, and there are "modern" subjects over other doorways in the Quadrangle: Hebrew, Greek, History, Medicine and Jurisprudence. Divinity was the oldest subject, and in the Renaissance the main disciplines in the curriculum of the humanities (*studia humanitatis*) were Grammar and Rhetoric (both continued from the medieval disciplines), Poetry, Moral Philosophy and History. Divinity and Moral Philosophy should be added to the seven medieval and Renaissance disciplines listed above, making a total of nine of each.

Bodley had restored Duke Humfrey's 1443 Library, and the three branches of philosophy found in, and central to the curriculum of, all medieval universities also have Latin lettering there: Moral and Natural Philosophy, and Metaphysics.

To sum up, we can say there were nine main medieval disciplines (Logic, Grammar, Rhetoric, Arithmetic, Geometry, Music, Astronomy, Divinity and Philosophy, which had three branches); and nine main Renaissance add-on disciplines (Hebrew, Greek, History, Medicine, Jurisprudence, Grammar, Rhetoric, Poetry, and Moral Philosophy).

Seven main disciplines in Universalist works

My Universalist works focus on seven disciplines: mysticism, literature, philosophy and the sciences, history, comparative religion, international politics and statecraft, and world culture. There are of course even more and different disciplines as we shall see on pp.28–32. But the seven disciplines listed above are the main disciplines for approaching a civilisation's Tree of Tradition, or the Tree of Tradition of all civilisations, the World Tree.

In my works, literature has seven branches: poems and poetic epics; verse plays, masques, prose plays and films; short stories, novellas, novels and satirical works; diaries; autobiographies and travelogues; letters and essays; and my statement of the fundamental theme of world literature.

I see the seven disciplines as a stag's seven-branched antler, and the branches of my literature as the stag's other seven-branched antler. The stag is my trademark and is on my coat of arms (see pp.3–4 and 181), which as I have said I was awarded by a former Garter, King of Arms, whose College of Arms is on the site of the College of Heralds Shakespeare visited to receive the coat of arms awarded to his father in 1597. I have said coats of arms go back to the battle of Agincourt in 1415. They were worn on English soldiers' armour to aid identification if they subsequently lay dead on the battlefield. Coats of arms have their place within the Tree of Tradition.

Universalists are at home in many disciplines and poets are cross-disciplinary. Like Donne they present images drawn from different disciplines. Donne's 'Love's Growth' draws his imagery from medical science, astronomy and scholastic philosophy, and in 'A Valediction: Forbidding Mourning' he draws on geographical ideas connected with compasses. He draws on Ptolemaic and Copernican teaching in astronomy, on alchemy and contemporary chemical ideas, and medical physiology. In 'The Exstasie' the idea of souls coming out of the body is derived from Plotinus. In the right hands, a poem can be cross-disciplinary and relate to traditions and influences within the Tree of Tradition of all civilisations that is a World Tree. Universalists work within the seven main disciplines.

Below is a list of 63 Universalist writers and thinkers taken from my work *A New Philosophy of Literature*.[14] They have all written in several disciplines and genres, which are in brackets, and many of these appear in my list of influences (see pp.153–154):

1. Homer (poetry, epic);
2. Xenophanes of Colophon (poetry, philosophy);
3. Parmenides of Elea (poetry, philosophy);
4. Plato (philosophy, teaching in Academy, statecraft, letters);
5. Aristotle (philosophy, logic, sciences, *Poetics*);
6. Demosthenes (political orations, statesman);
7. Julius Caesar (history, military leader, ruler, dictator, statecraft);
8. Cicero (political oratory, philosophy, law);
9. Virgil (poetry, epic);

10. Horace (poetry, criticism);

11. Ovid (poetry, *Ars amatoria*, *Metamorphoses*, poetic letters from Black Sea);

12. Omar Khayyam (astronomy, algebra, philosophy, jurisprudence, history, medicine, alchemy, poetry);

13. Dante (poetry, philosophy, statecraft, diplomacy);

14. Petrarch (poetry, epic poetry, essays, letters, ambassador);

15. Chaucer (poetry, romance/*Troilus and Criseyde*, translation, page, courtier, soldier, squire, diplomat, customs comptroller, Knight of the Shire, Clerk of the King's Works);

16. Leonardo (painting, sculpture, architecture, musician, science, mathematics, engineering, inventions, anatomy, geology, cartography, botany, writing);

17. Michelangelo (painting, sculpture, architecture, poetry, letters, engineering);

18. Ficino (Platonic scholarship, philosophy, letters);

19. Sir Thomas More (*Utopia*, statecraft, diplomacy);

20. Erasmus (writing, Biblical scholarship, theology, languages, diplomacy);

21. Sidney (poetry, novel/*Arcadia*, *An Apologie for Poetrie*, letters);

22. Shakespeare (plays, poems, sonnets);

23. Marlowe (plays, poetry, translation);

24. Donne (poetry, sermons, work as Dean of St Paul's);

25. Milton (poetry, polemical writing, work as Cromwell's Latin secretary);

26. Marvell (poetry, work as MP);

27. Dryden (poetry, plays, criticism, translation);

28. Pope (poetry, unfinished epic *Brutus*, prose 'Epilogue to the Satire', translation);

29. Swift (poetry, novels, polemical essays, sermons);

30. Johnson (poetry, literary criticism, lexicography in compiling the first dictionary, novel);

31. Voltaire (novel/philosophical satire, history, epic poetry, drama, criticism, letters);

32. Goethe (poetry, drama, literature, theology, philosophy, science);

33. Blake (printing, engraving, art, poetry);

34. Coleridge (poetry, literary criticism, philosophy);

35. Wordsworth (poetry, letters, prefaces [i.e. three versions of his Preface to *Lyrical Ballads* in the editions of 1798, 1800 and 1802]);

36. Shelley (poetry, verse drama, *A Defence of Poetry*, letters);

37. Tennyson (poetry, epic, verse drama, letters);

38. Dostoevsky (novels, stories, diaries);

39. Browning (poetry, long dramatic poems, verse drama);

40. Arnold (poetry, literary and cultural criticism, work as inspector of schools);

41. Tolstoy (novels, educational reform, writings on Christianity);

42. T.E. Hulme (poetry, essays, philosophy);

43. T.S. Eliot (poetry, verse drama, cultural history, social essays, literary criticism);

44. Yeats (poetry, verse drama, autobiography, Rosicrucianism, patterns of unified history in *A Vision*, letters);

45. Ezra Pound (poetry, literary criticism, cultural and social essays, letters);

46. H.G. Wells (literature, history, science);

47. Aldous Huxley (literature, mysticism);

48. Robert Graves (poetry, historical fiction, mythology, history of poetic inspiration);

49. Hesse (novels, poems, criticism, philosophy);

50. Arnold Toynbee (universal world history, classical history, Western civilisation, world religion, world travel);

51. Churchill (history, autobiography, biography, political oration, statesman, statecraft, painting);

52. Sartre (philosophy, novels, drama, essays);

53. Camus (novels, drama, philosophy, history);

54. Empson, who qualifies as a Universalist although on the Neoclassical side (criticism, poetry, letters);

55. Kathleen Raine, who qualifies as a Universalist although on the Romantic side (poetry, cultural criticism/statement);

56. David Gascoyne (poetry, journal fiction, literary criticism);

57. John Heath-Stubbs (poetry, epic poetry, plays, anthologies, critical study of later Romanticism);

58. E.W.F. Tomlin (philosophy, literature, travel);

59. Colin Wilson (social criticism, philosophy, fiction, criminology);

60. Ted Hughes (poetry, fiction, letters, occasional prose, mythological and critical Universalism);

61. Lawrence Durrell (poetry, novels, travel books);

62. Iris Murdoch (philosophy, metaphysics, novels); and

63. William Golding (novels, drama, poetry, essays).

This is the list that appeared in *A New Philosophy of Literature*. Now I might expand the list in the light of the 84 influences on pp.153–154, and include, for example, Anaximander of Miletus, an early physicist who was also aware of the infinite and had a Universalist perspective (see p.103).

Traditional and social approaches in the disciplines of world culture, and Universalism's blending

In *The Secret American Destiny* I presented America's destiny as being to create a political World State with a unified global culture. I say that Universalism, the study of the whole of humankind's activities, is in line to be the next American philosophy, and that American Universalism can challenge the social-secular approach that denies the traditional-metaphysical perspective in each discipline, and regards the universe as an accident.

In world culture, each of the seven disciplines has a traditional-metaphysical perspective that is challenged by a more modern social-secular approach. In *The Secret American Destiny* I devote chapter 1, 'Conflicting Approaches in Seven Disciplines',[15] to the conflict between the early rising traditional-metaphysical-based mysticism, literature, philosophy and the sciences, history, comparative religion, international politics and statecraft, and world culture, and a later more modern, declinist, social-secular approach to the seven disciplines.

I contrast the traditional-metaphysical mystics (such as St Augustine and St Hildegard of Bingen) who saw the inner, outwardly-invisible Fire or Light and the social-secular pantheism of visible Nature. I contrast the traditional-metaphysical writers and thinkers who quested for the

One Reality from the time of *The Epic of Gilgamesh* (texts in Akkadian on cuneiform tablets from c.2300BC) to the Metaphysical, Romantic and Modernist writers and thinkers, and the social-secular writers and thinkers who condemned social follies and vices. I contrast the traditional-metaphysical philosophers and scientists such as Plato and the materialistic social-secular, empirical and linguistic philosophers and scientists such as Locke, Hulme, Ayer, Hawking, and Dawkins.

I contrast the traditional-metaphysical historians such as Bossuet and social-secular, speculative historians such as Gibbon, Spengler and Toynbee. I contrast the traditional-metaphysical religions that put the Fire or Light into their religious goals, and the more social-secular religious expressions after 1889. I contrast the traditional-metaphysical international politics of Church-, Fire- or Light-dominated politicians of the Middle Ages and the social-secular relationships of sovereign nation-states and increasing nationalism. I contrast the traditional-metaphysical approach to world culture in the medieval and Renaissance art that featured the Fire or Light and the social-secular perspective after the 18th-century Enlightenment, and its 50 'isms' (see pp.17–18).

Universalism combines both the traditional-metaphysical and the social-secular perspectives and approaches in what I have called 'the Baroque' (a combination of Romanticism and Classicism), and both these traditions are branches on the Tree of Tradition. I combine traditional-metaphysical mystics who saw the Light, and social-secular movements in *The Light of Civilization*. I combine traditional-metaphysical poetry of Metaphysicals and Romantics and social-secular poetry in my Universalist Baroque work (which is a combination of Romanticism and Classicism) and in my fundamental theme of world literature in *A New Philosophy of Literature*. I combine traditional-metaphysical philosophy and modern social-secular science in *The New Philosophy of Universalism*. I combine traditional-metaphysical history and social-secular history in *The Fire and the Stones* and *The Rise and Fall of Civilizations*, and in my quartet on the West, and my American trilogy.

I combine metaphysical-traditional religion and modern social-secular religion in *The Fire and the Stones* and *The Light of Civilization*. I combine traditional-metaphysical international politics and social-secular, speculative international politics in *The World Government*,

World State and *World Constitution*. I combine traditional-metaphysical and modern social-secular world culture in *The Secret American Destiny*.

Card on which Junzaburo Nishiwaki wrote +A + −A = 0 on 5 October 1965.

Universalism blends and reconciles the two opposites in the Universalist formula which embodies the wisdom of the East, which the Japanese poet Junzaburo Nishiwaki wrote out for me on 5 October 1965: +A + −A = 0. Based on the Confucian *yang* + *yin* = the *Tao*, and in my *The Algorithm of Creation* part of the algorithm that offers a Theory of Everything, this algebraic formula reconciles all opposites and contradictions: day and night, life and death, time and eternity, finite and infinite. And in world culture it reconciles and unites the traditional-metaphysical and social-secular approaches.

The Tree of Tradition combines and reconciles all conflicting traditions and influences in English Literature

The Tree of Tradition has one trunk in which metaphysical sap flows from its roots in the infinite, and branches that include both the traditional-metaphysical and social-secular approaches to the seven disciplines, within which are many traditions and influences. In English Literature these include the narrative tradition of Chaucer, the lyric tradition of Wyatt and Surrey during the Renaissance, the verse plays of Shakespeare and masques of Ben Jonson, the Metaphysical poets of the 17th century and the epic poetry of Milton, the Classical Augustan poetry of Dryden and Pope in the 17th and 18th centuries, the Romantic and Victorian poetry of the 19th century, and the American-influenced Modernists of the 20th century.

Today there is more knowledge to absorb. A Theory of Everything is harder to assemble today than in the Renaissance time as there is much more scientific data to consider. It is helpful that scientific advances counterbalance the complexity of modern knowledge, and to those who have been through a centre-shift and seen the unity of the universe with instinctive unitive vision, the many traditions and influences are all within a pattern of unity to which one principle applies: behind all conflicts there is unity. Behind the many is the One.

The Tree of Tradition and the traditions and influences of conflicting genres

Today there are many more branches on the Tree of Tradition as World Tree than there were in the time of the Renaissance. In English Literature, the traditional genres of the Renaissance included lyric poetry, sonnets, satires, epic poetry, theatrical drama and comedies: six genre traditions. (See pp.20–21 for the 9 Renaissance disciplines.)

The four genres of classical (Greek and Roman) literature, focused on during the Renaissance, were poetry, drama, fiction and creative non-fiction, to which some add folk-tale; and poetry and drama had subdivision (epic, lyric, tragedy, comedy and pastoral).

Some lists assert there are broadly seven types of modern genre: action and adventure, comedy, fantasy, horror, mystery, drama and science fiction. There are 14[16] more exact types of literary drama: literary fiction, mystery, thriller, horror, historical, romance, Western, *Bildungsroman*, spectacular fiction (set in a world different from ours), science fiction, fantasy, dystopia, magical realism and realist literature.

Today there are 39 literary genres:

Fiction

1. action and adventure
2. *Bildungsroman*
3. comedy and humour
4. drama
5. dystopia
6. epic poetry

7. fable
8. fairy tale
9. fantasy
10. fiction: narrative literary works, novels
11. fiction in verse
12. folklore
13. historical fiction
14. horror
15. legend
16. letters
17. literary fiction
18. magical realism
19. masques
20. mystery
21. mythology
22. poetry: non-autobiographical poems
23. prefaces
24. realist fiction

25. romance
26. science fiction
27. short story
28. spectacular fiction (set in a world different from ours)
29. tall tale
30. thriller
31. verse drama
32. Western

Non-fiction
33. biography/autobiography
34. essay
35. narrative non-fiction
36. non-fiction: informational text with real-life subject
37. poetry: autobiographical poems
38. speech
39. travelogue

There are, in fact, an enormous number of contemporary literary genres. There are no fewer than 144 more specialised subdivisions for fiction writing.[17] There are more than 90 "movie genres"[18] which cover films. And so on. Contemporary writers' and film-makers' genres and subdivisions are on the Tree of Tradition.

The Tree of Tradition and the traditions and influences of 1,000 sub-classes of the Dewey Decimal and 228 sub-classes of the Library of Congress Classification systems

A good way of obtaining an overview of all the subjects in the Tree of Tradition as World Tree is to look at the two main classification systems used in the libraries in the Anglo-Saxon Western world.

The Dewey Decimal Classification (DDC) used by the British Library and many libraries in the Western world was first published in the US in 1876 and is used in 200,000 libraries in some 135 countries, and is structured round 10 main classes that cover all knowledge:

000	Computer science, information and general works;
100	Philosophy and psychology;
200	Religion;
300	Social sciences;
400	Language;
500	Natural sciences and mathematics;
600	Technology;
700	The arts; fine and decorative arts;
800	Literature and rhetoric; and
900	History and geography.

Each class is further structured into 10 hierarchical divisions, each of which has 10 subdivisions. There are therefore 1,000 entries on the list of Dewey classes. (See Appendix 2.)

If we look at the above main classes of the Dewey Decimal system, and its detailed sub-classes in Appendix 2, it is immediately clear that the Dewey Decimal Classification system's ten classes cover my seven disciplines: literature (800); philosophy (100) and science (500); history (900); comparative religion (200); international politics and statecraft (social sciences, 300). There is no obvious mention of mysticism or the Fire or Light, but these will be under religion (perhaps in 242, devotional literature); and there is no obvious mention of world culture. It is very much a social-secular approach to religion, concentrating on institutions rather than traditional inner mystical experience. The Dewey Decimal Classification system is too general to cover the detailed traditions within the Tree of Tradition.

The Library of Congress Classification (LCC) was developed by the Library of Congress in the US in 1897. It was always a practical classification of the books in that particular library, and is less categorial than the Dewey system. It is used in most research and academic libraries in the US and several other countries. Most public libraries and small academic libraries use the Dewey Decimal Classification system. The Library of Congress Classification system divides knowledge into

21 classes, with each beginning with a letter of the alphabet. Most of these sub-classes are identified by combinations of alphabetical letters. The 21 classes are:

A. General Works;

B. Philosophy. Psychology. Religion;

C. Auxiliary Sciences of History;

D. History: General and Old World, World History and History of Europe, Asia, Africa, Australia, New Zealand, etc.;

E.-F. History: Western Hemisphere

E. America;

F. US Local History, Canada, Latin America;

G. Geography. Anthropology. Recreation;

H. Social Sciences;

J. Political Science;

K. Law;

L. Education;

M. Music;

N. Fine Arts;

P. Language and Literature;

Q. Science;

R. Medicine;

S. Agriculture;

T. Technology;

U. Military Science;

V. Naval Science; and

Z. Bibliography. Library Science.

If we look at the Library of Congress Classification system's 21 classes (A to Z) and its detailed sub-classes in Appendix 2, it is immediately apparent that the disciplines do not stand out as clearly as in the Dewey system. Again, there is no obvious mention of mysticism or the Fire or Light. There is mention of literature (class P); philosophy (class B) and sciences (class Q); history (class D); comparative religion (class B); and international politics and statecraft (class J). There is no obvious mention of world culture. Much of the main disciplines are there but arranged differently. Again, the Library of Congress Classification system is too general to cover the detailed traditions within the Tree of Tradition.

In the Dewey Decimal Classification system there are 1,000 sub-classes. In the Library of Congress Classification system there are 228 sub-classes. In all these there are traditions and influences, but not the traditions and influences within *my* Tree of Tradition. (This explains the generalised and often inappropriate classifications on the back covers of some of my books.)

There are universal classification systems in English-speaking countries: Colon Classification (CC); and Universal Decimal Classification (UDC). There are also the Moys Classification Scheme used in UK and Commonwealth law libraries, including in the law library in Hong Kong; the Harvard-Yenching Classification, an English system for Chinese-language materials; the Vartavan Library Classification; the London Education Classification used at the University College London Institute of Education; the Garside Classification used in University College, London; the Bliss Bibliographical Classification; and the Gladstone Library Classification. Many of these classification systems are specialist and do not address the Dewey Decimal and Library of Congress Classification Systems' failure to reflect the traditions within my Tree of Tradition. (See pp.148–153 for a list of traditions based on my works.)

The Tree of Tradition as a massive Universalist World Tree

All writers and thinkers are confronted by a massive Tree of Tradition that includes (with some doubling up) the 1,000 broad-brush sub-classes of the Dewey Decimal system and the 228 sub-classes of the Library of Congress system. All writers and thinkers identify with and connect to a branch and offshoot, twigs, leaves, flowers and fruit and one or more influences within one of the traditions in the crown of this Tree of Tradition, in their own civilisation or in all civilisations (as World Tree).

2

The Tree of Tradition as World Tree: Traditions and Influences in a Universalist Writer's and Thinker's 60 Works

The Tree of Tradition's impact on a man of letters, poet and Universalist in its many forms

The Tree of Tradition as a massive Universalist World Tree contains millions of traditions and influences going back 5,000 years in 25 civilisations, many of which can be connected to the 1,000 broad-brush sub-classes of the Dewey Decimal and the 228 sub-classes of the Library of Congress systems. Only a relatively tiny amount of such a vast number of potential traditions and influences will impact on a contemporary writer's or thinker's works. The Tree of Tradition has many forms and can present itself to a man of letters, poet and Universalist as a pared-down Tree of Tradition on which every bough, branch and twig is a tradition that impacts on his past and future works.

It can also present itself as a pared-down Tree of Tradition that impacts on just one of the genres in which he writes and thinks. If the individual writer is an English man of letters and poet like me, for example, firstly the Tree of Tradition can present itself as the Tree of Tradition of the whole of English poetry that contains all the historical poems of his nation-state from *Beowulf* to his own contemporary works, the Tree of Tradition kept by the literary critic Christopher Ricks in my poem 'The Tree of Imagination' (1979–1980, see Appendix 1). So he can see what traditions and influences have inspired his past works and may inspire future works. A poet, especially a Universalist poet, is cross-disciplinary, and like the Metaphysical poets can draw on and reflect several disciplines in one poem, as Donne did in 'Love's Growth' (see p.22).

Secondly, the Tree of Tradition can present itself as the poetic Tree of Tradition of his own civilisation, the European civilisation, on which the British poetic tradition of English is one branch amid branches of all the European nation-states, with all European poems on its branches, twigs and buds.

Thirdly, the Tree of Tradition can present itself as the poetic Tree of Tradition of *all* civilisations, as the poetic World Tree, with poems from every nation-state or region in the world.

And finally, the Tree of Tradition can present itself as a reflection of the individual poet's works. Only the branches and twigs, the traditions and influences, that have already inspired his works are on this Tree, and any traditions and influences that have not already inspired his works are waiting to inspire a future work.

It can also present itself as a cultural Tree of Tradition of his own nation-state, showing (in my case) British history: the Roman conquest, the advent of Christianity, medieval Europe under Popes, the Renaissance, the Reformation and so on, all the stages in the growth, rise and decline of the European civilisation's spiritual roots and religious trunk, and its branches, twigs, leaves, flowers and fruit.

All this is for one discipline's subject in one nation-state (poetry within English Literature). There are forms of the Tree of Tradition for all the other subjects within that discipline, and all the subjects in the other disciplines. There may be two dozen forms of the Tree of Tradition that apply to one individual's work, all of which are forms of the Tree of Tradition of the individual writer's civilisation and of *all* civilisations.

To summarise, besides there being the Tree of Tradition behind an individual writer's or thinker's works, there is a Tree of Tradition that embodies a single civilisation and includes the traditions and influences on the individual writer's own civilisation during the 5,000 years of recorded history. Its branches are nation-states.

And there is also a Tree of Tradition that embodies *all* civilisations. The boughs of the Tree of Tradition as Universalist World Tree are the 25 civilisations, and the branches are nation-states and disciplines, which combine in a world culture. Within its crown are all universal traditions and influences of all civilisations, and it is therefore a Universalist World Tree.

The 25 civilisations shown in the Tree of Tradition as Universalist World Tree

If a writer or thinker reflects *all* civilisations universally, that writer reflects the Universalist Tree of Tradition or World Tree that includes the traditions and influences of all civilisations, and all the subjects and disciplines in the metaphysical and secular approaches in each living culture.

In my study of history *The Fire and the Stones,* partly updated as *The Rise and Fall of Civilizations,* I identified 25 civilisations:[1]

1. Indo-European Kurgan (perhaps builders of megaliths in Old Europe);
2. Mesopotamian (Sumerian-Akkadian and later Babylonian);
3. Egyptian;
4. Aegean-Greek (including Minoan and Mycenaean);
5. Roman;
6. Anatolian (including Hittite);
7. Syrian;
8. Israelite (Judaistic);
9. Celtic (including Irish-Celtic and Druid);
10. Iranian;
11. European ⎫ together forming Western civilisation
12. North-American ⎭ (now centred in Europe and USA);
13. Byzantine-Russian (Christian Orthodox);
14. Germanic-Scandinavian;
15. Andean (including Peruvian);
16. Meso-American (including Mexican and North-American Mississippian);
17. Arab (Islamic);
18. African;
19. Indian (Hindu);
20. South-East-Asian (mainly Mahayana and later Theravada Buddhist);
21. Japanese;
22. Oceanian (including Polynesian and Australian);
23. Chinese;
24. Tibetan; and
25. Central-Asian (including Mongolian) from c.500BC.

Of these 25 civilisations the first ten and no.14 are dead, and the other fourteen are still living. There are 11 dead and 14 living civilisations.

The Tree of Tradition as World Tree contains all the traditions and influences from all the civilisations.

The gods of the religions on the World Tree's trunk

On the trunk of the Tree of Tradition as Universalist World Tree are all the religions of all the above civilisations. I set out 21 civilisations with distinctive religions and four civilisations with related religions. The gods of the distinctive religions, and so the gods of all 25 civilisations, are all approached through the Light, and are on the Tree of Tradition as Universalist World Tree's trunk. They are:[2]

> Dyaeus Pitar/Magna Mater (Sky Father/Earth Mother); Anu/ Ogma/Utu, Shamash/Tammuz/Marduk, Shuqamuna/ Ashur; Ra/Amun/Aton, Horus/ Osiris/Apis; Zeus/Apollo, Anat/Athene (or Athena); Jupiter/Apollo, Gnostic God as Light; Mistress of Animals/Storm and Weather god Tarhun or Teshub/Sharruma/ Arinna, Cybele/Attis; El/ Dagon/Baal/Mot/ Resheph/Molech (or Moloch), Koshar/Astarte/Anath (or Anat), Adonis, Ashtoreth, Hadad/Rammon/Atargatis; El Shaddai/ Yahweh; Du-w ('Yoo-we', cf 'Yahweh')/Lug/Beli (cf Baal)/ Taran/Yesu; Mithras/ Zurvan (of Medes)/Ahura Mazda/Mani, Inshushinak/Kiririshna (cf Indian Krishna)/Nahhunte/Huban; God as Light; Wodan/Odin; Smiling god ('El Lanzon', 'the Great Image'), Inti/Quetzlcoatl/ Kukulcan (or Kukulan); Kinich Ahau/ Itzamna/Huitzilopochtli; Allah; Mwari/Nzambi/Cghene/ Ngai/Leza/Ndjambi Marunga/ Raluvhimba/Olodumare; Agni/ Brahman/ Atman/ Siva/Sakti, Visnu/Rama/Krishna/Om Kar, the Buddha; Kami/Amaterasu; Io (Maori); *Shang Ti/T'ien Ti*/T'ien Ti/the *Tao*.

The World Tree and its forms, Plato and literary genres

The many forms of the Tree of Tradition as Universalist World Tree are partial, particular, physical or actual shadows in relation to their One source, their Idea, Plato's 'Form' (a word with his specialised meaning of 'formed by Ideas of things that actually exist'). The Tree of Tradition as Universalist World Tree, the archetypal and unitive Tree of Tradition as Universalist World Tree that transcends time and space, embodies all civilisations as my unseen psychological Tree of Imagination, which is reflected by the seen physical Tree of Tradition as my poem says:

> The Tree of Tradition merely reflects
> A more unseen one which hangs from the sky.
>
> (lines 41–42)

All writers and thinkers when they set out are confronted by the massive Tree of Tradition as a Universalist World Tree of the traditions and influences in all civilisations, as I said on p.33. The single-discipline or single-tradition writer (such as the writer of detective novels) early on places himself or herself behind those that have gone before. There are as many as 39 different genres, as we saw on pp.28–29.

An example of the traditions that have influenced the works of a British man of letters, poet and Universalist

The British poet finds the branch off the bough of literature with which he feels a sense of continuity, and recognises his links to a number of poets who flowered there during their lifetimes and left the fruit of their works behind, fallen from the Tree to the ground as windfalls. The Universalist writer has links with more traditions and influences in seven disciplines than non-Universalist single-discipline writers.

Because there are so many forms of the One Tree of Traditions as Universalist World Tree, I need to set out an example of how an individual writer's and thinker's words reflect the traditions and influences of the Tree of Tradition as Universalist World Tree.

In this spirit of exemplification, and as the Universalist writer has more links to traditions and influences on the World Tree than other writers, I will now use my own works as an example of the works of all writers who are confronted by the traditions and influences of the massive Universalist World Tree.

I now set out my own works in seven disciplines and more subdisciplines, and relate each to the traditions (disciplines and literary genres) and influences on the archetypal Tree of Tradition as Universalist

World, and I will indicate the Universalist credentials of the influences and the way in which each has had an objective impact on my works. It is possible to set out a similar example using the work of any writer or thinker that has ever lived, and this exercise will demonstrate how all living and dead writers and thinkers that have ever been are all connected to the traditions and influences attached to the branches of this World Tree that is both within and transcendently outside time.

Each of my works follows traditions and influences within one or more disciplines, and each tradition or discipline has influenced one or more of my works, as I will now try to show.

Traditions and influences behind the seven disciplines in Nicholas Hagger's 60 Universalist works

I will proceed discipline by discipline, in the order of the seven disciplines I have already stated (see pp.21–22): mysticism; literature; philosophy and the sciences; history; comparative religion; international politics and statecraft; and world culture.

On p.25 I wrote:

> In world culture, each of the seven disciplines has a traditional-metaphysical perspective that is challenged by a more modern social-secular approach. In *The Secret American Destiny* I devote chapter 1, 'Conflicting Approaches in Seven Disciplines', to the conflict between the early rising traditional-metaphysical-based mysticism, literature, philosophy and the sciences, history, comparative religion, international politics and statecraft, and world culture, and a later more modern, declinist, social-secular approach to the seven disciplines.

In *The Secret American Destiny* I wrote:[3]

> We can now see that in each of the seven disciplines the original metaphysical approach has been challenged by, and now co-exists with, a social-secular approach. In each of the seven disciplines there is a '+A + –A' or pair of opposites that make for disunity in world culture.

I have said (see p.27) that Universalism blends and reconciles the two opposite traditions as in the algebraic formula +A (traditional-metaphysical) + −A (social-secular) = 0 (Oneness and unity of Universalism), and I now show Universalism reconciling the traditional-metaphysical perspective and the more modern social-secular approach in relation to my own works. In each discipline I will set out the two traditions and their Universalist reconciliation in relation to my own works, and will describe how I came to these two traditions and the influences that took me to them.

1. Mysticism
The Fire and the Stones, partly updated as *The Light of Civilization*.

Traditional-metaphysical and social-secular traditions of mysticism and their Universalist reconciliation
In *The Secret American Destiny* I wrote of the traditional-metaphysical and more secular pantheist mysticism:[4]

> For 5,000 years (from before the time of the Great Pyramid) mysticism has been dominated by two conflicting approaches: one inner, the other outer.
>
> The dictionary definitions of 'mysticism' convey the traditional, inner approach. A 'mystic' is defined as 'a person who seeks by contemplation and self-surrender to obtain unity or identity with or absorption into the Deity or the ultimate reality, or who believes in the spiritual apprehension of truths that are beyond the understanding' (*Concise Oxford Dictionary*). 'Mysticism' is 'belief in the possibility of union with the Divine nature by means of ecstatic contemplation; reliance on spiritual intuition as the means of acquiring knowledge of mysteries inaccessible to understanding' (*Shorter Oxford English Dictionary*).
>
> Evelyn Underhill set out the inner tradition of mysticism in *Mysticism* (1911). She defined the mystic union as a practical spiritual activity involving love and a psychological experience that is never self-seeking.[5] The mystic experiences unity – union with the Absolute – by contemplation and self-surrender, whereas the mystical philosopher reflects on the data and may not be a mystic.

The practical Mystic Way, which Underhill charts, begins with the awakening of the self to consciousness of Reality, and proceeds to purgation (which purifies the self) and detachment from the senses (which leads to illumination and visions). The self is enabled ('now it looks upon the sun')[6] and is then plunged into a Dark Night in which the sun of Reality is absent. After recollection, quiet, contemplation, ecstasy and rapture, the self achieves union with the Light and experiences unitive life as a permanent condition....

Alongside has always been present an alternative outer, 'extrovertive' mysticism that presents an awareness of the unity of the natural, social and outer universe without any inner vision. This is a form of pantheism in which the mystic experience of union is of an outer union with Nature in which stars, a heath, a lake or a pond are seen as part of the One, as I experienced in my four experiences of oneness in 1946, 1954, 1959 and 1963.[7] Wordsworth described the oneness behind his Nature mysticism:

A motion and a spirit, that impels

All thinking things, all objects of all thought,

And rolls through all things.[8]

This pantheistic mysticism is of the visible rather than the invisible (or seen shining behind closed eyes), of the seen rather than the unseen.

The social-secular view of the universe includes outer glimpses that all is a oneness in a system recognized by scientific Materialism. In this outer mysticism ultimate Reality is only implicitly present. There is no contemplation or spiritual vision, just a sense that Nature is one.

On p.25 I wrote:

I contrast the traditional-metaphysical mystics (such as St Augustine and St Hildegard of Bingen) who saw the inner, outwardly-invisible Fire or Light and the social-secular pantheism of visible Nature.

(Left) The earliest known portrait of St Augustine (in a 6th-century fresco, Lateran, Rome); and (right) Hildegard of Bingen receiving a vision of the Fire or Light (in an illumination from *Scivias*, 1151).

The less metaphysical, more secular 'extrovertive' pantheism is a form of mysticism that sees visual Nature rather than the invisible metaphysical Light.

Mystical Universalism unites both these traditions. As regards Universalism's reconciliation of the two traditions of mysticism, in *The Secret American Destiny* I wrote:[9]

> In mysticism Universalism presents the natural, social, outer universe which in the mystic state is pantheistically felt to be one within the context of ordering metaphysical Reality: the Light that I documented in all cultures and civilizations over 5,000 years in *The Fire and the Stones* and *The Light of Civilization*. The perception by the inner universal being that the infinite is behind the finite universe incorporates and contextualizes humanism, Materialism, Rationalism, Empiricism, skepticism, mechanism, positivism and

reductionism and many other 'isms' in all disciplines. We can know infinite Being, or the One, beyond and behind the phenomenal world of the senses, rationally via the image of the surfer on the crest of the surging wave of the expanding universe, whose feet are in finite space-time and whose upper body and head breast the infinite; and intuitionally via the vision of the 'ever-living Fire' or metaphysical Light....

This contextual approach of mystical Universalism can be summed up as –A (the finite and accidental) + +A (the infinite and order) = 0 (the reunification of mysticism). The inner experiences of the infinite of the individual Christian mystics [see pp.48–49] and of the mystics of all cultures and civilizations [see pp.47–48] – experiences of ordering metaphysical Reality – are therefore a context for all the contemplative pantheism and views on the finite universe of the rational, social ego.

As we have seen (on p.31), this traditional-metaphysical discipline of mystical Universalism has been relegated to a subdiscipline in our secularised time, and is not even overtly mentioned in the Dewey Decimal and Library of Congress classifications.

How I came to the two traditions of mysticism, and their influences
I summarised my Mystic Way in *My Double Life 2: A Rainbow over the Hills*.[10] It is as follows:

> First Mystic Life: 20 July 1964–18 October 1965;
> Dark Night of the Soul: 19 October 1965–2 September 1971;
> Second Mystic Life: 3 September 1971–28 April 1972;
> Dark Night of the Spirit, new powers: 29 April 1972–12 May 1979;
> Third Mystic Life: 13 May 1979–31 October 1981;
> Dark Night of the Spirit, ordeals: 1 November 1981–7 April 1990;
> Fourth Mystic Life: 8 April 1990–6 December 1993; and
> Unitive Life: 7 December 1993 to date.

The traditional-metaphysical tradition of mysticism is based on the experience of Fire or Light.

I was first aware of the Light in the poems of the Metaphysical poets at Oxford, and when I spent a year lecturing at the University of Baghdad in Iraq in 1961–1962 I used to pass Suhrawardi's medieval house on my way to work every day. Suhrawardi, an Iranian, lived in Iraq for some time and founded the Iranian school of Illuminationism.

While undertaking my research into mysticism between 1965 and 1990 (more or less the length of my 30-year-long Mystic Way which began on 20 July 1964 and ended on 6 December 1993),[11] I read St John of the Cross's *Dark Night of the Soul*, which was an influence within the mystical tradition on me, and encountered Dr R.H. Blyth, the authority on Zen Buddhism, who taught at my main university in Tokyo, Tokyo University of Education (where when it had a different name William Empson taught from 1931 to 1934). Blyth was ill and I only met him once, in a corridor, but we talked at some length and he arranged for me to go to a Zen meditation centre in Ichikawa City with my Japanese namesake Haga, and set me on my mystic path without my realising it.

I also met Professor Junzaburo Nishiwaki, a Japanese poet known as Japan's T.S. Eliot as his poem 'January in Kyoto' appeared in 1923, a year after Eliot's 'The Waste Land' (1922). (See p.27.) He was Professor Emeritus in one of my universities, Keio University, and I first met him on 21 December 1963.

Junzaburo Nishiwaki, Japanese poet, regarded as Japan's T.S. Eliot.

At that first meeting Nishiwaki spoke encouragingly. He was then 69, and he told me, "As a poet, you must teach the taste by which you will be relished, just as Wordsworth did," and he said of me to the Japanese who took me to him: "I want to kiss hands with Mr Hagger and toast his figure, his face, his hair, his knowledge and his mind. He is the greatest Englishman, a real scholar. I am seldom wrong in my intuition, but one day he will be the greatest man in England – and not only in England, all of Europe. One day he will get the Nobel Prize." Then he turned to me and said, "But never forget. Make the public come to you on your terms. Impose your will on the public. As Wordsworth said, teach the public the taste by which you are relished."

I met him again on 5 October 1965, when I asked him, sitting in a restaurant near Keio University with sawdust on the floor and drinking *saké* (Japanese rice-wine) what the wisdom of the East was. He took a business-reply card from my pile of books on the restaurant table, and wrote: +A + −A = 0. (See p.27.) He told me it was Confucius's algebraic thinking – he knew Ezra Pound, who was also a Confucian – and explained *yang* + *yin* = the *Tao*. As I said on p.27, I came to understand that *yang* and *yin* represented the opposites (light and dark, day and night, time and eternity, the finite and the infinite), and that the formula sets out all the conflicting opposites in the universe, which were reconciled in the One, the *Tao*: the Universalist unity of the universe and humankind, a vision of my unitive living ahead when all conflicts would be reconciled within an underlying unity. This formula expressed the essence of my Universalism, and it came to be the basis for the algorithm of Creation in my Theory of Everything.

In October 1965 I was writing 'The Silence', a poem that would take me 18 months to complete, about the development of Freeman (my Everyman), and I wrote Nishiwaki's algebraic formula into the poem:

An Eastern sage tempts:
"(+A) + (−A) = Nothing,
The Absolute is where there is no difference."

(lines 1245–1247)

That last line Nishiwaki said to me on 5 October 1965, before writing down the formula. It contained a truth I would instinctively recognise in the 1990s but was then a glimpse ahead to how I would be in the future. In the hot sun I had got to know my shadow, which kept me company during my walks to work and back, and I regarded my Shadow as my future self. Now I have become my Shadow and have my Shadow's perspective on the events in 1965 and my early contact with the Tree of Tradition as World Tree.

When I underwent my extraordinary experiences in Japan in 1965 and my first experience of the Mystic Light and found I was undergoing a centre-shift and was on a Mystic Way that would last nearly 30 years and take me from awakening to purgation, detachment from the senses and visions, a Dark Night of the Soul, full illumination, a Dark Night of the Spirit in which I would receive new powers, ecstasy and finally to unitive living with an instinctive vision of the unity of the universe and humankind, I looked for books in Tokyo bookshops that would help me. But there were none. I found tiny references to the Light in a number of books, but only Evelyn Underhill's *Mysticism* (1911), which I found in a Japanese bookshop (Kitazawa Bookstore), really helped me. Her book was an influence in helping me to understand the Mystic Way I was on and the tradition I was following.

In London I met Margaret Riley, an advanced Catholic mystic and artist who was living in the house where I had taken an advertised room in 1970 and who went to the Light every day, and she reinforced me. She embodied a Catholic Viennese tradition of mysticism on the Tree of Tradition, going back to Agnes Blannbekin (1244–1315, referred to as the Venerable Agnes Blannbekin), who had visions and whose revelations were written down by her anonymous confessor and published in 1731. Margaret influenced me. She inducted me into my full illumination on 11 September 1971, as my autobiography, *My Double Life 1: This Dark Wood*, narrates.[12]

(Left) Margaret Riley in 1971, sitting with her portrait of the Virgin Mary dressed as a nun to symbolise the call to the Mystic Way; and (right) Evelyn Underhill in 1926, 15 years after *Mysticism*.

Evelyn Underhill and Margaret Riley were the two influences on my mysticism, and Margaret Riley wrote no books but was an authoritative presence much older than me and pointing the way.

The first part of *The Fire and the Stones* (1991), updated in two books as *The Light of Civilization* (2006) and *The Rise and Fall of Civilizations* (2008), was about the Fire (in Indian mysticism) or Light (in Western Christian thought), and was in the Underhill tradition, as was my autobiographical work about my Mystic Way, *A Mystic Way* (1994).

Along the Mystic Way, while I researched the mystic tradition I had encountered the works of Pascal, who experienced full illumination in 1654. After his death in 1662 the following lines were found sewn into the lining of his doublet:

> The year of grace 1654,
> Monday, 23 November...
> From about half past ten in the evening until about half
> past twelve
> FIRE.[13]

I wrote in *The Secret American Destiny*:[14]

> The Light is a metaphysical experience.[15] It is 'beyond' or 'behind' (*'meta'*) the physical world of the five senses.

I encountered St Augustine of Hippo's eyewitness account of the Light in 400AD:[16]

> I entered [within myself]. I saw with the eye of my soul, above (or beyond) my mind, the Light Unchangeable.... It shone above my mind.... All who know this Light know eternity.

And I also encountered the 12th-century St Hildegard of Bingen's eyewitness account of the Light in her 1175 letter to Guibert Gembloux, written when she was 77 (before she died at the age of 81 in 1179):[17]

> From my infancy up to the present time, I now being more than seventy years of age, I have always seen this light, in my spirit [or soul, Jung's translation] and not with external eyes.... The light which I see is not located, but yet is more brilliant than the sun.... I name it 'the cloud of the living light'.... But sometimes I behold within this light another light which I name 'the living light itself'.

I have listed some of those who know the Light in all civilisations and cultures, who contributed to the metaphysical sap in the trunk of the World Tree and were my mystical forebears and, in a sense, influences:[18]

> Patanjali, Zoroaster, the Buddha, Mahavira, Lao-Tzu, Jesus, St Paul, St Clement of Alexandria, Plotinus, Mani, Cassian, St Augustine, Pope Gregory the Great, Mohammed, Bayazid, Al-Hallaj, Omar Khayyam, Suhrawardi, Hafez, Symeon the New Theologian, Hildegard of Bingen, Mechthild of Magdeburg, Moses de Leon, Dante, Angela of Foligno, Meister Eckhart, Tauler, Suso, Ruysbroeck, Kempis, Rolle, Hilton, Julian of Norwich,

St Catherine of Siena, St Catherine of Genoa, St Gregory Palamas, Padmasambhava, Sankara, Guru Nanak, Hui-neng, Eisai, Dogen, Michelangelo, St Teresa of Avila, St John of the Cross, Boehme, Herbert, Vaughan, Crashaw, Traherne, Norris, Law, Cromwell, Marvell, Milton, Bunyan, Fox, Penn, Naylor, Mme Acarie, Baker, Pascal, St Francis of Sales, Mme Guyon, John Wesley, Blake, Swedenborg, Shelley, Emerson, Tennyson, Browning, Arnold, Newman, Mme Blavatsky, Trine, Jung and T.S. Eliot.

In *The Light of Civilization* I collected the mystical experiences of the world's mystics civilisation by civilisation and presented the traditions of the Light within each of my 25 civilisations:[19]

The Indo-European Kurgan Light; the Mesopotamian Light; the Egyptian Light; the Aegean-Greek Light; the Roman Light; the Anatolian Light; the Syrian Light; the Israelite Light; the Celtic Light; the Iranian Light; the European Light; the North-American Light; the Byzantine-Russian Light; the Germanic-Scandinavian Light; the Andean Light; the Meso-American Light; the Arab Light; the African Light; the Indian Light; the Southeast Asian Light; the Japanese Light; the Oceanian Light; the Chinese Light; the Tibetan Light; and the Central Asian Light.

The headings in the long section on the European Light cover the experiences of individual European mystics and their sources:[20]

The *New Testament* Jesus: Transfiguration and Parables of Light; Jesus as the Gnostic Light of the World, God as Light; Paul's Blinding Light: the Gentilized Light in the 'Epistles'; the Light of the Christian-Gnostic Alexandrian School: Clement's Gnosis of Light, the Logos of Light; the New Roman Light in the Early Middle Ages; the Christian Neoplatonist Light: St Augustine's Unchangeable Light, Dionysius's Darkness beyond Light; the Benedictines: Pope Gregory's Unencompassed Light; the West Roman Empire's Christian Light; the Cistercian Light: St Bernard's Consuming Fire; the Living Light of Hildegard and Flowing Fire of Mechthild; the Late Medieval Brightness; the Italian Franciscans' Light Supreme of St Bonaventura; the Energizing Fire, Infinitesimal Point of Light and Light of Glory of Dante; the German Dominican Light of Wisdom and Spark of the Soul of Meister Eckhart; the Flemish Eternal Brightness or Light; the English and Late Italian Fire of Love of Rolle and St Catherine of Siena; the Renaissance Dimming; the Reformation Light; the Light of the Jesuits and Carmelite Counter-Reformation: St John of the Cross's Supernatural, Burning Light and St Teresa of Avila; the Protestant Lutheran Light of Boehme; the Church of England Light of the Metaphysical Poets Donne, Herbert, Vaughan, Traherne; the Puritan or Non-Conformist Light of Marvell, Milton and Bunyan, the Quaker Inner Light of Fox; the Later Counter-Reformation: the Jansenist Fire of Pascal, the Light of Quietism of Mme Guyon; the Light of the Evangelical Revival of John Wesley; the Dimming Christian Light; Secularized Established Church; the Victorian Dimming of the Christian Light in European Literature c.1880 after Tennyson, Browning, Arnold and Goethe; Secularization of English Hymns between 1889 and 1951; the Vanishing Light; the Christian Light Today; and the 20th-century Mystic Reawakening and T.S. Eliot.

The section on the North-American Light draws on the following headings:[21]

Transcendentalism of Emerson and Thoreau; New Thought and Trine; and Protestant Evangelism

After presenting the tradition of the Light in *The Light of Civilization* I presented as a tradition the heretical Light in Western civilisation under the following headings:[22]

The Essene Light; the British Druid Light; the Gnostic Light and the Spark; the Hermetic Light and Alchemy; the Manichaeist Light; the Templar Light; the Grail Light; the Kabbalist Light; the Esoteric Light, Including the Freemasonic, Rosicrucian and

Romantic Neoplatonist Light; the Theosophical Light and the Spiritual Sun; and the New Age Light.

I have referred to Confucius's algebraic thinking, $+A + -A = 0$, *yang* + *yin* = the *Tao*. It is this algebraic thinking that unites the traditional-metaphysical and the social-secular traditions of mysticism (see pp.44–45) in the Confucian reconciliation of opposites: uniting the inner vision of the Fire or Light with the outer pantheism within Nature that Wordsworth knew, and which I experienced, a Oneness I experienced six times between 1954 and 1974 as I set out on p.912 of *My Double Life 2: A Rainbow over the Hills*:

Jul/Aug 1954	Experiences the Oneness of the universe on Merrow golf course.
Mar 1959	Experiences the Oneness of the universe by Worcester College lake.
13 Nov 1963	Experiences the Oneness of the universe by Strawberry Hill pond.
5–6 Jan 1965	First experience of the Oneness of the universe at Kyoto's Ryoanji Stone Garden.
11–12 Aug 1965	Second experience of the Oneness of the universe at Kyoto's Ryoanji Stone Garden.
4 Aug 1974	Experiences the Oneness of the universe in the fusion of clouds and ground in Earl's Path pond on Strawberry Hill.

Since my first glimpse of the mystic Light in 1965 and my full illumination in 1971 I have recorded 112 experiences of the Light.[23] (Blake had two, separated by 20 years; the second one was on the day after his visit to the Truchsessian Gallery in October 1804, according to his letter to William Hayley on 23 October 1804.)

I have recently regularly seen at night, behind closed eyes in the dark, an oval cloud that comes towards me, seemingly made of swansdown, very soft, which I regard as my soul. This oval cloud has replaced the Light in recent years. I have recorded 17 experiences of this oval cloud between 22 April 2020 and 24 April 2021 (see *The Promised Land*, pp.213–215), and I have written 15 poems based on my 'oval cloud' between 25 April 2020 and 10 April 2021, and another seven added in 2023, until 5 March 2023, making 22 in all (see *The Oak Tree and the Branch*).

Mysticism should be a foremost discipline today, but in our secular time the metaphysical Light has been forgotten, and though I have written about it in my works, few readers have had the experience and consequently the Light in my works has had a muted reception, something that people are curious about but do not take up.

Mysticism's traditions and influences

Mysticism's 14 traditions on the Tree of Tradition that influenced me include 3 main traditions (1–3) and another 11 sub-traditions (4–14):

1. the tradition of the Mystic Way;
2. the tradition of inner illumination by the Fire or Light, the metaphysical Reality, the One;
3. the tradition of extrovertive mysticism;
4. the tradition of Viennese mysticism;
5. the tradition of Underhill's *Mysticism*;
6. the tradition of Pascal's Fire;
7. the tradition of St Augustine's Light Unchangeable;
8. the tradition of unitive vision, instinctively seeing the unity of the universe, at the end of the Mystic Way;
9. the tradition of world mystics (see pp.47–48);
10. the tradition of the Light within 25 civilisations;
11. the tradition of the European mystics (see pp.48–49);
12. the tradition of the North-American Light;
13. the tradition of Zen Buddhist *satori* (Enlightenment); and
14. the tradition of Confucian reconciliation of opposites.

Mysticism's 11 forebears and influences on me (in the order mentioned in the text) were:

1. Evelyn Underhill
2. Margaret Riley

3. Pascal

4. St Augustine

5. Hildegard of Bingen

6. Suhrawardi

7. St John of the Cross

8. R.H. Blyth

9. Junzaburo Nishiwaki

10. T.S. Eliot

11. Blake

2. Literature

Traditional-metaphysical and social-secular traditions of literature in its seven genres or subdivisions, and their Universalist reconciliation in the Baroque

I have already said (on p.21) that I have written within seven subdivisions of literature: poems and poetic epics; verse plays, masques, prose plays and films; short stories, novellas, novels and satirical works; diaries; autobiographies and travelogues; letters and essays; and my statement of the fundamental theme of world literature. I have also said (on p.22) that the seven disciplines and seven subdivisions of literature are symbolised in my works as the two seven-branched antlers of a stag.

On pp.25–26 I wrote:

> I contrast the traditional-metaphysical writers and thinkers who
> quested for the One Reality from the time of *The Epic of Gilgamesh*
> (texts in Akkadian on cuneiform tablets from c.2300BC) to the
> Metaphysical, Romantic and Modernist writers and thinkers,
> and the social-secular writers and thinkers who condemned
> social follies and vices.

In *The Secret American Destiny* I wrote of the traditional-metaphysical and more social-secular traditions of literature, and I set out 12 Universalist characteristics of the metaphysical tradition within literature:[24]

1. The infinite (*to apeiron*) that surrounds the universe;

2. The metaphysical Reality perceived in all cultures as Light (or Fire, which is a universal cosmic energy);

3. The universal principle of order in the universe (universal in the sense that its effects are found in all aspects of Nature and its organisms);

4. The oneness of known humankind behind its apparent diversity;

5. The similarities in cultures and civilizations;

6. The universal being (or self) that opens to the Light behind the rational, social ego;

7. Universal virtue, a standard by which to measure human follies, vices, blindness, corruption, hypocrisy, self-love and egotism in relation to an implied universal virtue (when human interaction is considered from a secular perspective, separated from its context of Reality);

8. The promise of immortality of the universal being or spirit;

9. An inner transformation or centre-shift from ego to universal being;

10. The quest of the purified soul to confront death – in the ancient cultures by journeying to the Underworld – and to receive the secret Light of infinite Reality;

11. A sensibility that approaches Reality through more than one discipline, the sensibility of a polymath; and

12. A new perspective of unity in key disciplines: seeing world history as a whole; seeing the common essence (the inner experience of the Light) of all world religions; seeing the One that can be revealed by philosophy and science; seeing the World State that can unify international politics; and seeing the unity of world literature.

In *The Secret American Destiny* I show how eight of these Universalist characteristics of literature are reflected in the world literature of ten historical periods within the Tree of Tradition – the ancient world; the classical world; the Middle Ages; the Renaissance; the Baroque; the Neoclassical, Romantic, Victorian and Modernist periods; and the 20th-century anarchy:[25]

For 4,600 years world literature has displayed two conflicting literary approaches.

In *A New Philosophy of Literature: The Fundamental Theme and Unity of World Literature* I showed that ever since literature appeared in the Mesopotamian civilization c4600BC and threw up, over several centuries, successive versions of *The Epic of Gilgamesh*, there has been a tradition describing the hero's quest for metaphysical Reality. The literary Gilgamesh (based on a historical king who ruled Uruk in modern Iraq in the 27th century BC) wants immortality and the theme of the questing hero in literature originated in works associated with him....

We can form a bird's-eye view of the metaphysical aspect of the fundamental theme of world literature by following eight of these characteristics through the ten periods and noting the religious texts, poets and literary authors in which they are expressed:

- The infinite (*to apeiron*) that surrounds the universe – Heaven/Elysian Fields and Underworld; Iranian light and dark; Fire of Brahman; the *Tao* 'infinite and boundless'; Yahweh; Homer, Anaximander's *to apeiron*, Plato, Virgil; the *Koran*; Grail legends, Dante; Ficino's letters, Marlowe's *Dr Faustus*; Donne, Milton's *Paradise Lost*, Bunyan's *Pilgrim's Progress* and Dryden; Pope, Johnson and Goethe; Blake's infinite, Coleridge, Wordsworth's One, Shelley's One; Tennyson, Arnold, Emily Brontë and Emerson; Eliot, Yeats and Rilke's 'We are bees of the invisible'; and the Neo-Romantics;
- Metaphysical Reality perceived as Light – Utu-Shamash, Ra, Ahura Mazda, Agni-Brahman, T'ien and Yahweh; Pindar, Parmenides's One, Xenophanes's 'one god', Plato's 'universal' light, Socrates's 'pure light', the *New Testament*, the Essene Dead Sea Scrolls, Gnostic, Manichaean and Neoplatonist texts, *The Golden Ass*, St Augustine's *Confessions* and Pope Gregory the Great; Perceval, Dante, *Piers Plowman*, the *Koran*, Sufi, Buddhist, Hindu and Tibetan texts, Neo-Taoist Clear Light and Japanese Zen; Donne, Cervantes, Milton's *Paradise Lost*, Vaughan, Traherne and Bunyan's *Pilgrim's Progress*; Pope and

Goethe; Blake, Coleridge, Wordsworth, Shelley and Keats; Tennyson, Emerson and Thoreau; Eliot and Yeats; and Dylan Thomas and David Gascoyne;

- The universal principle of order in the universe – gods who ordered the universe: Anu and Utu-Shamash, Ra, Ahura Mazda, *rta* (harmony in Nature), the *Tao* and Yahweh; Zeus and Jupiter in Homer, Greek myths and Sophocles, Plato, Virgil's Fate, Caesar's omens, Horace, Ovid, the *New Testament*, the Essene Dead Sea Scrolls and Gnostic texts; the *Elder Edda*, the *Kalevala*, the *Nibelungenlied*, Dante and Buddhist, Hindu and Neo-Taoist texts; Ficino's letters and Shakespeare's 'Great Chain of Being'; Donne, Milton's *Paradise Lost*, Bunyan and Dryden; Pope and Goethe; the One of Blake, Coleridge, Wordsworth and Shelley, and the Truth of Keats; Tennyson, Emily Bronte, Emerson and Tolstoy; Hulme, Eliot, Pound, Yeats and Hesse; and Iris Murdoch and Solzhenitsyn;

- The oneness of known humankind – oneness in *The Epic of Gilgamesh*, the Egyptian *Book of the Dead*, the *Avesta*, the *Rig Veda* and *Upanishads*, the *Tao Te Ching* and the *Old Testament*; the Athenian Empire, Plato, the Roman Empire and the *New Testament*; Augustine's *De Civitate Dei* and Dante's *De Monarchia*; More's *Utopia* and Marlowe's *Tamburlaine the Great*; Donne's 'No man is an island' and Bunyan; Pope's 'stupendous whole'; Blake; Emerson and Whitman; Eliot and Hesse; and Heidegger, Eliot and Churchill;

- The universal being (or self) that opens to the Light – the *akh*, Atman and soul; Plato's soul as charioteer, Virgil's Aeneas who 'shone in the bright light', the *New Testament* and Gnostic texts; Dante, St Catherine of Siena and the Neo-Taoist *The Secret of the Golden Flower*; Ficino and Erasmus; Marvell; Pope, Johnson and Goethe; Blake, Coleridge and Wordsworth; Emerson, Dostoevsky and Tolstoy; Eliot, T.E. Lawrence and Hesse; and Heidegger;

- The promise of immortality of the universal being or spirit – the rituals of Dumuzi/Tammuz, the Egyptian *Book of the Dead*, Agni, Gilgamesh, the *Rig Veda*, *Avesta*, Brahmanism, Taoism and the Shekhinah's covenant with the Israelites; Homer's Underworld and Elysian Fields, Pindar, Plato, Virgil's Elysium and the *New Testament*; Beowulf's journey to Valhalla, 'The Dream of the Rood', Dante, Everyman's quest, and Buddhist, Hindu and Neo-Taoist texts; Ficino's letters, More and Erasmus; Donne's *Sermons* and Milton's *Paradise Lost*; Johnson and Goethe; Blake, Wordsworth and Shelley; Tennyson's *In Memoriam* and Tolstoy; Eliot, T.E. Lawrence and Hesse; and Greene and Waugh;

- An inner transformation or centre-shift from ego to universal being – Tammuz's dying and rising, the birth of the *akh* in 'Making the Transformation into a Living Soul' in the Egyptian *Book of the Dead*, 'end to all Duality' in the *Avesta*, the innermost self in the *Upanishads*, the Chinese transformation from sense-perception, the Israelite transformation from the ego to the soul in prayer; the Mycenaean mysteries at Eleusis, Plato, the Roman rites of Vesta, Ovid, the *New Testament*, St Augustine and Pope Gregory the Great; Dante and St Catherine of Siena; Ficino and Erasmus; Marvell; Pope's 'Eloisa to Abelard'; Blake, Coleridge and Wordsworth; Dostoevsky (Victorian Europe); Eliot and Hesse; and Jaspers and Pasternak; and

- The quest of the purified soul to confront death by journeying to the Underworld, and to receive the secret Light of infinite Reality – Gilgamesh's quest for immortality, the rituals of the Egyptian *Book of the Dead*, the *Avesta*'s 'place of Everlasting Light', the quest of the *rsis* (inspired poets), Arjuna, Buddha and Mahavira, the quest for the *Tao*, the quest for the Light of Yahweh in the Tabernacle; the Greek mysteries, Odysseus's visit to the Underworld, Plato's assertion that earthly life is one episode of a long journey, Aeneas's visit to the Underworld, the rites of Roman religion, and the *New Testament*; *Beowulf*, Sir Galahad's quest for the Grail, Dante and Zen; Ficino, More and Spenser's *The Fairie Queene*; Donne, Milton and Dryden; Goethe; Blake, Coleridge, Wordsworth and Shelley;

Tennyson's *Idylls of the King*, Arnold's 'The Scholar-Gipsy'; Joyce's *A Portrait of the Artist as a Young Man* and T.S. Eliot; and Durrell's *Alexandria Quartet* and Golding.

On p.52 we saw that the fundamental theme of world literature has metaphysical and social aspects. In *The Secret American Destiny* I show how another of these Universalist characteristics is reflected in the social aspect of the fundamental theme of world literature in each of the ten historical periods within the Tree of Tradition:[26]

> Alongside this traditional, metaphysical aspect of the fundamental theme of world literature from early times co-existed a social aspect: condemnation of social follies and vices in terms of an implied universal virtue. We can form a bird's-eye view of this social aspect of the fundamental theme of world literature by following another of the Universalist characteristics through the ten periods:
> * Universal virtue, a standard by which to measure human follies, vices, blindness, corruption, hypocrisy, self-love and egotism in relation to implied universal virtue (when human interaction is considered from a secular perspective, separated from its context of Reality) – the stories of Gilgamesh, Dumuzi/ Tammuz, the people in the Egyptian *Book of the Dead*, Mithras, Arjuna, Lao-Tze and the *Old Testament* prophets; Homer's criticism of Achilles, Aeschylus, Sophocles, Euripides and Menander, Plato, Plautus, Terence and Seneca, Horace and the *New Testament*; Dante, *Everyman* and *Sir Gawayne and the Grene Knight*; Donne, Milton, Corneille, Racine, Molière and Restoration comedy; Pope, Swift, Johnson, Jane Austen and Goethe; Blake, Shelley's *Prometheus Unbound* and Byron's *Don Juan*; Pushkin and English, French and Russian novelists; Ibsen, Shaw and Forster; and Greene, Waugh, Orwell and Solzhenitsyn.

I concluded:[27]

> The two aspects of the fundamental theme are in a dialectic and are present throughout the history of world literature. My study shows that the conflicting metaphysical and social aspects – the quest for Reality and immortality and the condemnation of social vices in relation to an implied virtue – each dominate some of the ten periods. All works of literature draw on one or other of these two aspects of the fundamental theme of world literature, or combine both. When the civilization is growing, the quest for Reality predominates; and when it turns secular, condemnation of follies and vices is to the fore. Literature that describes the quest is mostly found in the literature of the ancient world, the Middle Ages and the Baroque, Romantic and Modernist periods, while literature that condemns social vices is mostly found in the classical world and in the Renaissance, Neoclassical, Victorian and 20th-century periods.

Universalism seeks to combine and reconcile the metaphysical and social aspects of the fundamental theme, and I have reflected it in my own works. My literary Universalism reconciles the two traditions in what I have called my Baroque, a mixture of Classicism and Romanticism, sense and spirit.

As regards Universalism's reconciliation of the two traditions of literature, in *The Secret American Destiny* I wrote:[28]

> In literature Universalism presents condemnation of the follies and vices of humankind which can be found in the literature of the classical period within the context of the quest for the One, the literary theme of the quest for Reality that goes back to c.2600BC. The balance between condemnation of follies and vices and the quest for the One, which I document in *A New Philosophy of Literature* as a tussle for dominance through ten literary periods, is now restored through Universalism....
>
> Universalist literature appeals to the intuitive faculty and reflects the oneness of the universe, but it also appeals to the reason as it interprets intuitive experience rationally in a blend of

the intuitional and rational, Romanticism and Classicism and the opposites of sense and spirit in the Baroque Age....

The works of the Universalist man of letters reveal Being, as do my own *Collected Poems* and *Collected Stories*. They investigate the universe with precise language and catch intimations of unity, of the presence of the One, Being. They offer sudden revelations of Being and capture Being in the moment. Universalist epic relates the extremities of war and peace to notions of Heaven and Hell, as I have attempted to in my two poetic epics, *Overlord* and *Armageddon*. Universalist verse plays link order to government and the Being behind the divine right of kings, as do Shakespeare's history plays and as do the five plays in my *Collected Verse Plays*. Diaries and autobiography link the everyday to growing awareness of Being and contact with Being, as do my *Awakening to the Light* (diaries) and *My Double Life 1: This Dark Wood* and *My Double Life 2: A Rainbow over the Hills* (autobiography).

The Universalist man of letters uses a variety of forms to probe and investigate the universe.

The 12 Universalist characteristics (see pp.52–53), including the nine shown, are all found in my own literary works, and in all seven literary genres or subdivisions, which reflect the fundamental theme of world literature, as we can now see in (1)–(7) below:

How I came to the two traditions of literature in seven genres or subdivisions, and their influences
(1) Poems and epic poems

Poems
2,001 poems (1,478 in *Collected Poems*, 317 in *Classical Odes* and 206 in *Life Cycle*).
34 published volumes of poems. 4 Selected Poems (*A Metaphysical's Way of Fire, Quest for the One, Visions of England, A Baroque Vision*); two *Collected Poems* (volumes 1–30, 1994, 2006); *Classical Odes* (2006); *Life Cycle and Other New Poems* (volumes 31–34, 2016). Awaiting publication: *The Oak Tree and the Branch* (due in 2024).

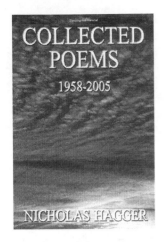

I came from a musical family in which my mother gave violin recitals in the 1930s and my father, a tenor, sang in Handel's *Messiah* at The Royal Albert Hall. They attended local musical evenings in the 1940s and 1950s. The music came out in me as musical words: writing, and eventually poetry.

At Chigwell School I was taught English parsing, grammar and Latin at the age of nine by Arnold Fellows (AF), a Victorian master of great character. He dominated our classroom and insisted on perfect spelling, punctuation and grammar and was undoubtedly an early influence. Later I read classical poetry under the Headmaster Donald Thompson, who also taught Classics, and David Horton (Homer's *Iliad* and *Odyssey*, Virgil's *Aeneid* and pastoral poetry, *Eclogues* and *Georgics* book 4, a few of Horace's odes and extracts from Ovid's *Metamorphoses*) and English poetry (from Chaucer to Shakespeare, the Metaphysicals, Milton, the Romantics and the Victorians) over the years under The Rev. George Davenport. I knew all the metres in Greek, Latin and English verse.

I knew I would be a poet in March 1957. My call to be a poet came after I had got into Oxford, when I was sitting on a garden bench in Chigwell School's Lower Field. I had been reading Donne and Coleridge, and I was reading Hopkins' 'Wreck of the *Deutschland*' in *The Faber Book of Modern Verse*, sitting in warm sunshine. I thrilled to the language and took my eye off the book and glimpsed my future and I felt a call to become a poet and reflect the unity of the universe. (Nearly 40 years later I would write my first epic poem, *Overlord*, which would be about the wreck of Deutschland, Germany, in the Second World War.)

A still stretch of the Bandusian spring at Horace's villa in Licenza where Nicholas Hagger sipped the "water of the Muses".

I left Chigwell later in March 1957 and spent three weeks in April visiting Italy and Sicily. I went to Horace's villa at Licenza in the Sabine hills, and found his "Bandusian spring" ("*fons Bandusiae*"), and cupped my hands in the limpid spring and sipped the water – and imagined I had sipped the water of the Muses' spring and had become a poet.[29]

I began writing poems in the solicitors' office I worked in for a year from the end of June 1957, before going up to Oxford. In early March 1959 I changed from Law to read English Language and Literature under the literary critic Christopher Ricks.

When I had my first tutorial with Christopher Ricks at Oxford he asked me, "What literature do you like?" I said, "Mystical literature, for example Blake and Wordsworth." He said, "I shall teach you to like social satire." He meant Dryden and Pope. Later I taught Dryden's political satire 'Absalom and Achitophel' and Pope's 'The Rape of the Lock'. In putting me in touch with the tradition and influences of Dryden and Pope Ricks was himself an influence, and later became my mentor for more than 40 years.

In June 1959 Arnold Fellows, the master who taught me grammar and Latin at Chigwell, visited Oxford, and Old Chigwellians were invited to meet him. I had just changed to English Language and Literature, and, standing by the mantelpiece in an Old Boy's room, white-haired and Victorian, he asked me what I would do. Without hesitation I said I would be a writer. He (the author of *The Wayfarer's Companion*) said without hesitation, "Whatever you write, send it to me. I may not understand it, but I will proofread it for you and make sure it's in accurate English." He died before I could take him up on his offer.

The Oxford course stopped at 1860. Being more interested in writings after then and knowing I would become a poet and writer, I attended lectures outside my course on Yeats by J.I.M. Stewart (a.k.a. the writer of crime fiction Michael Innes). I was fascinated by Yeats' involvement in the Irish Uprising of 1916, his 'Easter 1916', the execution of the Irish patriots, some of whom he knew, in Dublin's Kilmainham Gaol and his later semi-metaphysical poems such as 'The Second Coming' (1919) and 'Among School Children'. J.I.M. Stewart said at the end "If you become a writer, call one of your books 'The Chestnut Tree'." He meant, Answer Yeats' question in his poem 'Among School Children':

> O chestnut tree, great rooted blossomer,
> Are you the leaf, the blossom or the bole?
> O body swayed to music, O brightening glance,
> How can we know the dancer from the dance?

I am sorry, J.I.M. Stewart, whose lectures on Yeats were more interesting than Tolkien's on *Beowulf*, but I am calling this work 'The Tree of Tradition' rather than 'The Chestnut Tree'. However, the Tree of Tradition is a great-rooted blossomer (see the front cover), and it has roots in the infinite and a metaphysical trunk (or "bole"), and it blossoms amid the branches of its traditions into influences that leave behind the fruit of their works – and the answer to Yeats' first question is that the Tree of Tradition is the leaf, the blossom *and* the bole, but in particular the branches, which he omitted. And although J.I.M. Stewart's lectures were outside my course I needed to attend his lectures more than the lectures within my course. Yeats said, "Man can embody truth but he cannot know it" (letter to Lady Elizabeth Pelham, 4 January 1939). Like Yeats' chestnut tree, the Tree of Tradition embodies truth and, as I have just explained, its truth can also be known.

To carry Yeats' words further, to a writer who is asked "Why did you not do more to promote your own works?" I would advise a reply along these lines: "I grew as a tree, rooted myself in the infinite and produced a crop of fruit, my works, and I did not have time to do other than root myself, grow and bear fruit, and if I had done other things I would not have rooted myself and grown and there would have been no fruit."

Mystical poems. In 1962–1963 I went several times to the Dulwich Group of Poets in a room above The Crown and Greyhound pub and regularly heard poets read and recite some of their poems. My early volumes reflect the beginning of my Mystic Way, my First Mystic Life

(20 July 1964 – 8 October 1965, see p.42): *A Stone Torch-Basket, The Early Education and Making of a Mystic, The Silence,* and *The Wings and the Sword.*

Yeats in 1914, two years before the
Irish Uprising.

I went to Japan having read the poetic tradition from *Beowulf* to 1860. In Japan in 1964 I had lunch with Edmund Blunden, a First-World-War poet (author of 'Report on Experience', which begins "I have been young, and now am not too old/And I have seen the righteous forsaken"), and having been primed to do so whacked him on his back when he began to wheeze and gasp for breath. He had been gassed as a soldier in the First World War, and the gassing affected him for the rest of his life. He asked me to look for Shakespeare's last works in Stratford lofts. I arranged to meet him in The Owl (then thatched) in Lippitts Hill, High Beach when I was back in the UK on leave, which we discussed in Tokyo, but he was ill and cried off at the last minute. It was just as well as the escaped police murderer Harry Roberts stormed into the pub when we would have been there and made everyone hand over their wallets.

'The Silence' was written in Japan in abbreviated narrative in a sequence of images in the Modernist manner in 1965–1966, and I was influenced by T.S. Eliot at this time (having read him from 1957 and taught him in Japan from 1964), as his mystical thread surfaced at the end of the *Four Quartets* in 'Little Gidding': "And the fire and the rose are one." Eliot visited Little Gidding church in 1936. I visited it in 1966, and the rose is perhaps the rose-window of Little Gidding church, suggesting that there can be a mystical experience of the Fire or Light beneath the rose-window within the church.

I did not know while I was writing 'The Silence' that at the very time Eliot died in 1965 my boss in Japan, the Representative of the British Council, the philosopher E.W.F. Tomlin who would later write *T.S. Eliot: A Friendship* about the 100 letters he received from T.S. Eliot, was arranging for me to visit Eliot in London when I was next on leave. Tomlin asked me to contribute to a book he organised in Japan, *T.S. Eliot: A Tribute from Japan* (1966), and I wrote 'In Defence of the Sequence of Images'. The novelist and short-story writer Frank Tuohy, who was teaching at another university in Japan, and lived near me, read a draft of 'The Silence' and said it needed glosses, as in Coleridge's 'The Ancient Mariner', which I added. 'The Silence', then, was a narrative poem in the tradition of 'The Ancient Mariner' and its glosses.

I recall a visit to Watchet and the church ("kirk") that appears in 'The Ancient Mariner', whose narrative tradition and tradition of glosses I followed in 'The Silence'.

In March 1966 I went to China and visited Russia twice, on my way to England on leave and on my way back to Japan, at the height of the Cold War. In the UK I wrote 'Archangel' about Communism, and in 'Old Man in a Circle' (1966) I saw European civilisation as having grown old and entered a decline following the beginning of decolonisation after the Suez crisis.

I took the Old Man in a Circle from a circular representation on a medieval miniature of the signs of the Zodiac and their correspondence to the Great Year's labours, the cyclic process of living through a cycle of darkness and death, and returning as light and life (see p.65). The Spanish J.E. Cirlot in *A Dictionary of Symbols*, which contains the medieval miniature I found, wrote: "The year was usually represented by the figure of an old man in a circle." I saw the Old Man as the embodiment of the European spirit going through darkness and death, and light and rebirth; and the Great Year as the ending of the European empires and the birth of what would become the European Union.

The Old Man in a Circle within a circular representation of the signs of the Zodiac and the Great Year's labours in J.E. Cirlot's *A Dictionary of Symbols* (see p.64).

I also wrote 'Blighty', about an old lady (Britannia) in decline. I wrote a lot of poetry in Japan, then stopped and spent a year in England living in West Dulwich. I then went out to lecture in Libya. I wrote few poems and I lived through the Gaddafi Revolution of 1969. I was asked to work for British Intelligence and I lived in permanent danger, a situation that made my wife want to escape the world of spies and return to England. I underwent a Dark Night of the Soul when my marriage broke up.

Catullus from a manuscript c.1400AD, reputed to have been copied (like his poems) from a succession of manuscripts that have not survived.

Catullan poems. I entered what I call my Catullan phase. I lived on in Tripoli and then, still in great danger in London, alone, I wrote poems in a range of emotions (as did Catullus) that were wrung out of me. *The Gates of Hell* is full of short poems and sonnets that drew on many conflicting emotions and feelings within an overall narrative, amid the agony of being separated from my wife and daughter. These poems were raw. (In 1998 I visited Verona, the town where Catullus was born, and sought out the Roman bridge, the Ponte Pietra, completed c.100BC, that he would have known.)

On my way back to London after Libya I drove to Rapallo and visited Ezra Pound. I had written to him from Libya, addressing the envelope 'Ezra Pound, Rapallo'. The envelope was delivered to him, and I spent an evening with him. I raised abbreviated narrative in a sequence of images, told him I planned an epic poem, and asked if, as the author of *The Cantos* for the last 55 years (1915 to 1970), he recommended abbreviated narrative. From his answer I decided to turn away from Modernism and return to the narrative of Wordsworth and Tennyson. My turning-away from the method I had used in 'The Silence' impacted on my lyrical and other poems, and my method became increasingly classical.

In my Second Mystic Life (3 September 1971 – 28 April 1972) I experienced full illumination, and towards the end of *The Gates of Hell* my poems were filled with visions and images.

I needed to get away from going abroad to teach at overseas universities. I stopped my intelligence work after four years of being an agent, and wrote a lot of poems and I now wanted to teach poems in class. I became a no.2 in the English Department in a school in Clapham, London, and then a Head of English at a large girls' comprehensive in Wandsworth. I was able to spend a term on one set book and look at the writing in detail. I was able to read Wordsworth's *Prelude*, books 1 and 2; and Milton's *Paradise Lost*, books 1 and 2, and 9 and 10.

Metaphysical poems. Slowly I had begun to write metaphysical poems in volumes such as *The Pilgrim in the Garden* (1973–1974) and *Visions near the Gates of Paradise* (1974–1975). I kept writing poems with new powers from my Dark Night of the Spirit (29 April 1972 – 12 May 1979), and I read Raleigh, Donne and Marvell in class, all Metaphysical poets. Raleigh was the first Metaphysical poet, and I taught his 'Give me my scallop-shell of quiet'.

In 1973 I had visited the house where Marvell taught the daughter of Sir Thomas Fairfax in Nun Appleton, Yorkshire from 1650. It looked deserted. I walked in the garden to the pool and looked at the plants Marvell might have seen in 'The Garden', and walked back to the house, which had been rebuilt since Marvell was there, and through the window saw an elderly piano-tuner playing ping-ping-ping on a piano. I wrote 'In Marvell's Garden, at Nun Appleton' on 28 October 1973. I reworked the poem in *The Fire-Flower* as 'A Metaphysical in Marvell's Garden' on 4, 16–17 February 1980, during my Third Mystic Life. It includes the following stanza:

> With drowsed eyes glance at solid grass and be
> In whirlpools of energy like a sea.
> Breaths heave the light, and answering currents pour
> Through spongy stones and stars, or seaweed tree.
> Now see with eye of mind into swelled form,
> Imagine sap wash, oak wave in acorn.
> Knowers are one with known, and are soaked by tides
> That foam and billow through an ebbing lawn.

(lines 33–40)

Marvell between c.1655 and c.1660, shortly after living at Nun Appleton House to tutor Fairfax's daughter, c.1650–1652.

The title of the second poem influenced the title of my first Selected Poems, *A Metaphysical's Way of Fire* (1991).

My Third Mystic Life (13 May 1979 – 31 October 1981) expressed itself in *Lady of the Lamp* (1979), *The Fire-Flower* (1980) and *Beauty and Angelhood* (1981).

Lyrical poems. The next phase of my Dark Night of the Spirit (1 November 1981 – 7 April 1990) plunged me into ordeals, and I was now writing more and more lyrical poetry, and read Wyatt and Tennyson at school to feed into my poetry. My lyrical poetry focusing on Nature in *A Rainbow over the Spray* (1981–1985) came from my teaching of Blake's *Songs of Innocence and Experience*; Wordsworth's Nature poems; Housman's Nature poems such as 'Loveliest of Trees', beginning "Loveliest of trees, the cherry now/Is hung with bloom along the bough" (which I knew by heart soon after I read it for the first time in the "lounge" at 'Journey's End', in late 1957); Brooke's 'Grantchester'; Keats' sensuous Nature poems, including 'Ode to Autumn'; Shelley's *Adonais*; and Hardy's late poems on his first wife. Ted Hughes' poems on rivers were in exact metres and in stress metre, and although he wrote to me and I corresponded with him throughout the 1990s, I was not conscious that he was a direct influence. I was already writing my Nature poems before Hughes wrote to me in 1994.

In my Fourth Mystic Life (8 April 1990 – 6 December 1993) I wrote the Nature poems in *A Sneeze in the Universe* (1989–1992). I brought out *Selected Poems: A Metaphysical's Way of Fire* in 1991 – David Gascoyne and Kathleen Raine, two more influences, spoke at the launch (which included launching *The Fire and the Stones*).

On 3 May 1993, after walking by Pisa's River Arno to the wall behind which Shelley wrote *A Defence of Poetry* in March 1821, crossing the river and walking back along the Lung'arno Mediceo and sitting with a coffee in the open air and near a bridge, I had a vision, a revelation (which I put in my classical ode, 'After the Pisan Arno') of two completed works: *Classical Odes* and my epic poem *Overlord*. Assembling these would take the next twelve years. I had discussed *Overlord* with Ezra Pound, and completed this work in the course of the mid-1990s. It initially came out in four separate volumes. At the same time I began writing classical odes, seeing European culture as a unity, and 317 were published in

Classical Odes (2006), many of which were on visits to historical places in Europe, to which the UK had drawn close.

At the end of my Mystic Way, at the beginning of my Unitive Life (7 December 1993 to date), I wrote *Sojourns* and *Angel of Vertical Vision*, and I compiled my first *Collected Poems 1958–1993: A White Radiance* (1994).

Baroque poems. Since the early 1990s my poems have continued to be a combination of Romanticism and Classicism in the Baroque. I brought out *A Baroque Vision* (2024, delayed by lockdowns). My poems have had Universalist themes, and *A Baroque Vision* shows how my approach developed into Universalist poems in 100 poems based on 50 poetic volumes (including verse plays and masques), just as *The Essentials of Universalism* (see p.111) would show how my Universalism developed in 75 selections from 25 of my prose works. I brought out *Selected Poems: A Quest for the One* (2015) and *Selected Poems: Visions of England* (2019), 102 poems on places in England chosen by the Earl of Burford (my Literary Secretary at the beginning of the new century).

Social, satirical poems. I have already said (on p.61) that Ricks introduced me to Dryden and Pope at Oxford, and prepared the way for my satirical verse. In my social, satirical verse such as 'Zeus's Ass' (2000), 'Zeus's Emperor' (2009, 2015), *Fools' Paradise* (2020) and *Fools' Gold* (2022), I have looked back to Dryden and Pope, and also Swift, whose 'Verses on the Death of Dean Jonathan Swift' I followed in 'Verses on the Death of Mr Nicholas Hagger' (2015).

In July 2004 Ricks sent me a 1944 copy of *Horizon* that contained Eliot's essay, 'The Man of Letters and the Future of Europe' (see p.19), with a comment: "Apt to your thinking, no?" It was very apt. In this essay Eliot recommended that the man of letters should hold the leaders of Europe to account for damage caused to the cultural health of Europe. There was obvious damage they caused during the Second World War, at the end of which Berlin was in ruins. Eliot had tapped into a tradition that includes Swift's criticism of the British Lilliputian leaders in *Gulliver's Travels* and in 'A Modest Proposal' (on solving Irish poverty by a policy of eating Irish babies).

Nicholas Hagger with Christopher Ricks at Worcester College, Oxford, on 1 July 2019.

I widened Eliot's holding the leaders of Europe to account to all Western leaders, including those of America, and the damage they caused to include Brexiteers' leaving their own European civilisation (see *Fools' Paradise* and *Fools' Gold*). Eliot's 'The Man of Letters and the Future of Europe' became a tradition of holding Western leaders to account for their policies that damaged the cultural health of Europe, and also became an influence.

I have also, in my condemnation of follies and vices, looked back to Horace. I again visited Horace's Bandusian spring near his villa at Licenza in the Sabine Hills (see p.60) in September 1996 and recalled how I cupped my hands in the limpid stream in 1957, and sipped the water from what I thought of as resembling the Pierian spring of the Muses near Mount Olympus in Macedonia, the fountain of knowledge that would make me a poet, hailed by Pope in his 1711 'An Essay on Criticism': "A little learning is a dangerous thing;/Drink deep, or taste not their Pierian spring." (Not to be confused with the Castalian spring near the oracle at Delphi.) I had read bits of Horace at school and emulated his four books of odes with my four books of classical odes.

I have increasingly been influenced by Tennyson, who lived near where I live in Essex at one stage in his life, Beech Hill Park, High Beach, deep within Epping Forest. In 2008 I visited Farringford on the Isle of Wight and stayed five days in what used to be Tennyson's house. To go out involved walking through the sitting-room where Tennyson read or recited his poems to his wife in the evenings. I went to an upper room, room 17, to write. It overlooked the hollow beneath the wood that the 'I' of 'Maud' loathed. I went to the library at dusk, Tennyson's large new study (c.1861), and did half an hour's work there after supper. There was a presence in the room. I slept in his bedroom.

When I returned to Essex Tennyson came with me, and I often sense his presence in my study and see him as the editor who tells me each morning to look at a particular page number, where I always find there is an improvement to be made.

Epic poems
Overlord (books 1–2, 3–6, 7–9, 10–12, 1994–1996; and one-volume edition, 2006); *Armageddon* (2010) in 41,000/26,000 lines of blank verse

My daily diaries (begun in 1963) reveal that I had writing an epic poem on my mind from 5 May 1968 (when I considered going into Old Norse epic) to my beginning of *Overlord* on 2 June 1994. A more certain start date in my thinking may be 30 July 1968 when I was thinking in my diary about writing an epic in the tradition of Homer, Virgil and Milton. An Appendix in the one-volume *Overlord*, 'The 25-year Gestation and Birth of *Overlord*', pp.932–942, sets out the diary entries of the relevant 'thinking' passages. They are:

5 May 1968	Intention to write an Old Norse epic.
30 Jul 1968	Definition of classical epic, mention of Homer, Virgil, Milton.
13 Sep 1969	Visionary poem, after World War Two a settled way of life broke up.
20 Oct 1969	"Think about epic".
19 Feb 1970	Visit to El Alamein, thought of Montgomery's role in the Second World War (not in diary).
11 Jun 1970	Epic battle poetry, mention of Homer, Virgil, Milton.

20 Jun 1970	Reflection on all epics, mention of Homer, Virgil, reference to Milton.
16 Jul 1970	Visit to Pound in Rapallo, "I outlined my poetic epic and asked 'Why can't you compress at length?'" As a result, rejection of compression in epic.
20 Jul 1970	Mention of *Paradise Lost*.
24 Jul 1970	Mention of *The Iliad*, *The Aeneid*, and Milton.
6 Dec 1975	Decided to call my epic *Overlord*.
28 Dec 1975	"It is my destiny to write a 12-book epic about the Second World War.... I have planned the twelve books."
15 Apr 1976	Visit to D-Day beaches, Bayeux tapestry "an epic in pictures; mine to be in words".
22 Jul 1979	"*Overlord* is about the Second Coming of Christ and a united Europe."
12 Jan 1993	"My epic will be like *Paradise Lost*, with a reference to the New World Order."
27 Jan 1993	Told Ricks in Oxford of "my desire to write an epic post-Virgil-Dante-Milton".
3 May 1993	Vision in Pisa of a finished epic "as great as Homer's, Virgil's, Dante's, Milton's."
21 Jun 1993	Walk round Oxford with Ricks, agreed *Overlord* should be in blank verse.
29 May 1994	Decision to have Eisenhower as hero, rather than Montgomery.
31 May, 1 Jun 1994	With D-Day veterans in Lisieux.
2 Jun 1994	"On the way out in the coach, started writing the epic, on my knee."
21 Oct 1994	Properly started the epic, having stopped to write *The Warlords* from 1 to 31 Aug 1994.

The idea crystallised in my diary entries of 11 and 20 June 1970. That was when I decided to consult Ezra Pound (who had written, "Genius is the capacity to see ten things where the ordinary man sees one"), and I wrote to him from Libya.

The reason I visited the main Modernist Ezra Pound (who edited Eliot's 'The Waste Land', acted as Yeats' secretary and got Joyce's *Ulysses* published) on 16 July 1970 was to consult him as to whether I could use Tennysonian narrative as in *Idylls of the King* rather than the compression of abbreviated narrative as in Pound's *The Cantos* (begun in 1915 and still being written in 1970) in my coming epic poem, which would continue the tradition of poetic epic (Homer, Virgil, Dante, Milton).

I spent a long evening with Pound (from 7pm until after midnight), during which he urged me to make a start: "If you can see it you can do it. Seeing it's half the battle." I took this as his blessing that after using abbreviated narrative in 'The Silence' I should use blank verse in my coming epic poem on the last year of the Second World War, my hero, the American Eisenhower, being my Aeneas. And this decision was later confirmed during a long walk round Oxford with Christopher Ricks on 21 June 1993. As I have said, that decision prepared the way for my Neo-Baroque poetry, a combination of Classicism and Romanticism, sense and spirit, that is a Universalist reconciliation of opposites (+A + −A = 0), and influenced all the poems I would write after 1970, during the last 52 years.

Ezra Pound in 1963.

Another influence on my poetic epic tradition was the blind poet John Heath-Stubbs, who I met on 30 July 1970 and had several subsequent meetings with in 1970, after my visit to Pound. On 17 August 1970 Heath-Stubbs and I walked round the corner from where he was living in Sutherland Street, London to the Pavistock public house and discussed my visit to Pound. At our first meeting he gave me a signed copy (his name in squiggly writing because he was blind) of *Artorius* book 1, the mythological epic he had begun on King Arthur. It was in blank verse; I had told him I would be writing my epic poem. I met him again at a centenary service for T.S. Eliot in Eliot's church, St Stephen's, Gloucester Road, London, at which Sir Laurens van der Post spoke, an event which led to my visiting van der Post at his home. (Valerie Eliot, T.S. Eliot's widow, approached us outside the church as Heath-Stubbs and I were in conversation some time before the service began, and I broke off to say Hello to her.)

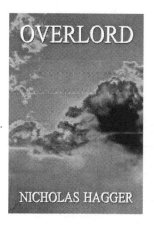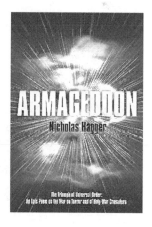

I had read Dante's *Inferno, Purgatorio* and *Paradiso*. I had read them in my bedroom in Loughton during the autumn of 1957, when I read so many classics of European and Russian literature while working as an articled clerk to a solicitor in a legal firm in London. I went to Dante's house in Florence in 1993, and stood outside its massively thick walls. In both *Overlord* and *Armageddon* (which is about the War on Terror against bin Laden following 9/11), my American heroes Eisenhower and George W. Bush both visit the Underworld as did Aeneas, and in October 1995 during my visit to Italy I made sure I went to old Baiae and visited the entrance to the Underworld where Aeneas (and Virgil) entered.

It took me 25 years to do my research and begin writing my epic *Overlord* – a little longer than Milton spent after having the idea in 1637 before he started *Paradise Lost* in 1658 (and finished it in 1663). I finally began after my vision in Pisa on 3 May 1993 when, sitting in the café across the River Arno from where Shelley lived in a riverside house and wrote *A Defence of Poetry* in 1821 (see pp.69–70, and my poems 'The Pisan Arno' and 'After the Pisan Arno'), I saw my epic poem *Overlord* as a finished book along with my *Classical Odes*, a vision requiring me to put in twelve years' work on these two texts.

Milton, engraving by William Faithorne,
1670 (three years after the first publication
of *Paradise Lost*).

I had read Milton's *Paradise Lost*, the last epic in the English language, on the tow-path by the River Seine in Paris during the Easter vacation in 1959. Christopher Ricks had asked me to read *Paradise Lost* to catch up with the others, who had read it while I was reading Law. I went to

Chalfont St Giles in December 1994. Milton's 1580 cottage was specially opened for me. The curator knew I had written about Milton and he showed me three rooms and facsimile editions of his work books. I sat in the room where blind Milton dictated 50 lines a day of *Paradise Lost* to his daughter, wife, two nephews or to amanuenses, being "milked" during the plague, from which his family were isolating. They had a cow that kept them in milk and blind Milton saw himself as being milked like a cow in his daily dictation. I thought of his daughter doubling up as a milkmaid and an amanuensis. I had followed Milton's blank verse in epic poetry, and had admired his flow.

Milton had spent 21 years after 1637, when he first had the idea of *Paradise Lost*, researching and preparing for his coming work. As we have seen, I had spent more than 25 years (from 30 July 1968 to 2 June 1994, properly starting on 21 October 1994) researching and preparing since I first had the idea.

(Left) Bust of Homer in the British Museum (Roman copy of a lost Hellenistic original from Baiae, 2nd century BC); and (centre) bust of Virgil at the entrance to his tomb, known as a *columbarium*, in Naples (right).

Ezra Pound and Christopher Ricks were technical influences on both my epic poems on war, but the main influences were Homer's *Iliad* and Virgil's *Aeneid*, books of both of which I read at school in the original Greek and Latin. I visited Troy on 15 July 1995 and sat on the wall where Helen might have sat. I climbed a mountain opposite the range of Mount Taygetos across the valley of the River Eurotas 5kms from Sparta, and saw the 'Menelaion' where Menelaos lived with Helen before Paris ran off with here, causing the Trojan War. I wrote 'At Menelaos's Palace, Sparta' and 'At Troy VI' in *Classical Odes*. I went on to Ithaca and visited Pilikata, the site of Odysseus's palace, and walked to the museum and looked down at three seas beneath the cliff (the Ionian and Tyrrhenian seas and the Gulf of Patras).

I wrote *Armageddon* between 22 May and 5 September 2008, and 21 January and 22 July 2009. It was about 9/11 and George W. Bush's attempt to hunt down bin Laden. During my research for the book I made a discovery that achieved what Bush failed to achieve.

Armageddon contains an Appendix (titled 'Bin Laden's/Al-Qaeda's Historical Attempts to Acquire Weapons of Mass Destruction and Unleash Armageddon in the United States') based on my research which sets out the 69 attempts by bin Laden to buy nuclear weapons between 1992 and 2005, including nuclear suitcase bombs to be planted in ten American cities. I put the same Appendix at the back of *The Secret American Dream* and sent it, flagged, to President Obama on 5 April 2011. On 2 May 2011 bin Laden was killed. I believe I had met bin Laden (my Turnus) on 4 November 1986 when two Afghans gatecrashed a gathering of Eastern Europeans I was hosting in the Jubilee Room at the Palace of Westminster. The Afghan I believe was bin Laden told me that he and his "brother" (half-brother) were staying at the Dorchester Hotel in London to buy anti-aircraft missiles to send into Afghanistan to pro-American fighters seeking to oust the Russians. At that time bin Laden was working for the CIA, and it is now known that bin Laden and his half-brother Salem *did* stay at the Dorchester in mid-1986, and did buy anti-aircraft missiles.

(2) Verse plays and masques; unpublished prose plays and films

Verse plays
5 verse plays: *The Warlords*, parts 1 and 2 (1995); *The Tragedy of Prince Tudor* (1999); *The Rise of Oliver Cromwell* (2000); *Ovid Banished* (2000); *Collected Verse Plays* (2007)

I began my verse plays in 1994. I made visits to France and Germany to see sites I would need for *Overlord*, and I thought in April it would help my coming poetic epic if I put the last year of the war on stage. I wrote the first line sitting on the floor of the ferry terminal in Calais on 1 August 1994. *The Warlords* became two parts, in the tradition of Marlowe's *Tamburlaine the Great* Parts 1 and 2, Shakespeare's *Henry IV* Parts 1 and 2 and Goethe's *Faust* Parts 1 and 2. I envisaged an empty stage and created the scenery in the words, as did Sophocles: an unrealistic approach to the theatre.

I had read Aeschylus's *Agamemnon*, Sophocles' *Oedipus Tyrannus* and Euripides' *Alcestis* in Greek at school under David Horton, and all of them were influences. In July 1995 I visited Athens and from the Acropolis looked down on the Theatre of Dionysus, where the works of Aeschylus, Sophocles and Euripides were first performed, and later that month I visited the Theatre and stood on the stage and realised there was no scenery. The scenery was in the words they wrote, that invited the audience to imagine their setting. Only in their writing's appeal to the imagination of the audience was there any scenery.

The Theatre of Dionysus, Athens, where Aeschylus, Sophocles and Euripides created the scenery for their first plays in their characters' words, as did Shakespeare.

On 24 January 1998 I stood on the Globe Theatre's stage and spoke with Mark Rylance, the Artistic Director of the Globe, and later arranged for him to come with his wife and have lunch at Otley Hall. In due course Rylance brought four casts to stay for three days each at Otley Hall, sleeping in sleeping-bags, and I was invited to join their rehearsals and their evening dinners. I spoke with two Globe directors and questioned them on how they went about putting on the works they were directing. Like the three Greek dramatists, Shakespeare created the scenery for the stage in his words, as can be seen from the Chorus's plea to the audience to use its imagination in the Prologue of Shakespeare's *Henry V*:

> And let us, ciphers to this great accompt,
> On your imaginary forces work.
> Suppose within the girdle of these walls
> Are now confined two mighty monarchies,
> Whose high upreared and abutting fronts
> The perilous narrow ocean parts asunder:
> Piece out our imperfections with your thoughts;
> Into a thousand parts divide one man,
> And make imaginary puissance;
> Think when we talk of horses, that you see them
> Printing their proud hoofs i' the receiving earth;
> For 'tis your thoughts that now must deck our kings.

That reinforced my resolve to set the scenes in my verse plays in the characters' spoken words – just as Aeschylus, Sophocles and Euripides did.

There were 237 characters in *The Warlords*. I was concerned to show the last year of the war on stage, not with how actors' salaries could be afforded. I followed *The Warlords* up with three plays I wrote while I owned Otley Hall and ran it as a historic house – and had four casts of the Globe to stay.

The Tragedy of Prince Tudor was based on an attempt by an *élite* of mega-rich families (which elsewhere in my works I called "the Syndicate") to take over the UK and control the Royal family. This came out of my discussions in 1998 with the Earl of Burford, my Literary Secretary, who on 26 October 1999 would leap onto the Woolsack at the House of Lords in an attempt to block the abolition of hereditary peerages, including his own.

I followed it up with *The Rise of Oliver Cromwell*, which grew out of the book I was writing at the time, *The Secret History of the West*, and letters I found that claimed that Cromwell was funded by Dutch Jews to behead Charles I.

Ovid Banished was about Ovid's banishment for life to Tomis for knowing too much during Augustus's rule.

All five plays have a common theme of world government. In *The Warlords*, first Hitler and then Stalin dream of ruling the world; Prince Tudor and his family suffer at the hands of the Syndicate's world-government-in-waiting; Cromwell is taken over by Dutch Jews, who pay for his New Model Army in return for Cromwell's beheading of Charles I and his allowing the Jews back in the UK after more than three centuries; and *Ovid Banished* shows Ovid colluding with Augustus's world government.

In the 1990s I was aware of attempts to form a world government by the Bilderberg Group, which I had found during my research into the Second World War for the historical part of *The Fire and the Stones*, and discussed with the Earl of Burford. During my research into Eisenhower I had discovered that he referred to the "military-industrial complex" (my "Syndicate"). I saw the politics of the 1990s as being affected by a coming world government that sought to take over British institutions, and the Earl of Burford, my Literary Secretary at Otley Hall from 1998 to 2000, encouraged me into taking what would later be called a pro-Brexit view of the European Union, into which the European Community developed in 1993, and more fully in 1997 when legislation passed from national Parliaments to Brussels. Some of my Classical Odes reflect a concern for what Europe was doing to the UK. My five verse plays in the 1990s came out of this Brexiteer concern.

During the next decade I saw the benefits of a world government, and in *The World Government* (2010) I set these out and wrote favourably of a world government in my subsequent poems. By the time of the 2016 referendum I was a Remainer, and significantly my verse plays stopped.

My verse plays looked back to those of Eliot and Fry, and further back to Aeschylus, Sophocles and Euripides and to Shakespeare's historical plays on the Globe stage and, as I have said, to Marlowe's historical *Tamburlaine the Great*. But I cannot locate a tradition for my theme of world government, which came out of my original research, reinforced by the Earl of Burford's corroborating research on my behalf. This, then, was a case of a new sprig on a branch of the Tree of Tradition that was not there before.

Masques

3 masques: *The Dream of Europa* (2013); *King Charles the Wise* (2018); *The Coronation of King Charles* (2021)

My three masques came out of my satirical poems 'Zeus's Ass' (2000, about Blair); and 'Zeus's Emperor' (2009, revised in 2015, about van Rompuy), in both of which I wrote about Zeus's horror at the way the world was progressing (or as he sees it, regressing).

The Dream of Europa is about Zeus's horror at Brexit.

In *King Charles the Wise* Zeus sends Minerva to Prince Charles (as he was then), and goddesses present the US, European and British perspectives on Brexit, and after his speech accepting humanitarian concerns Minerva declares that he will be known as 'King Charles the Wise'.

The Coronation of King Charles presents the Carolingian Age – I prefer this adjectival version of the Age of Carolus (the Latin for Charles) to Carolean – after King Charles has watched three historical pageant entertainments (in the tradition of those performed on street corners for the coronations of Elizabeth I and James I) in the Banqueting House, which was built on the site of the old Banqueting Hall where Ben Jonson's masques were performed.

On 8 July 1966, while on leave from Japan, I stood in the Banqueting House and followed the route Charles I walked to be beheaded on a scaffold reached by stepping through a first-floor window and noted that he stopped and looked up at the Rubens picture of his father

James I which is now on the cover of my *A Baroque Vision,* and I thought of Ben Jonson in the Banqueting Hall on this site. My masques were rooted in his tradition, which I was very aware of in 1966.

Portrait of Ben Jonson by Abraham Blyenberch, c.1617, National Portrait Gallery.

Ben Jonson inspired the tradition of masques (a genre or subdivision within literature). The bungled Brexit, which ended in an economic crisis following a fall in the UK's balance of payments and a rise in UK indebtedness, precipitated the three masques. The setting of the Coronation masque came from that visit I made to the Banqueting House.

The idea of the Coronation masque grew out of my being asked, after *King Charles the Wise* appeared, to join seven courtiers to celebrate Prince Charles's 70th birthday near Canterbury Cathedral on 17 November 2018. It was suggested that at the level of long-term planning I should write a masque for the Coronation while I was still well and could do it. I discussed the idea with the then Garter Principal King of Arms Thomas Woodcock (later Sir Thomas Woodcock) in the course of meetings at the College of Arms. During these he awarded me my own coat of arms (see p.3, 22, 181), which includes a stag (see p.22) and two oak trees, on one view perhaps the Tree of Tradition and the Tree of Imagination (or Tree of Tradition as World Tree).

Unpublished prose plays and films
After I had my full illumination in 1971 and found myself on a Mystic Way, my unpublished works all seemed juvenilia and irrelevant to my new mainstream literary effort, and work on them was discontinued. During the 1970s I was groping my way forward with experimental forays, and my unpublished works from the 1960s and 1970s were put aside as wrong turnings. However, they were within traditions, and they should be included in this study of my works in relation to their traditions to make it clear that these other traditions were available to me and influenced me.

Prose plays
3 plays: *The Molten Owl's Song* (1960–1961); *Great King Werig* (1962); *The Noddies* (1967)

The three plays were literary forays into tortured states of mind. *The Molten Owl's Song* (written when I was at Oxford) was about Caban's seeking to break away from his family. *Great King Werig* is about an industrialist who renounces capitalism. *The Noddies* is about a paranoiac gardener who feels watched by his boss's imaginary spies, who he calls "Noddies".

Films
3 films: *Tristy* (1962); *The Busman* (1968); *Gosnold's Hope* (1998)

Tristy is about a young man who loves life and wants to experience everything. He is full of hope, and is in a tradition of youthful enthusiasm and energy reflected in *Bildungsroman*s.

The Busman is about an old lady who suffers from hallucinations and believes she has an intruder.

Gosnold's Hope was written as an American film epic about the founding of America following the Jamestown voyage in 1607. It was written in conjunction with advice from Jack MacAdam of Mediterranean Film Studios between 1997 and 1998, just after I had arrived at Otley Hall, for the 400th anniversary of the founding of America in 2007. The film's hero Bartholomew Gosnold helped recruit the crews for three ships during interviews at Otley Hall, and travelled to America as Admiral Newport's no.2. He was killed by Indians inside the fort at Jamestown and was buried there.

I helped the discoverer of Jamestown and its 3 million artefacts, Bill Kelso, find his body. I sat with him by the River James and told him to locate the centre of the fort as that would be equidistant from the Indian arrows fired from the other side of the walls of the triangular fort. I said out of respect for the dead they would bury their no.2 in as safe a place as possible. After years of digging Bill Kelso located one end of the fort in the River James and found Gosnold's skeleton wrapped in an English flag about 50 feet from where we had been sitting when I started the hunt. The skeleton was removed to the archaeological laboratory at Jamestown. Kelso came to England to find Bartholomew's sister's body at Shelley church, near Hadleigh in June 2005, and take a sample of DNA that would prove the skeleton he had found in the Jamestown fort was Bartholomew's.

However, he was misadvised on the whereabouts of her grave, and the wrong body was dug up from under the ancient church floor. I was there during the digging-up of the body. Kelso was still convinced he had found Gosnold, who is now on display at Voorhees Archaearium, Jamestown.

One day a film will be made of the voyage, but when I left Otley Hall getting a film made was overtaken by the many books I was writing. The main influence was the guidebook I wrote for Otley Hall c.2001, which is still on sale there and details Bartholomew Gosnold's role in the founding of America. This has now been widely accepted.

(3) Short stories; unpublished novellas, novels and satirical works

Short stories

1,202 short stories in six volumes (1,001 in *Collected Stories*, volumes 1–5, and 201 in *The First Dazzling Chill of Winter*, volume 6): *A Spade Fresh with Mud* (1995), *A Smell of Leaves and Summer* (1995), *Wheeling Bats and a Harvest Moon* (1999), *The Warm Glow of the Monastery Courtyard* (1999), *In the Brilliant Autumn Sunshine* (2007) (all in *Collected Stories*, 2007), *The*

First Dazzling Chill of Winter (2014). *Selected Stories: Follies and Vices of the Modern Elizabethan Age* (2015). Awaiting publication: *The Still Brimming Twilit River* (due in 2024); *The Building of the Great Pyramid* (due in 2024).

I read Somerset Maugham's and Ernest Hemingway's short stories on the tube when travelling to London and back to work in a solicitors' office in 1957–1958. I met Hemingway in Malaga, Spain in 1959. I was told that he would be in the Miramar Hotel bar there on 16 August 1958 and I went there and told him I would write stories in the tradition of his Nick Adams stories. He looked at me with still eyes and nodded. (My Nick Adams has been Philip Rawley.)

He told me I must attend the *mano e mano* the next day, 17 August 1959. I queued for a ticket before the heat got up. I saw the legendary Antonio Ordonez compete against his brother-in-law Luis Dominguín, who was badly gored. Hemingway, who wrote about the fight in *Death in the Afternoon*, was waving his arms in a maroon short-sleeved shirt.

Hemingway in 1954 (five years before
Nicholas Hagger met him in 1959).

I taught some of Hemingway's short stories at the University of Libya in 1969. I followed Hemingway's sparse dialogue which revealed hidden thoughts.

I had written a few stories before, but I wrote my first very short story, 'Limey', on 15 July 1966 while on leave from Japan in the UK. Many of the early stories were told to me by Brian Buchanan ('Brewer'), my colleague at my main university in Tokyo, with whom I shared a room. He had led an eventful life. He had grown up in Ireland as Mrs. Patrick Campbell's godson and had met the Easter-1916 martyrs including John MacBride (who Yeats wrote about), and many of Ireland's greatest writers, including Joyce, Shaw and Synge. (He was dandled on Shaw's knee.) He was in Scotland when Hess, the Führer's no.2, landed, and co-interrogated him on that first night.

He had been in many extreme situations. He often invited me to stay in his Pacific seaside retreat at Nobe for the weekend during my first year in Japan (before I leased a nearby house in Nobe with a view of the Pacific), and over *saké* (rice wine) at night he would yarn about his life and I would later turn his tales into stories alongside my own. I wrote about Philip Rawley who in the course of the seven volumes grows old in the course of seven decades. I trace his development from a raw youth to a "still brimming" elderly man with much wisdom.

There is a tradition of short stories in English Literature that is mainly 20th-century, and includes H.G. Wells and Katherine Mansfield, and later Frank Tuohy, with whom I went to China and who had an accurate social-secular eye. Tuohy discussed the techniques of short-story writing with me during weekly visits for dinner, and in China. But Hemingway brought something fresh to the tradition: vividness, dialogue and significant content.

I look back to Brian Buchanan as having influenced me into becoming a short-story writer, and to Hemingway, who showed me a way. But I have managed to introduce metaphysical as well as secular content. In 2015, at the same time as I brought out *Selected Poems: A Quest for the One* (2015), I brought out *Selected Stories: Follies and Vices of the Modern Elizabethan Age* (2015), and these two volumes between them reflect the fundamental theme of world literature, a metaphysical quest for the One that alternates down the generations with a social and secular condemnation of follies and vices (see (7)).

Unpublished novellas, novels and satirical works

Novellas
3 novellas: *Juben* (1961–1962); *The Eternicide* (1963); *The Lost Englishman* (1964)

These works I have also withheld as juvenilia, literary forays into different disciplines when my mature works would present seven disciplines as wholes. They were written from my rational, social ego rather than my deeper self and were overtaken by my centre-shift and illumination. I took the view that they should be held back until the development I was undergoing was completed, which turned out to be my progress towards Universalism. They were explorations of genres and traditions on my way to Universalism, and may one day have interest as early gropings. As with my unpublished plays and films, when I dip into them I am struck by how well they read and how they hold my attention.

The three novellas were looking for signs of a metaphysical Reality in the materialistic secular world: Juben in Iraq (a literary foray into the archaeology of Iraq's ancient civilisations); Dr Vassily Zabov in London (a literary foray into science's denial of survival after death as a scientist uses the then new science of EEGs to prove that there is no soul within brain function and that death is the end, and conducts an experiment on the living brain of a homeless tramp which leads him to question his materialism – Zabov weirdly lives in London's Cecil Court, where my future publisher would be based); and *The Lost Englishman*, rewritten in two variations as *The Confessions of a Rationalist* and *The Tree of Knowledge* (a literary foray into a disappearance to search for metaphysical truth). All of these three works were in the shortened novella tradition of Camus' length, and were still not in their final state when I had my illumination in 1971, and after then seemed irrelevant to my main theme and work on them was discontinued.

These works show the tension within me between secular/materialistic and metaphysical perspectives with heroes who are floundering. I read many European works in 1957–1958, including the

18th-century *Bildungsromans Adolphe* by Constant, and *The Wayward Head and the Heart* by Crébillon fils, and the novellas are all in the *Bildungsroman* tradition, with a hero (or rather anti-hero) seeking truth and being defeated.

Novels

4 novels: *Mandalas* (1962–1963); *The Age of Cartoon* (1968); *Chains* (1970–1971); *The Desert Rose* (1977)

The four novels are about the pressures of the outside world on men who are seeking Reality.

In *Mandalas* Dr Truffer contemplates before his mandalas, tapestries from Tibet of a courtyard and a central One (a literary foray into Eastern religion), and ends up drowning himself in a Forest pond.

In *The Age of Cartoon* George Thompson is a youthful revolutionary who wants to overthrow British society in the 1960s (a literary foray into contemporary British politics and industrial relations).

In *Chains* the hero's life falls apart in Libya (a literary foray into the international politics of the Libyan Revolution).

In *The Desert Rose* the hero, called West, takes part in Western espionage in Libya (a literary foray into espionage).

These four novels, like the three novellas, were explorations of some of the seven disciplines I would later explore.

Satirical works

4 fictional satirical works: *The Fountain* (1974); *The Garden* (1974); *The School* (1974); *High Hopes* (1977)

The four satirical prose works explore satirical themes.

In *The Fountain* people shrink, and size is an indication of stature. I was clearly influenced by Swift's *Gulliver's Travels* and this work anticipates my satirical poems involving Zeus.

In *The Garden* weeds are given the same rights to grow as flowers, a satire on educational mixed ability.

The School satirises unexpected freedom given to the pupils, which predictably results in deteriorating discipline.

High Hopes satirises the rugged educational attitude and social idealism of the 1970s. It is about a teacher who runs a small property business from his school and inadvertently sells the school to some Arabs, with disastrous results.

All these four works reflect the influence of Swift, and gave me a way of looking that led to 'Zeus's Ass', 'Zeus's Emperor', *Fools' Paradise* and *Fools' Gold*.

(4) Diaries
Awakening to the Light, Diaries 1958–1967 (1994)

David Gascoyne showing Nicholas Hagger a poem
in April 1991.

Diary-writing had been a tradition since Pepys' *The Diary of Samuel Pepys* and Franz Kafka's *Diaries 1910–1923*. Also David Gascoyne's *Collected Journals, 1936–42*, which were assembled by Gascoyne and Kathleen Raine, who both spoke at my first launch in 1991. I was aware of David Gascoyne's Journal 1937–1939, written under the shadow of the looming Second World War, when I had dinner with both of them on 22 April 1991. Gascoyne sat next to me and asked me many questions about my metaphysical approach to literature.

I had kept a daily diary since 1963, and kept it throughout my time in Japan and beyond, and as during that time I underwent my centre-shift and had my first experience of the Light I released key entries from 1958 to 1967 that showed my awakening to the Light. I have continued to keep a diary since 1967 to the present, but it is for others to bring out key entries in more volumes in the future. I have been asked several times when volume 2 of my *Diaries* will appear. Bringing out further volumes is an ongoing project. At 83 now I have little time to do this, and it would be wrong to prioritise this over my current contracted works. But if someone would like to raise this as a project, I could oversee a plan for bringing out further volumes.

(5) Autobiographies and travelogues
A Mystic Way (1994); *My Double Life 1: This Dark Wood* (2015); *My Double Life 2: A Rainbow over the Hills* (2015); *The Promised Land* (2023)

Autobiographies
Autobiographical writing has been a tradition since St Augustine's *Confessions*, 397–400AD, and in Europe since Rousseau's *The Confessions* (books I–VI, 1782; books VII–XII, 1789). I read Kierkegaard's *Journals* (1834–1854), and T.E. Lawrence's autobiographical *The Seven Pillars of Wisdom*, which I found through Colin Wilson (see p.121). Poets tend to write autobiographies, and I read Yeats' *Autobiographies*.

My 29-year-long Mystic Way ended on 7 December 1993, and *A Mystic Way* (1994) enabled me to see its impact on my life and the development of my Universalism. In 2015 I updated it and left bits out to reveal the pattern of my life in 30 episodes in *My Double Life 1: This Dark Wood* and *My Double Life 2: A Rainbow over the Hills*. I do not think I was influenced into writing my first autobiography by Gascoyne and Kathleen Raine, both writers of autobiographical works. It came naturally as I sought to find the beginnings of Universalism in my life. I was, however, aware of the tradition of autobiographies that preceded me, and the need to be balanced, factual and objective where possible.

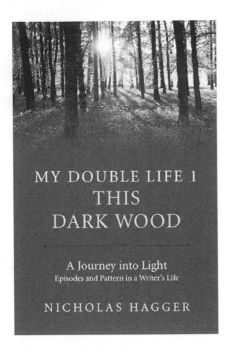
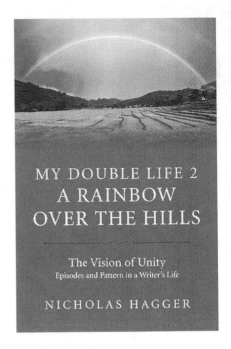

Travelogues
The Last Tourist in Iran (2008); *The Libyan Revolution* (2009)

The tradition of writing about one's travels goes back to the ancient world, and at least to Pausanias (2nd century AD). As the European nation-states expanded there was travel-writing in the 16th–18th centuries. T.E. Lawrence's travels in Arabia were widely known after the First World War, and I taught his *Seven Pillars of Wisdom* to postgraduates in Japan (see p.121), which must have influenced me.

Iran was reflected in Robert Byron's *The Road to Oxiana* (1937, written 1933–1934). My work *The Last Tourist in Iran* is subtitled *From Persepolis to Nuclear Natanz*, and covers both ancient Persia and modern Iran.

The Libyan Revolution covers Gaddafi's Revolution, of which I was an eyewitness, in 1969 and subsequent events during the next 40 years. Immediately before Gaddafi's *coup* I was an eyewitness of a *coup* planned by Libyan ministers for 5 September 1969, which was overtaken by Gaddafi's *coup* on 1 September 1969.

The ministers' *coup* leaders said they would insist that I would be made British Ambassador, and that I would be put in charge of all Libyan oil and would deal with all wanting to buy Libyan oil fields. They urged me to go to London and interview the Libyan Ambassador to the UK, Dr Omar Muntasser, who they wanted to become the President of Libya after their *coup*. I duly did this. I interviewed Dr Muntasser and got comments from the British Foreign Office via the Minister of State Goronwy Roberts. I wrote an article which appeared in the now defunct English-language Libyan newspaper *The Daily News*, titled 'Libyan-British Relations', on 24 August 1969. My article was translated into Arabic and appeared in the Libyan press. I was later informed that Gaddafi read my article and immediately organised his *coup* for 1 September 1969. When I later informed Asa Briggs of this, he said this was very important as it gave an entirely new perspective on the Libyan Revolution, and I *must* put it in a book on Libya.

(6) Letters and essays
Selected Letters (2021); *Selected Prefaces* (2022)

Letters

The tradition of letters existed in ancient India, Egypt (papyri) and Sumer, and in Rome, Greece and China. The first handwritten letter

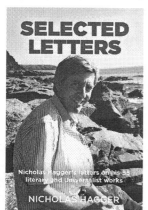

seems to have been sent by Queen Atossa of Persia, c.500BC. In Rome 900 letters by Cicero have survived, and Pliny the Younger wrote 247 letters and sent letters about the eruption at Pompeii, which killed his uncle Pliny the Elder. Alexander Pope collected and edited his letters, and my *Selected Letters* is in the epistolary tradition of Pope. The letters of Keats, Pound, Yeats and T.E. Lawrence had all had an impact on me.

In my *Selected Letters*, letters were only included if they refer to one or more of my works, which are listed at the end of each letter. All my works are mentioned, some many times, and the idea was that my *Selected Letters* would throw light on my works.

Essays

'In Defence of the Sequence of Images' in *T.S. Eliot: A Tribute from Japan* (1966); *Collected Prefaces* (2022); and 'A Spiritual Awakening and Turning-Point in 1965' in *Spiritual Awakenings*, ed. by Marjorie Woollacott and David Lorimer, AAPS Press (2022)

'In Defence of the Sequence of Images' is on abbreviated narrative in a sequence of images, the Modernist method I used in 'The Silence' (January 1965 – June 1966), which Eliot and Pound also used.

My *Collected Prefaces* draw together my first 55 Prefaces as essays so the development of my Universalist thinking can be clearly seen. In 1991 I revived the Preface in the tradition of Wordsworth's editions (and versions) of his 'Preface to *Lyrical Ballads*' (1798, 1800 and 1802 editions). I wrote version 5 of the Preface to *Selected Poems: A Metaphysical's Way of Fire* entitled 'Preface on the New Baroque Consciousness and the Redefinition of Poetry as Classical Baroque', and in all my 60 books I have written a Preface. In a letter to Tony Little, later Headmaster of Eton, of 3 May 1991, sending him a copy of *Selected Poems: A Metaphysical's Way of Fire* for his school library, I said I had revived the Preface, which has "fallen into disuse since Wordsworth and Shelley". Wordsworth and Shelley were both influences on my following the tradition of writing a Preface (sometimes called a Prologue) to all my works. Collecting all the Prefaces offers an opportunity to see the development of my thinking in my 60 works.

In July 2022 I gave a PowerPoint presentation on Zoom to India, and one of the audience, who was close to the Indian government, said he was then reading my *Collected Prefaces* and it was an excellent idea to collect them as the essays enabled him to track the development of my thinking on Universalism within one book.

'A Spiritual Awakening and Turning-Point in 1965' focuses on the centre-shift and first experience of the mystic Light I experienced in Japan in 1965, and its influence on all my works.

(7) The fundamental theme of world literature

A New Philosophy of Literature: The Fundamental Theme and Unity of World Literature (2012); *Selected Poems: Quest for the One* (2015); *Selected Stories: Follies and Vices of the Modern Elizabethan Age* (2015)

A NEW PHILOSOPHY OF LITERATURE

THE FUNDAMENTAL THEME AND UNITY OF WORLD LITERATURE

The Vision of the Infinite and the Universalist Literary Tradition

NICHOLAS HAGGER

Universalism sees world literature as a whole, and in *A New Philosophy of Literature* I examined all literature during the last 5,000 years and concluded that the fundamental theme of world literature is a quest for the One (which began with *The Epic of Gilgamesh* from c.2100BC and continued to the Romantics, Eliot and my metaphysical works); and also a condemnation of the social follies and vices of humankind (which began with Horace and continued to the Augustans, Dryden and Pope and my social satirical works).

In *The Secret American Destiny* I summarise the quest for the One in a passage I have already quoted (see p.56):[30]

> The quest of the purified soul to confront death by journeying to the Underworld, and to receive the secret Light of infinite Reality – Gilgamesh's quest for immortality, the rituals of the Egyptian *Book of the Dead*, the *Avesta*'s 'place of Everlasting Light', the quest of the *rsis* (inspired poets), Arjuna, Buddha and Mahavira, the quest for the *Tao*, the quest for the Light of Yahweh in the Tabernacle; the Greek mysteries, Odysseus's visit to the Underworld, Plato's assertion that earthly life is one episode of a long journey, Aeneas's visit to the Underworld, the rites of Roman religion, and the *New Testament*; *Beowulf*, Sir Galahad's quest for the Grail, Dante and Zen; Ficino, More and Spenser's *The Fairie Queene*; Donne, Milton and Dryden; Goethe; Blake,

Coleridge, Wordsworth and Shelley; Tennyson's *Idylls of the King*, Arnold's 'The Scholar-Gipsy'; Joyce's *A Portrait of the Artist as a Young Man* and T.S. Eliot; and Durrell's *Alexandria Quartet* and Golding.

I also summarised condemnation of the follies and vices of humankind in a passage I have already quoted (see p.57):[31]

Universal virtue, a standard by which to measure human follies, vices, blindness, corruption, hypocrisy, self-love and egotism in relation to implied universal virtue (when human interaction is considered from a secular perspective, separated from its context of Reality) – the stories of Gilgamesh, Dumuzi/Tammuz, the people in the Egyptian *Book of the Dead*, Mithras, Arjuna, Lao-Tze and the *Old Testament* prophets; Homer's criticism of Achilles, Aeschylus, Sophocles, Euripides and Menander, Plato, Plautus, Terence and Seneca, Horace and the *New Testament*; Dante, *Everyman* and *Sir Gawayne and the Grene Knight*; Donne, Milton, Corneille, Racine, Molière and Restoration comedy; Pope, Swift, Johnson, Jane Austen and Goethe; Blake, Shelley's *Prometheus Unbound* and Byron's *Don Juan*; Pushkin and English, French and Russian novelists; Ibsen, Shaw and Forster; and Greene, Waugh, Orwell and Solzhenitsyn.

These two aspects of the fundamental theme are in a dialectic, and one of the two is dominant in every generation. Very often one is dominant in a generation and gives way to the other in the next generation or two, and then returns to dominance in the following generation or two, and then gives way in the following generation. Thus Augustan poetry gave way to Romantic poetry and was succeeded by Victorian social poetry, which was later succeeded by Modernism, whose main theme was the quest rather than follies and vices (see below).

In *The Secret American Destiny* I wrote of my own works and my consistency of outlook since 1963:[32]

My study shows that the conflicting metaphysical and social aspects – the quest for Reality and immortality and the condemnation of social vices in relation to an implied virtue – each dominate some of the ten periods. All works of literature draw on one or other of these two aspects of the fundamental theme of world literature, or combine both. When the civilization is growing, the quest for Reality predominates; and when it turns secular, condemnation of follies and vices is to the fore. Literature that describes the quest is mostly found in the literature of the ancient world, the Middle Ages and the Baroque, Romantic and Modernist periods, while literature that condemns social vices is mostly found in the classical world and in the Renaissance, Neoclassical, Victorian and 20th-century periods. We shall see that Universalism seeks to combine and reconcile these two aspects. I reflect the metaphysical and social aspects of the fundamental theme in my own works. I have described my earliest use of this approach:

> I was asked to write an article on contemporary English literature for the Japanese magazine *The Rising Generation* (*Eigo Seinin*). In the coming weeks I wrote 'The Contemporary Literary Scene in England: The Missing Dimension', which eventually appeared in the July 1964 issue. I distinguished the many writers who had a social and secular vision (such as the Angry Young Men) from the few who had a metaphysical perspective (such as Eliot). From the outset in December 1963 I was aware of the conflict between sceptical and metaphysical writers that I would later reflect in *A New Philosophy of Literature*.[33]

The 'missing dimension' was the metaphysical aspect. In 1991 my *Selected Poems: A Metaphysical's Way of Fire* divided my poems into two Parts:

> I had the idea for splitting the *Selected Poems* into social and metaphysical poems and wrote: 'Does the social/metaphysical split help the Baroque idea or hinder it? The metaphysical and the social, they are together, not

in opposition.' I implemented this idea: Part One of my *Selected Poems* had 'Social World' in its title, and Part Two had 'Metaphysical World'. And the contradiction between the social and metaphysical can be found in the theme of *A New Philosophy of Literature*.[34]

In 2015 I presented my poems and stories in relation to these two aspects. In my *Selected Poems: Quest for the One*, Part One is entitled 'Quest for the One' and Part Two 'Follies and Vices' – and 220 vices are listed in the Preface.[35] And in my *Selected Stories: Follies and Vices of the Modern Elizabethan Age*, Part One is entitled 'Follies and Vices' and Part Two 'Quest for the One' – and 150 vices are listed in the Preface. It can be seen that there has been a consistency of outlook in my works stretching from 1963 to 2015.

As with mysticism, the traditional literary quest for the One – for metaphysical Reality, the infinite and the Light – has dwindled, and in the 20th century only a few poets have continued it. One of them was T.S. Eliot, whose last line of 'Little Gidding' is 'And the fire and the rose are one.' [See p.64 on the rose-window at Little Gidding.] Frank Warnke's *European Metaphysical Poetry* stated the European metaphysical tradition in poetry. In contrast, the alternative condemnation of social follies and vices is relatively widespread and has expressed itself in modern satire. Many practising poets have an exclusively social-secular perspective, and the social aspect of the fundamental theme of world literature currently coexists with its traditional metaphysical aspect.

The tradition of seeing world literature as a whole is a recent one. So far as I am aware it can be traced to T.S. Eliot's essay 'Tradition and the Individual Talent' (1919), in which Eliot urged poets to cultivate a historical sense and feeling for "the whole of the literature of Europe from Homer", and to be aware of "the mind of Europe" as "no poet... has his complete meaning alone".

I have followed Eliot in *The Tree of Tradition* but have widened the Tree of Tradition to the World Tree of all civilisations, and have carried the idea of tradition beyond our civilisation, the European civilisation as

Eliot agrees, to the whole world. My study is the first truly Universalist study of literature, and so I have extended the tradition in *A New Philosophy of Literature*. My main influence in doing this was Eliot, who stopped at seeing the whole of European literature from Homer.

Literature's traditions and influences

Literature's 46 traditions on the Tree of Tradition that followed my Mystic Way and influenced me include:

1. the tradition of questing for metaphysical Reality in literature;
2. the tradition of condemning the social follies and vices of humankind, social satires, in literature;
3. the tradition of a man of letters in several disciplines like Swift and T.S. Eliot holding European and Western leaders to account for the damage of their policies to the cultural health of Europe and the West (in accordance with T.S. Eliot's 'The Man of Letters and the Future of Europe');
4. the tradition of mystical poems (in my First Mystic Life);
5. the tradition of social poems;
6. the tradition of narrative poems, some with glosses;
7. the tradition of Modernist poems;
8. the tradition of poems on decline;
9. the tradition of Catullan poems (range of emotions in my Dark Night of the Soul);
10. the tradition of poems on illumination and visions in my Second Mystic Life;
11. the tradition of metaphysical poems (quest for the One in my Dark Night of the Spirit);
12. the tradition of lyrical poems (in my Third Mystic Life);
13. the tradition of Nature poems (during my Dark Night of the Spirit's ordeals, and in my Fourth Mystic Life);
14. the tradition of Baroque poems (blend of Romantic and Classical in my Unitive Life);
15. the tradition of epic poems (in my Unitive Life);
16. the tradition of writing in trimeters, tetrameters and pentameters;

17. the tradition of writing alternately-rhymed lines in trimeters;
18. the tradition of writing in blank verse;
19. the tradition of rhymed stanzas of 4, 8 or 10 lines;
20. the tradition of writing alternately-rhymed lines in 8-line stanzas;
21. the tradition of writing rhymed sonnets from Wyatt to Wordsworth and beyond;
22. the tradition of writing classical odes (from Horace to Keats and beyond);
23. the tradition of blank verse in epic poetry;
24. the tradition of narrating warfare in epic poetry;
25. the tradition of questing for metaphysical Reality, including visiting Hell/the Underworld and Heaven in epic poetry;
26. the tradition of unrealistic verse drama on a stage without scenery;
27. the tradition of scenery in verse drama;
28. the tradition of masques ending in revels;
29. the tradition of paranoia in plays;
30. the tradition of crisis and choice in films;
31. the tradition of epic founding a new civilisation;
32. the tradition of questing for metaphysical Reality in short stories;
33. the tradition of condemning follies and vices in short stories;
34. the tradition of questing for metaphysical Reality in novellas;
35. the tradition of questing for proof of atheism in novellas;
36. the tradition of forays into disciplines in novels;
37. the tradition of satirical works in prose;
38. the tradition of literary diaries;
39. the tradition of autobiographies about a quest for metaphysical Reality;
40. the tradition of writing travelogues about remote places;
41. the tradition of writing letters about literary works;
42. the tradition of essay-writing;
43. the tradition of writing Prefaces to literary and thinking works;
44. the tradition of one fundamental theme of world literature;

45. the tradition of questing for the One in world literature; and

46. the tradition of condemning follies and vices in world literature.

Literature's 49 forebears and influences on me (in alphabetical order) were:

1. Aeschylus
2. Blake
3. Blunden
4. Brooke
5. Buchanan
6. Camus
7. Catullus
8. Chaucer
9. Clare
10. Coleridge
11. Dante
12. Davenport
13. Donne
14. Dryden
15. Durrell
16. Eliot, T.S.
17. Euripides
18. Gascoyne
19. Hardy
20. Heath-Stubbs
21. Hemingway
22. Homer
23. Horace
24. Hughes
25. Jonson
26. Keats
27. Lawrence, T.E.
28. Marlowe
29. Marvell

30. Milton
31. Nishiwaki
32. Ovid
33. Pope
34. Pound
35. Raine, Kathleen
36. Raleigh
37. Ricks
38. Shakespeare
39. Shelley
40. Sophocles
41. Swift
42. Tennyson
43. Thompson
44. Tuohy
45. Virgil
46. Wilson, Colin
47. Wordsworth
48. Wyatt
49. Yeats

3. Philosophy and the sciences

The Universe and the Light (1993); *The One and the Many* (1999); *The New Philosophy of Universalism* (2009); *The Algorithm of Creation* (2023); *The Essentials of Universalism* (2024)

Traditional-metaphysical and social-secular traditions of philosophy and the sciences, and their Universalist reconciliation

In philosophy and the sciences there has been a metaphysical tradition and a social empirical tradition. In *The Secret American Destiny* I wrote:[36]

For 2,700 years philosophy and the sciences have had two conflicting approaches.

In *The New Philosophy of Universalism: The Infinite and the Law of Order* I showed[37] that ever since the pre-Socratic Greek philosophers of the 6th and 5th century BC there has been a tradition describing the inner quest for metaphysical Reality. Anaximander of Miletus wrote of 'the eternal, infinite boundless' (*to apeiron*). Xenophanes and Parmenides wrote of space being a plenum, a fullness, and of the One, which Xenophanes called god (or God). Anaximenes wrote of *aither* (ether) and Heraclitus of a moving 'ever-living Fire'. To the Greeks, the *kosmos* was an 'ordered whole', and the universe was ordered and unified.

The early religions spoke of an ordered universe. The Indo-European Kurgan shamanism saw the Underworld, Earth and Sky united in the World Tree, and the early Indian *rta*, or harmony in Nature, reflected metaphysical harmony. The *Upanishads* wrote of supreme good as being One. Zoroastrianism sought to 'gain the reign of the One'. The Chinese *Tao* was like an ocean, a sea of moving energy 'infinite and boundless'.

Plato carried on the metaphysical tradition of a hidden Reality. It was continued in Plotinus's One, Augustine's 'Intelligible Light' and Grosseteste's metaphysical 'Uncreated Light'. In the 15th century Christian philosophers such as Ficino turned to Neoplatonism. Rationalism took over the metaphysical tradition....

Alongside this quest for metaphysical Reality co-existed from early times a social, empirical view of reality, a scientific tradition which was begun by Aristotle. His *Metaphysics* was in three parts: ontology (the study of Being and existence), natural theology (the study of the prime mover, his equivalent of God, the existence of the divine) and universal science (the study of first principles and laws). He laid the groundwork for science, 'which studies Being'.[38]

His early students spoke of metaphysics as '*ta meta ta phusika*', 'what comes after physics'. Originally metaphysics was on an equal footing with physics and came after it chronologically in Aristotle's works. The Atomism of Democritus and Lucretius developed scientific awareness. Aristotelianism was taken up by Aquinas and triumphed over Platonism in the 13th century. After 1500 Renaissance Humanists saw the universe as pluralistic, mechanistic and ruled by mathematical laws and subject to physical causes, not ruled by God and subject to divine interventions; and philosophy fragmented. Humanism and Empiricism took up the scientific tradition. John Locke, George Berkeley and David Hume turned away from metaphysics (in its sense of 'the study of Being') and led to Utilitarianism and Pragmatism, logical positivism, linguistic analysis and the anti-metaphysical utterances of the Vienna Circle.

In our time the two conflicting approaches have expressed themselves in philosophy as: intuitionism versus logical and linguistic analysis....

Scientists' theories have impressively been confirmed by experiments; and reductionism, which sees the universe in purely physical and materialistic terms, does not merely co-exist with the tradition of metaphysical Reality, but now claims to have superseded it. Empirical science has risen high and there are claims that it is on the verge of a Materialistic Theory of Everything, although more sober scientists who have worked on the Standard Model that unites forces and particles deny that this is near. Contemporary science is dismissive of the traditional metaphysical outlook, and has led to the views of the British academic I described at the end of the Prologue, who would not look beyond materialist evidence and regarded a whole view of the universe as ambitious.

In our time the two conflicting approaches have expressed themselves in the sciences as holism versus reductionism.

As regards Universalism's reconciliation of the two traditions of philosophy and the sciences, in *The Secret American Destiny* I wrote:[39]

In philosophy Universalism presents empiricism within the context of evidenced and ordering metaphysical Reality. On the empirical side Universalism reunifies linguistic and phenomenological philosophies.... On the metaphysical side Universalism reunifies rational and intuitional metaphysics....

Philosophical Universalism balances trust in the reason – with its emphasis on the finite universe, a view of Nature as order, clarity, balance, restraint, sense of duty, a social view of humans via the rational, social ego – and trust in the intuition and the imagination: awareness of the infinite behind the finite, revolt against reason, the philosophical tradition, a view of Nature as organic dynamic process and a view of humans as individuals. In bringing together the conflicting traditions of reason and intuition Universalism brings together the objective and the subjective empirical/scientific and the metaphysical, Classicism and Romanticism. Universalism sees the rational within the context of the intuitional. They complement each other for they describe the whole from different parts of the self, one emphasizing the finite universe, the other the manifesting infinite in accordance with $+A + -A = 0$....

In this reunification intuition is fundamental and reason works in the service of intuition. Intuition sees but does not know how to say what it sees. Reason says but is limited in what it says, and is reinforced by the perception's intuition.

How I came to the two traditions of philosophy and the sciences, and their influences

I read books of Plato's *Republic* in Greek for exams at school under Donald Thompson and David Horton, and knew about his world of Forms, or Ideas, at an early age. I read Socrates' question-and-answer technique in some of Plato's dialogues, and in his *Symposium* (*Banquet*) under Donald Thompson.

Socrates' approach to the universe was an early influence on me. I visited the *agora* in Athens in July 1995 and spent time in the prison next to the court-house where Socrates (see pp.106 and 136–137) is thought to have died by drinking hemlock after being sentenced to death. It is open to the air without a roof, not the large prison with barred doors officially described as 'Socrates' prison' visible on Philopappou Hill from the path to the Acropolis. The prison in the *agora* now has low internal walls. The two rooms to the right of the entrance conform to Plato's description in *Phaedo* of Socrates' quarters in the State prison.

A gutter I recall standing by formed Socrates' urinal, and poison has been found in the extreme right-hand room, the room where Socrates allegedly lay on the prison bed to drink poison. Like Raleigh 2,000 years later (see pp.120–121) Socrates occupied two rooms, and I wrote in my 'In Plato's Athens and Eleusis: The Mysteries of Death', in *Classical Odes* (poems about treasured places in the European and North-American civilisations – the West):

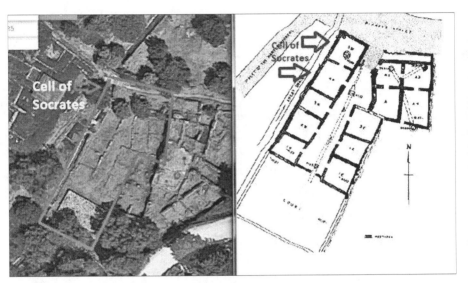

Enclosure in the south-west corner of the agora containing Socrates' prison on (above) map.

The two rooms of Socrates' prison with (left) the room where Socrates drank hemlock to the right between the two walls; and (right) the same room with Nicholas Hagger standing in 1995 where Socrates drank hemlock.

I enter the *agora*, and walk down
The hot Panathenaic Way and view
Ruins and find the law-court (*helaia*),
Simon the Cobbler's house Socrates knew
And the stones thought to be the state prison,
And stand in Socrates's two-room suite,
Now ankle-high, where, walled, in 399
Socrates spent his last month in great heat.

I look at the north-western room. A large
Water-jar and basin set in the floor   10
Were found here. This was the bathhouse where calm
Socrates took his last bath just before
Drinking poison hemlock, perhaps from one
Of thirteen terracotta jars, their lees
Dried now, used for drugs, found in the cistern
With a marble statue: of Socrates.

I stand on the nearby bridge by the drain
Into which bathwater flowed, see the two
Low-walled rooms to the right of the entrance
Abut the long square stone drain. I go through   20
The bathhouse to the largest cell next door
Where prison cups were found, stand on the ground
Where Socrates drank hemlock as Plato's
Phaedo witnessed, his pupils gathered round.

I read Aristotle's scientific approach in Greek, and the transition of medieval scholastic, metaphysical philosophy into Descartes' Rationalism. Via Colin Wilson's introduction I read A.N. Whitehead and the small group of philosophers – that included Bergson, T.E. Hulme, Husserl, William James – who offered a Vitalist alternative to the materialism and linguistic analysis of the anti-metaphysical philosophers of the Vienna Circle. I read Whitehead's *Process and Reality*, his process metaphysical philosophy reconciling intuitions into a holistic scheme, and Whitehead was a philosopher I looked up to.

At Oxford, in my third year, in 1960–1961 I had permanently by my bed *Great Philosophers of the East* and *Great Philosophers of the West* by the metaphysical philosopher E.W.F. Tomlin, which I read bits of every night, not knowing that in 1963 he would be my boss in Japan. He had me to lunch at his large house the day after I arrived in Tokyo, and it was a treat to discuss Kierkegaard and metaphysical Reality with him. There were perhaps a dozen others round the long table, but all stopped talking while we had our philosophical discussion. I was then 24. (Later, when I had a short spell in publishing in the 1980s I brought out Tomlin's two 'Great Philosophers' works in one volume as *Philosophers of East and West*.)

I had been very interested in Existentialist philosophy. I read H.J. Blackham's *Six Existentialist Thinkers* at Oxford – it too was by my bed for a long while – and I was delighted when Blackham came and gave an outside lecture in the Provost's Courtyard at my college, Worcester College, in the summer of 1960, before rows of chairs on the uneven flagstones, and I was able to go up afterwards and have a long discussion with him about the Existentialists, and by arrangement with him wrote to him. My visits to Colin Wilson in 1960 and 1961, before and after my talk with Blackham, further cemented my interest in Existentialism.

When I was in Paris in 1959, going there to read Milton's *Paradise Lost* by the Seine, I had called on Sartre. I went up the stairs to his apartment on the first floor and he came to the door, and after a few words went back inside. I believe I disturbed him while he was working, but it was important that I should have made eye contact with the man whose books preached freedom of choice, the choice of the rational, social ego. Before my centre-shift freedom of choice was important to me, and I used to comment on my Existentialist free choices that I believed were shaping my destiny. I called my hero of 'The Silence' Freeman because of the free choices of his destiny (as I saw it in those pre-Providential days) that derived from Sartre. And I also, via Colin Wilson, read all Camus' novellas, and relished his philosophy of the absurd.

After my centre-shift and full illumination, Sartre and Camus fell away, they were no longer a way forward. They had not been along the Mystic Way and dwelt on the workings of Providence. Later on I saw them as not having even begun the experience that was the desirable way forward. Sartre came to Japan in 1966 and spoke to a crowded hall at my second university. I found him obsessed with Marxism. He seemed to see free choice as supporting Communism and opposing the West.

In the early 1990s I met some key scientists, starting with David Bohm, who had worked with Einstein and written *Wholeness and the Implicate Order*. He had me to Birkbeck, University of London, a research university where he taught, on 27 March 1992 and gave me 40 minutes to discuss Einstein's universe, its origin in the Big Bang and how he saw the emergence of the universe in relation to the quantum vacuum. I had further dealings with him and when he fell ill with another heart attack in later 1992 his wife was in touch with me. I rang him in September 1992 and talked with him for 45 minutes, and at the end of October was sad to hear that he had died very shortly after writing a favourable comment for the back cover of my book *The Universe and the Light*.

I had been invited to speak for the whole of a Friday evening at a conference in Winchester on 'The Nature of Light' on 10 April 1992, and the next morning had breakfast with John Barrow, author of *Theories of Everything*, which I had read. I asked him over breakfast, "Where do love and order come into your mathematics? Do love and harmony feature in your view of a Theory of Everything?" He said, "No, I stay within my subject, cosmology." I made the point to him that a Theory of Everything could not be confined to cosmology but must include *all* experience of the universe, including the metaphysical Reality as well as a materialistic, secular, scientific view of the universe.

I had been writing *The Universe and the Light* since 31 December 1991 and I finished it on 9 September 1992. On 23 April 1992 cosmic microwave background (CMB) radiation, discovered in 1964 and mapped by NASA's COBE (Cosmic Background Explorer), was revealed by Smoot and Mather. I returned to Anaximander of Miletus, who was the first to see the earth suspended in space in the early 6th century BC and who saw the earth and perceived universe as coming out of *to apeiron*, the "limitless" or "boundless" or "infinite". He saw an endless movement, a Reality from which the universe began as a germ (*gonimon*), and influenced my Form from Movement

Theory. He was an influence, and I drafted the maths for my Form from Movement Theory in the dining-hall at Jesus College, Cambridge on 4 September 1992, watched by Roger Penrose who would later win the Nobel Prize for Physics, during a conference on Reductionism from 1 to 5 September 1992.

The philosopher Anaximander of Miletus (died c.546BC) holding a sundial; Roman mosaic from Johannisstraße, Trier (early third century AD).

I had been invited to contribute a paper to this conference, and very early on Roger Penrose, wearing a red jacket, came and sat next to me. We talked at some length. I had brought a completed typescript of my book *The Universe and the Light* to read through during the evenings of the conference, and when I told him he asked if he could borrow it, and later gave me an endorsement for the back cover. That night he and I set off round Jesus College to try and find a phone – that was in the days before there were mobiles – and we lost our way in the dark corridors and found ourselves opening the door of a don's room – with the don inside by a desk lamp. We eventually found a phone and took it in turns to ring home. During the time we were walking together in Jesus College I was able to ask him about his singularity, about the two pre-particles that gave rise to the Big Bang and feature in my Theory of Everything in *The Algorithm of Creation*.

Penrose is now regarded as one of the few scientists who can be mentioned along with Einstein. He worked with Hawking, and by reversing his proof that the universe gave rise to a singularity he and Hawking came up with the Big Crunch, a contraction of the universe, the reverse of the expansion that follows the Big Bang. He had his theory of understanding "the trapped surface" while crossing a road in the 1960s. He worked out the solution in his mind before he crossed the road, and forgot the solution when he reached the other side. I said he should have gone back to the side of the road he crossed from in the hope it would come back into his mind, and he roared with laughter at the basic common sense in my idea.

All these three contacts with scientific traditions and influences – the traditions of singularity, the Big Bang and the quantum vacuum via the influences of Bohm, Barrow and Penrose – came in useful when I came to write up my Theory of Everything in *The Algorithm of Creation* (2023).

Universalism takes the whole universe – everything – into account, and covers all disciplines. My anthology *The Essentials of Universalism* contains 75 prose selections from 25 volumes, key passages from all the works showing the development of Universalism. Colin Wilson signed to me *The Essential Colin Wilson*, and I believe his gift was an influence on my following an anthologising tradition.

Philosophy's and the sciences' traditions and influences

To sum up, philosophy's and the sciences' personalised traditions on the Tree of Tradition that influenced me should include:

- the tradition of Socrates' dialogues;
- the tradition of Plato's *Republic*;
- the tradition of Whitehead's process metaphysical philosophy;
- the tradition of E.W.F. Tomlin's *Philosophers of East and West*;
- the tradition of H.J. Blackham's *Six Existentialist Thinkers*;
- the tradition of Sartre, Camus and French and German Existentialism;

- the tradition of David Bohm's *Wholeness and the Implicate Order*;
- the tradition of John Barrow's *Theories of Everything*; and
- the tradition of Roger Penrose's work on a singularity.

A more generalised and fuller version of philosophy's and the sciences' 13 traditions on the Tree of Tradition that influenced me include:

1. the tradition of Anaximander's view of the earth as suspended in space, *to apeiron*, the boundless or infinite;
2. the tradition of Socrates' dialogues;
3. the tradition of Plato's *Republic*;
4. the tradition of Whitehead's process metaphysical philosophy;
5. the tradition of philosophers of East and West;
6. the tradition of Existentialist thinkers;
7. the tradition of French and German Existentialism;
8. the tradition of writing within many disciplines (as in Universalism);
9. the tradition of an implicate order in the universe;
10. the tradition of seeking a Theory of Everything;
11. the tradition of singularity in the universe;
12. the tradition of seeing the unity of the universe and humankind; and
13. the tradition of an anthology of essentials in Universalist philosophy.

Philosophy's and the sciences' 10 forebears and influences on me, then, were:

1. Socrates
2. Plato
3. Whitehead
4. E.W.F. Tomlin
5. Blackham
6. Colin Wilson
7. Sartre

8. Bohm
9. Barrow
10. Penrose

4. History

The Fire and the Stones (1991); *The Rise and Fall of Civilizations* (2008). Current affairs: *The Syndicate* (2004); *The Secret History of the West* (2005); *The Fall of the West* (2022); *The Golden Phoenix* (2023). American trilogy: *The Secret Founding of America* (2007); *The Secret American Dream* (2011); *The Secret American Destiny* (2016). Eyewitness history: *The Libyan Revolution* (2009); *The Last Tourist in Iran* (2008). Local history: *A View of Epping Forest* (2012).

Traditional-metaphysical and social-secular traditions of history, and their Universalist reconciliation

In history there has been a metaphysical/Providential tradition of St Augustine and Bossuet, and the speculative linear tradition of Herodotus, Thucydides and Livy.

In *The Secret American Destiny* I wrote of the two traditions:[40]

> For 5,000 years history has had two conflicting approaches.
>
> Attempts to describe and interpret the events of history by philosophical reflection belong to speculative philosophy of history. Speculative philosophy assumed that history is linear, that it has a direction, order or design and is not a random flux without a pattern. In my work to prepare the ground for my study of civilizations[41] I reviewed the traditional approach of describing world history in terms of metaphysical Reality (as expressed in religions) and the pattern of all civilizations.
>
> In the religious texts of the ancient cultures there was always an attempt to explain the direction of human events and to interpret them. In the classical world the *Bible* interpreted human events in relation to Providence. St Augustine of Hippo saw history as being influenced by Providence in *City of God*. His approach was metaphysical and theological. Thomas Aquinas synthesized Aristotelian philosophy and Christianity, and saw historical

events in relation to the eventual significance of history. Jacques-Bénigne Bossuet's *Discours sur l'histoire universelle* (Discourse on Universal History, 1681) attributed the rise and fall of empires to Providence. He tried to reconcile the existence of God with the existence of evil, and saw history as having a progressive direction. Leibniz raised the question of why a good God permits evil – he called the attempts to answer this question 'theodicy' in 1710 – and he and Bossuet grappled with the involvement of God in evil historical events, just as I did in my poetic epic *Overlord*, which in book 5 asks why a good God permitted Auschwitz. The involvement of Providence was not considered deterministic as leaders had free choice, which either furthered the Providential purpose or caused a reaction against their own policies – which furthered the Providential purpose.

Alongside this speculative linear tradition was another tradition of history, that it is a study of past events connected with individuals, individual countries, specific empires and social movements. In the classical world Herodotus, Thucydides and Livy narrated historical events and tried to assess their significance in a linear way, but were secular evidence-gatherers, realistic students of human nature who regarded human intelligence and judgement as contributing to cause and effect, rather than the will of the gods. Herodotus investigated events, and the Greek word for 'inquiry' (*historia*) passed into Latin and became our subject of 'history'. He is today considered to have been largely reliable in reporting what he was told, even though that was sometimes fanciful. He narrated the events of the Persian invasion of Greece in the 5th century BC, while Thucydides told of the events of the Peloponnesian War and Livy the expansion of the Roman Empire. Machiavelli, in his *Discourses on Livy* (c.1517), about the expansion of Rome to the end of the Third Samnite War, saw political greatness such as Rome's as a phenomenon that appeared in cycles.

With the Enlightenment came a more secular speculative approach that ignored Providence. The Rationalist Enlightenment Deist philosopher Edward Gibbon, influenced by Hume's scepticism, put the linear direction of history in reverse in *The History of the Decline and Fall of the Roman Empire* (1766–88). The history of the Roman civilization was a retrogression rather than a progress, owing to moral decadence, barbarism and religion (to which Gibbon was hostile). Georg Wilhelm Friedrich Hegel saw history as a dynamic dialectic between spirit and matter – which can be seen as a conflict between the Light and Materialism – and there were traces of the traditional linear Providential view of history in his secular speculative approach. Marxist history saw history as a dialectic between the workers and the ruling class. In *The Decline of the West* (1922) Oswald Spengler saw civilizations as organisms with life cycles from youth to old age and a limited span of life. He asserted that the soul of the West had died and that decline into dictatorship was imminent. It *was* in Germany, but the West is still a positive force and in the wider European perspective he was wrong.

Yeats in *A Vision* (1925), which he wrote while reading Gibbon (bought with money from his 1923 Nobel prize) and influenced by his wife's automatic writing, saw history as cycles of 2,000-year-long ages, which, it has to be said, do not relate to the dates of the rise and fall of empires. His 'rough beast' slouched towards Bethlehem at the end of the Christian 2,000-year-long Age, an arbitrary date; but with IS (or ISIL) attacking Christians, Yeats's lines now seem prophetic. Arnold Toynbee's comparative study of the cycle of civilizations in *A Study of History* (1934, 1939, 1954, 1959, 1961) was inductive and deemed unscientific – he identified 21 different civilizations in 1934, changed the figure to 23 in 1954 and to 30 in 1961[42] – but it continues the more secular speculative approach and again there are traces of the traditional Providential view of history. Toynbee wrote of a civilization's growth and decay and was acutely aware of religions' role in the cycle of civilizations.

Recent histories have continued the secular speculative approach. Paul Kennedy's *The Rise and Fall of the Great Powers* (1987) studied the Great Powers from 1500 to 1980 and their decline through imperial overstretch. Francis Fukuyama's

The End of History and The Last Man (1992) saw the post-Cold War world becoming a permanent liberal democracy. He asserted that liberal democracy had triumphed and that history had ended in the Hegelian sense: a dialectic had ceased and there was now permanent stability. However, though a World State is desirable and America will build it, wars in Afghanistan and Iraq and Russia's revival of a Cold War policy in the Ukraine meant that the Hegelian end of history did not happen in the aftermath of 1992. Samuel P. Huntington's *Clash of Civilizations and the Remaking of World Order* (1993, 1996) argued that post-Cold War conflict is for cultural, not ideological reasons. So Ukraine might split into Catholic-western Ukraine and Orthodox-eastern Ukraine, an event that has nearly happened. With a secular speculative approach he argued that the West should abandon democratic universalism and military interventionism. But the World State will be based on democratic universalism.

Along with the secular speculative approach many historical works present events connected with individuals, asserting that Napoleon Bonaparte and Winston Churchill were great men who changed the course of history by their strength of will rather than being swept along by linear or cyclic patterns of history whose power they expressed. Pericles, Augustus, Napoleon and Churchill may have believed that they controlled history, but it can be argued that they were in fact the creation of their civilization's stages. In my verse play *The Rise of Oliver Cromwell* I examine Oliver Cromwell's life and see him as the creation of stage 30 of the European civilization (seceders from the 'new people'). Many contemporary works have abandoned traditional attempts to interpret the events of history and merely record the evidential secular and social facts regarding individual countries, empires and social movements.

In *The Secret American Destiny* I wrote of my own work in continuing the two traditions:[43]

I have continued both the metaphysical/Providential and secular/ speculative traditions in my own study of history, *The Fire and the Stones*, Part Two updated as *The Rise and Fall of Civilizations* (1991, 2008). I taught Gibbon, Spengler and Toynbee to postgraduate students in Japan and to Emperor Hirohito's second son from 1965 to 1967, and saw a fourth way, of seeing world history as a 'whole history', a common historical process in different cultures, which I describe as Universalism. As I have said, I see 25 civilizations going through 61 stages. Each civilization then passes into a younger civilization. The growth takes place through the importing of a metaphysical vision, as I have shown,[44] and when this vision begins to fail the civilization turns secular and declines. I see history as both linear and cyclical:[45] cyclical because the Light recurs in different rising and falling civilizations, but linear because it spirals in a linear direction like a spiral staircase towards one worldwide civilization, the coming World State. My rise-and-fall patterns are cyclical, but the direction of each civilization's metaphysical vision is linear – progressing towards a World State.

As regards Universalism's reconciliation of the two traditions of history, in *The Secret American Destiny* I wrote:[46]

In history, historical Universalism presents past events and social movements within the context of the ordering pattern of civilizations, which owe their genesis and growth to visions of metaphysical Reality. As all history emerged from one point that preceded the Big Bang and then from the first cell and the first human historical event, historical Universalism perceives history as one, an interconnected unity, a whole. The history of a particular country cannot be studied in isolation from the history of the rest of the world as that would be partial history. History is the combined events that have befallen humankind as a whole from the recorded beginnings to the present. And so history has a worldwide pattern....

In all civilizations, cultures and times, human beings have encountered similar problems. In the early stages of civilization, metaphysical visions of Being have been numerous. In the later stages of civilization, Being tends not to be seen. The prevailing climate is one of skepticism, secular atheistic Materialism. Thinkers keep their civilization alive by reminding their fellow-citizens of the 'ever-living Fire' or metaphysical Light that inspired it. They are against the trend of their day, the social approach, but they ensure that the civilization's fundamental vision is handed on to the next generation within the amalgam of Universalism. In the long term, such mystical thinkers are fundamental to the health of their civilization. This view can be traced in my works.

How I came to the two traditions of history, and their influences

At school I absorbed the history of the Greeks, the Romans, the Norman Conquest, the Tudors and the growth of the British Empire. In studying Classics for A-level I read the Greek history of the 5th century BC via Thucydides' writings on the Peloponnesian War, and Roman history from the origins of Rome to the establishment of the Roman Empire via Livy and other Roman historians, in Greek and Latin texts.

My teachers of Ancient History at Chigwell School, Godfrey Stott, who fought in the war and made me translate Caesar as Montegomerius to drive home a comparison between Roman and British history, and David Horton and Headmaster Donald Thompson, who steered me through A-levels and university entrance, set me on my way.

I found that I had encountered contemporary history by living through the bombing of London and its environs, the *Blitzkrieg*, of the Second World War. I had heard Churchill speak in Loughton near the War Memorial on 16 June 1945, on his way to Potsdam, and I shook hands with Churchill and got his autograph in my autograph album in October 1951.

On 19 April 1956 I saw Khrushchev and Bulganin, who were running Russia after Stalin's death in 1953, arrive in Downing Street. And my MP, John Biggs-Davison, got me a ticket to the main Suez debate on

12 September 1956 after Prime Minister Eden, with Churchill sitting beside him, announced the collusion with France and Israel that would result in disaster.

I was very aware of ancient history: I toured Italy (in 1957) and Greece (in 1958 and 1960), and I was very aware of contemporary history as the UK's decolonisation gathered speed and the *Pax Americana* filled the gap left by the dwindling British Empire, a process I recognised in the decline of the Athenian and Roman Empires during my study of ancient history. A parallel was drawn between the two Roman Punic Wars against Carthage and the two World Wars against Germany.

When Horton retired in 2003 after 50 years in the classroom, I was invited to a retirement dinner in the open air in the Head's garden, Haylands, presided over by the Head, Tony Little, who would go on to be the Head of Eton. I was seated next to Horton, and he told me he would have to give a speech and had written out notes on separate pieces of paper, would I hand them to him one at a time as he spoke. He was not asked to speak until dusk, and in fading light it was then too dark for him to read what he had written. I improvised by reading the headings out to him while he stood, and he got through his speech that way. When he sat down in near-dark he thanked me profusely for preventing him from drying up. He had already retired in 1991 and had returned to work, and after this retirement party he came out of retirement again and taught at Chigwell for ten more years.

In Japan I was asked to teach Emperor Hirohito's second son Prince Masahito Hitachi from July 1965, and at the request of the chamberlains, who wanted me to improve the Prince's knowledge of world history, I bought two copies of Stewart Easton's *A Brief History of the Western World* and from 1965 to 1966 taught him the history of many individual American and European countries.

I had a group of around eight Japanese postgraduate students at my main university, and in September 1966 the professor in charge of me, Professor Irie (in the 1930s a pupil of the poet and critic William Empson, one of my predecessors at that university), presumably having had reports on the world history I was teaching the Prince, asked me to teach them a course entitled 'The Decline of the West'. I asked, "What if I think the West is *not* declining?" He said, "Professor Hagger, we would like you to teach a course entitled 'The Decline of the West'."

Toynbee in 1967.

Privately I agreed that the West was declining, and I put together a course for the autumn of 1966 to the summer of 1967 based on Gibbon's *The History of the Decline and Fall of the Roman Empire*, Spengler's *Decline of the West* and Toynbee's *A Study of History*. I knew I was straying outside English Literature, which the British Council wanted me to teach, but my employer had asked for it. I can now see there was a Providential significance behind this request as Irie was shifting me away from English Literature into history and towards the development of my Universalism. I did not tell Tomlin I was teaching the course, and was mortified to learn that Toynbee had arrived at Yokohama, Japan on 9 November 1966, and that Tomlin had visited him – and might have taken me with him if he had known I was teaching Toynbee to my postgraduate students.

While teaching world history I saw a fourth way of understanding it, and put it in my book *The Fire and the Stones*, which was published in 1991. I spent 25 years (1965–1990) researching my theme of 25 civilisations growing out of their founder's vision of the Fire or Light. I often thought of my history of the world as following the tradition of Sir Walter Raleigh's *History of the World* (down to 146BC), which he wrote while imprisoned in the Bloody Tower (in two rooms on the upper floor) from 1603 to 1616, while awaiting execution. He was the first Metaphysical poet, a historian and entrepreneur in America, and I saw myself as following his Universalist tradition. I went to the Bloody Tower. In October 2018 plaster and paint were removed and revealed a self-portrait with a laurel wreath Raleigh had drawn on a wall of his prison (see above).

A wall-painting discovered in the Bloody Tower within the Tower of London in October 2018, thought to be a self-portrait with a laurel wreath by the occupant of that room from 1603 to 1616, Sir Walter Raleigh.

I also taught my Japanese postgraduate students T.E. Lawrence's *Seven Pillars of Wisdom*, which I first heard of via Colin Wilson. I modelled some of my writings on eyewitness history and current affairs on Lawrence. I had seen the film *Lawrence of Arabia* when it came out in 1962. I had met Peter O'Toole at Oxford in 1959, and he came back to my room at Worcester College with his chauffeur to drink a bottle of vodka with me while waiting for his actress wife Siân Phillips to finish playing at the Oxford Playhouse. He asked me to go through *The Merchant of Venice*, in which he was currently playing Shylock at Stratford-upon-Avon, to see if my academic approach would help him understand his lines.

T.E. Lawrence in 1918, soon after
his exploits in Arabia.

We forgot the time, and at midnight I realised the College gates
would be closed and that though he was semi-drunk I would have to
make him climb over the nine-foot-high gates. We went out into the
dark and had to hide when the History tutor, dressed in DJ, climbed
in from outside. O'Toole called from a bush in the dark, quoting
Shylock, "How like a fawning publican he looks!/I hate him for he is
a Christian," and the History tutor scuttled off in terror into the night.
Then the chauffeur and I got O'Toole to the top of the gates and pushed
him over and he fell heavily, but unhurt, the other side. I then helped
the chauffeur climb out.

Fifty years later, in 2010, I met Peter O'Toole again on a cruise. The
first evening I caught up with him after a lecture. I said, "Greetings
from 50 years ago," and I recounted how I had to get him to climb
out. I told him step by step what a struggle I had had and he laughed
his way through my story, helpfully adding the chauffeur's name and
embellishing bits I left out. A small crowd from the lecture audience
had gathered round us and it was clear that O'Toole remembered
everything that had happened that night in great detail. I ended by
saying to laughter, "Then you went off and played Lawrence among
pretend Arabs while I went to Iraq and taught real Arabs."

Later still, in 2020, I visited Wadi Rum in Jordan where O'Toole filmed *Lawrence of Arabia*, and sat where he, and many years earlier Lawrence, had meals. I saw where Lawrence slept.

While I was teaching the *Seven Pillars of Wisdom* I realised that some events recorded in the book were treated very differently in the film. I counted (speaking from memory) 46 places in the book which the film had changed. For example, in the book Lawrence helps an Arab escape and in a separate incident has to execute an Arab. In the film the two events are combined, and Lawrence has to execute an Arab he earlier helped to escape.

Over the years I had acquired a knowledge of current affairs. I wrote features for *The Times* for *The Times* Features' Editor from 1970 to 1972, specialising in the African liberation movements, and I focused on America after acquiring Otley Hall in Suffolk, UK, where the crew of the Jamestown Voyage that founded the United States in 1607 were recruited. I ran Otley Hall as a historic house and had many American visitors, including the wife of the Governor of Virginia. I visited the US and gave a lecture in Virginia about the founding of America and met Charlie Bryan, the curator of the Richmond Museum. He urged me to write about the founding of America, as did Bill Kelso, the archaeologist who discovered Jamestown and unearthed 3 million artefacts.

My American trilogy came out of this, and as I have already said (see p.81), my knowledge of the Syndicate came out of the research I did for *The Fire and the Stones* (1991), but was deepened by the end of the 1990s from my research into America while I was based at Otley Hall. This research led to my Syndicate quartet.

The historian Asa Briggs (Lord Briggs) had attended the launch of *The Fire and the Stones* (see p.69) and made a speech along with David Gascoyne and Kathleen Raine. We stayed in touch. He urged me to write *The Libyan Revolution*, as the attempted *coup* I was involved in when I was in Libya explained Gaddafi's decisions in 1969. I wrote it as eyewitness history at his urging, and I also wrote *The Last Tourist in Iran* as eyewitness history. Briggs also urged me to write *My Double Life 1: This Dark Wood*, about my intelligence work. He too had been involved in intelligence work during the war, at Bletchley Park, as had the previous Provost of mine Sir John Masterman, who was Chairman of the XX Committee during the war that turned round German agents with false information as to where D-Day would take place.

Sir William Addison, author of *Epping Forest: Its Literary and Historical Associations* (1945).

I also wrote local history, *A View of Epping Forest*. I visited the bookshop owned by our local author William Addison in May 1945, and guided by him (tall, in a dark suit, balding), spent a book token on a book on trees, *The Observer's Book of Trees*, which included a picture of an oak tree, a tree that would be in the badge of my four schools and become their symbol, and would also become the Tree of Tradition (as on the front cover). At Easter 1945 he had brought out *Epping Forest: Its Literary and Historical Associations*, and I last met him at the entrance to Queen Elizabeth's Hunting Lodge in 1987. He was in a wheelchair. I am in his tradition of looking at the history of the Forest which predates the Romans. I have followed a tradition of looking at Epping Forest from a historical perspective, and Sir William Addison (as he became) is my main influence.

History's traditions and influences

History's 14 traditions on the Tree of Tradition that influenced me include:

1. the tradition of Bossuet's metaphysical view of the Light as fundamental to the rise of civilisations;
2. the tradition of the speculative history of Gibbon, Spengler and Toynbee;
3. the tradition of classical history;
4. the tradition of the founding of America;
5. the tradition of American history;
6. the tradition of the future of America;
7. the tradition of world history;
8. the tradition of world federalism;
9. the tradition of a World State;
10. the tradition of current affairs;
11. the tradition of the Syndicate's New World Order;
12. the tradition of English social history;
13. the tradition of the eyewitness history of Iran and Libya; and
14. the tradition of local history (Epping Forest).

History's 14 forebears and influences on me were:

- William Addison, who got me interested in local history;
- Godfrey Stott and David Horton, who got me comparing the Athenian, Roman and British Empires;
- Prof. Irie (Empson's pupil), who persuaded me to prepare a year's lectures on 'The Decline of the West';
- Charlie Bryan and Bill Kelso, who urged me to write about the founding of America;
- Asa Briggs, who got me to write about Libya and my intelligence work, and wanted me to send him *The Secret American Destiny*;
- Gibbon and Spengler who influenced me regarding the decline of the West;

- Raleigh and Toynbee who influenced me into working on world history; and
- T.E. Lawrence who interested me in Middle-Eastern history.

They are numbered as follows:

1. Addison
2. Stott
3. Horton
4. Irie
5. Bryan
6. Kelso
7. Briggs
8. Gibbon
9. Spengler
10. Raleigh
11. Toynbee
12. T.E. Lawrence

5. Comparative religion

The Fire and the Stones (1991); *The Light of Civilization* (2006)

Traditional-metaphysical and social-secular traditions of comparative religion, and their Universalist reconciliation

In comparative religion there has been a tradition of an inner quest for metaphysical Reality, and a tradition focusing on the outer observance in services in places of worship. In *The Secret American Destiny* I wrote:[47]

For 5,000 years all religions have had two conflicting approaches.

In the traditional ancient religious texts, from the Egyptian *Book of the Dead* to the *Upanishads* and the Neo-Taoist *The Secret of the Golden Flower*, there was an inner quest for metaphysical Reality, the Light. I have shown (in Part One of *The Fire and the Stones*, 'The Tradition of the Fire', and Part Two of *The Light of Civilization*, 'The Tradition of the Light'; and also in *The Universe and the Light*

and *The Rise and Fall of Civilizations*[48]) that all the early religions –
the religions of the Mesopotamian, Egyptian, Aegean-Greek,
Roman, Anatolian, Syrian, Israelite, Celtic, Iranian, Germanic-
Scandinavian, Indian, Southeast Asian, Japanese, Chinese and
Tibetan civilizations – had a common experience of the Light or
Fire, as did (judging from their 'stones', their megalithic ruins
and statues) the religions of the Indo-European Kurgan, Oceanian
and Central Asian civilizations. (The other seven civilizations I
do not regard as 'ancient'.)

I have shown (in *The Universe and the Light*)[49] the influence of
religions as the driving force of the history of civilizations. I have
described how the Light or Fire enters and takes hold in new
civilizations:

> A contemplative mystic has a vision of the Fire which
> migrates to a new area and forms a new religion. This
> becomes associated with the State, and increases the power
> of a priestly class who performs its rites. Peoples are attracted
> to the Fire and a political unification takes place around
> it. The Fire inspires the civilization's expansion. Foreign
> invaders create a revival of a past culture, the religion turns
> worldly and undergoes a Reformation and a new people
> adopt a heresy as the new orthodoxy. There is another
> expansion. Eventually the religion declines. This decline is
> associated with the decolonization. The Fire is now absent,
> the civilization enters a conglomerate and is increasingly
> secularized. Eventually after a period of federalism, the
> civilization is occupied and it ends up passing under its
> successor's religion.[50]

This vision happened in all 25 civilizations, and the one Light
or Fire was seen by a contemplative before it passed into
each civilization. The Light or Fire is therefore common to all
rising-and-falling civilizations. For how the Fire spread from
civilization to civilization, see the chart of 25 civilizations and
cultures in Appendix 3.

I then described the experience of the Fire, the growth of
the religion and the consequent growth and development of

the civilization as a result of its driving force, in ten religions: the Egyptian, Islamic, Hindu, Chinese, Japanese, Orthodox, Christian, Buddhist, Tibetan Buddhist and Judaistic religions.

I have set out (in *The Light of Civilization*)[51] 21 civilizations with distinctive religions and four civilizations with related religions (that are early phases or later branches of the 21 distinctive civilizations). It is worth listing [relisting, see p.36 regarding the gods on the trunk of the Tree of Tradition] the gods of the distinctive religions of all 25 civilizations to make the point that in their worship within these religions and sects contemplatives all see the common Light:

Dyaeus Pitar/Magna Mater (Sky Father/Earth Mother); Anu/Ogma/Utu, Shamash/Tammuz/Marduk, Shuqamuna/ Ashur; Ra/Amun/Aton, Horus/ Osiris/Apis; Zeus/Apollo, Anat/Athene (or Athena); Jupiter/Apollo, Gnostic God as Light; Mistress of Animals/Storm and Weather god Tarhun or Teshub/Sharruma/Arinna, Cybele/Attis; El/Dagon/Baal/ Mot/ Resheph/Molech (or Moloch), Koshar/Astarte/Anath (or Anat), Adonis, Ashtoreth, Hadad/Rammon/Atargatis; El Shaddai/ Yahweh; Du-w ('Yoo-we', cf 'Yahweh')/Lug/Beli (cf Baal)/ Taran/Yesu; Mithras/Zurvan (of Medes)/Ahura Mazda/Mani, Inshushinak/Kiririshna (cf Indian Krishna)/ Nahhunte/Huban; God as Light; Wodan/Odin; Smiling god ('El Lanzon', 'the Great Image'), Inti/Quetzlcoatl/Kukulcan (or Kukulan); Kinich Ahau/Itzamna/Huitzilopochtli; Allah; Mwari/Nzambi/ Cghene/ Ngai/Leza/Ndjambi Marunga/ Raluvhimba/ Olodumare; Agni/Brahman/ Atman/Siva/ Sakti, Visnu/ Rama/Krishna/Om Kar, the Buddha; Kami/ Amaterasu; Io (Maori); *Shang Ti/T'ien* Ti/the *Tao*.

We can get close to the common Light the contemplatives saw during their quest for metaphysical Reality within all these religions and sects by studying the invocations to Ra in the Egyptian *Book of the Dead* and the experiences of the European Christian mystics, including Augustine and Hildegard [see pp.25, 40–41 and 47].

Alongside comparative religion's emphasis on the inner quest for metaphysical Reality is another approach which focuses on outer observance in the services in their churches, temples and mosques. This approach concentrates on rituals in places of worship and emphasizes social religion. I have shown evidence[52] that this social approach secularized English hymns after 1889: the Light or Fire has more or less vanished from hymns and been replaced by social, humanist subjects.

I have also set out[53] the times in each civilization when the Light weakens during religions' and civilizations' times of decline under foreign threat or rule. In North America the only time of decline was during the period before and after the Civil War, c.1854–96. In Europe the most recent time of decline was c.1880 to c.1991 when the Germans subjected Europe to two world wars and the Russians occupied Eastern Europe until the fall of the Berlin Wall. I believe that the incorporation of Eastern European nation-states into the EU and the ratification of the Lisbon Treaty in the first decade of the 21st century have ended this European time of decline – and weakening of the Light in Europe.

As a Universalist I see all religions as different routes up an inner mountain, at the top of which there is one sun, and so I am on the side of the metaphysical tradition of an inner quest rather than on the side of the tradition of social observance.

As regards Universalism's reconciliation of the two traditions of comparative religion, in *The Secret American Destiny* I wrote:[54]

In comparative religion, Universalism presents the social observance of religions within the context of ordering metaphysical Reality, the Light. We saw [on pp.126–127] that the Light is common to all religions. As all religion emerged from the point that preceded the Big Bang, from the first cell and from the first appearance of organized religion, religious Universalism[55] affirms that all humankind will eventually be saved from the finite universe of time into infinite timelessness, not just members of one particular religion. Religious Universalism sees the prospect of all religions becoming merged into a one-world religion based on what all religions have in common: the infinite timeless Being that has been intuitionally glimpsed by mystics of all religions as the Light. All human beings are equal in relation to metaphysical Light that can fill their souls and order Nature's ecosystem.

The vision of metaphysical Light of Being is found in every generation and culture. It is a universal experience received in the universal being or intellect, and brings together Catholic, Protestant and Orthodox Christianity, Islam, Judaism, Hinduism, Buddhism, Jainism, Sikhism, Taoism and many other religions such as Zoroastrianism, which all share the experience. The universal experience of the Light can have regional and local applications. In the Greek time Zeus became identified with the local gods of religions in Asia Minor, and in the Roman time Jupiter became identified with local gods such as Zeus and Sol (who had taken over from Mithras in Asia Minor). A one-world religion based on the one experience of the 'ever-living Fire' or metaphysical Light which all religions have in common, would merge God, Allah, Yahweh, Brahman, the Enlightened Buddha, Nirvana, Om Kar, the *Tao* and Ahura Mazda. The words of their prophets would be regional and local variations of the universal experience: the words of Christ, Mohammed, Moses, Siva, the Buddha, Mahavira, Guru, Nanak, Lao-Tze (or Lao-Tzu).

How I came to the two traditions of comparative religion, and their influences

I was a Christian in my youth, from a Methodist family who moved to Anglicanism and sent me to an Anglican school. I taught in Iraq and Libya and encountered Islam. I encountered Zen Buddhism and Buddhism in Japan; Hinduism, Jainism and Sikhism in India; and Zoroastrianism in Iran. I encountered the Russian Orthodox Church and the Catholic Brompton Oratory (through Margaret Riley). In the course of my life I encountered most religions, and, having embarked on my Mystic Way, found the common essence of all religions was the Fire or Light, of which I had 112 recorded experiences until 24 April 2021 (the last 19 of which are listed in *The Promised Land*).

Key influences were Evelyn Underhill; and Margaret Riley, who helped me achieve full illumination and progress along my Mystic Way to instinctive unitive vision. Margaret Riley opened my way to the Light which shines into all religions, and in my last masque I have referred to the God of the One who, as the Light, is in all religions. Each religion has its own clerics who apply to it rather than to all other religions, just as a nation-state can be remote from the United Nations and not relate to other nations.

The traditions of inner quest and a Mystic Way, and outer observance have Dewey classes 204 (religious experience) and 290 (other religions) – 291, formerly comparative religion, is no longer used; and Library-of-Congress classes BL (religions, mythology), BM (Judaism), BI (Islam, Bahaism, Theosophy, etc.), BQ (Buddhism) and ER (Christianity).

Comparative religion's traditions and influences

Comparative religion's 7 traditions on the Tree of Tradition that influenced me include:

1. the tradition of Methodism;
2. the tradition of Anglicanism;
3. the tradition of Zen Buddhism;
4. the tradition of Buddhism;
5. the tradition of the Mystic Way;
6. the tradition of the Fire or Light; and
7. the tradition of Universalist religious experience of the One.

Comparative religion's main forebears and influences on me regarding the inner quest for metaphysical Reality were the mystics on pp.47–48 and especially the following 4:

1. St Augustine of Hippo
2. St Hildegard of Bingen
3. Evelyn Underhill
4. Margaret Riley

6. International politics and statecraft

The World Government (2010); *Peace for our Time* (2018); *World State* (2018); *World Constitution* (2018)

Traditional-metaphysical and social-secular traditions of international politics and statecraft, and their Universalist reconciliation

In *The Secret American Destiny* I wrote of a tradition of early states' international politics and statecraft being controlled by their priests' vision of metaphysical Reality as they were dominated by religious rites connected with the Fire or Light; and also of a tradition that emphasised the social-secular relationships of sovereign nation-states:[56]

> For 2,600 years – and probably for 5,000 years – international politics and statecraft ('the art of conducting affairs of state', *Concise Oxford Dictionary*) have been conducted by two conflicting approaches.
>
> In the early stages of the ancient civilizations when the Fire or Light within their religion was managed by a priestly class who performed State rites, the State was dominated by the Fire or Light, and the vision of metaphysical Reality attracted surrounding peoples and led to political unification and expansion. The growing, expanding civilization's diplomacy maintained the metaphysical vision enshrined in its religion, and in ancient Egypt, Mesopotamia, Iran, India, China and the other early civilizations the Pharaoh or priest-King or Supreme Ruler derived his authority from the chief god of the new religion. International politics and statecraft, and diplomacy, maintained the *status quo* of the unifying vision of metaphysical Reality, which saw the oneness of surrounding humankind, and perpetuated its local forms....
>
> In the kingdoms of Europe during the Middle Ages the State was dominated by the Church: the Pope or (as in the case of Henry II) his Archbishop. During the time of the Crusades, religion and the vision of metaphysical Reality led diplomacy in Europe. The Renaissance brought a new outward-looking spirit of intellectual

inquiry, opened up by the flow of classical texts from the libraries of Constantinople and renewed interest in geography. Cities grew and prospered, leagues of states formed: the Hanseatic League and Habsburg Empire flourished, and little by little politics grew away from religion. England broke with the Pope, and the Reformation loosened the Catholic grip on politics. Revolutions against the monarchy in England and France weakened religion's control over the State. My study of all the revolutions from 1453 to 1920, *The Secret History of the West*, showed that secret societies were behind the growing revolutionary nationalism. Coinciding with advances in map-making, nations emerged, and slowly nations of city-states turned into nation-states in which the State was secular. Following the unifications of Germany and of Italy, the State was secular in much of Europe.

Alongside the tradition of international politics and statecraft being controlled by religion's vision of metaphysical Reality, affirming a vision of unified peoples and acknowledging the religion of local groups, there now co-existed a new approach to international politics and statecraft that emphasized the secular and social relationships of sovereign nation-states as they competed with each other in continental wars. From the 19th century on, nationalism was a force, which swiftly expressed itself through rival imperialisms in Africa and elsewhere....

Nationalism was challenged by a plan for a New World Order. Conceived by self-interested élitist families I have described collectively as 'the Syndicate' (most notably the Rothschilds and Rockefellers) who created the Bilderberg Group, they worked to bring in a world government that would loot the Earth's resources.... The Syndicate are motivated by their own business profits, increasing their trillions into quadrillions at the expense of the peoples of the Earth, and are not interested in perpetuating a vision of metaphysical Reality that embraces the oneness of humankind....

There has long been a yearning for a genuine World State as opposed to one that would enable families of an *élite* to become quadrillionaires....

In *The World Government* I set out a blueprint for a democratic World State,[57] and we shall return to this in due course. The point now is that there is an honourable tradition of respected thinkers calling for a World State that would recognize the oneness of humankind as perceived in the unifying vision of metaphysical Reality. The World State is an ideal that would abolish war, famine, disease and poverty and see off the greed and self-interest of *élites* who care more about their family fortunes than the whole of humankind.

Nelson Rockefeller's *The Future of Federalism* (1962) is behind the ideas of world federalism.

As regards Universalism's reconciliation of the two traditions of international politics and statecraft, in *The Secret American Destiny* I wrote:[58]

In international politics, Universalism presents nation-states within the ordering context of regional empires and one World State that transcends nationalism.... A democratic World State with elected representatives from world constituencies would incorporate and subsume all the nation-states and solve the world's problems. As all politics emerged from one point that preceded the Big Bang, from the first cell and from the first human political organization, political Universalism[59] sees the whole world as being ordered as one political entity, an interconnected unity, a whole. As all humans are world citizens they have human rights, which includes a human right to live under a world government that has abolished war, famine and disease. Political Universalism affirms a world government that is not totalitarian, respects the human right of all humankind to have a democratic vote and allows each human being the maximum freedom, and attacks property.

Our global identity is reinforced by the web created by Tim Berners-Lee, which theoretically allows each world citizen to communicate with all others (provided they are on email). The web symbolizes the interconnectedness of humankind just as the distinctive DNA signature of all world citizens symbolizes the uniqueness of each individual.

Political Universalism minimizes the conflict that divides people. It eliminates divisions by negotiation. National borders in a World State would be like state borders in the US. Steps have already been taken towards a world government. Many trade institutions have been founded, and there is a structure of American, European and Pacific Unions, in different stages of advancement, which, it is intended, will eventually merge and form a one-world political structure with its own currency.

The age of global governance was ushered in when on 6 September 2000 149 heads of government and officials from other nations, representing 189 member states of the UN, attended the UN Millennium Assembly and Summit of World Leaders in New York and adopted a revised version of the UN Charter, the Charter for Global Democracy. In September 2005 there was another UN Summit, when a total of 191 UN states were represented. In September 2010 there was a further UN Summit on the millennium development goals, and in September 2015 there was yet another UN summit to adopt the post-2015 development agenda.

How I came to the two traditions of international politics and statecraft, and their influences

While writing contemporary history and current affairs, I have researched a coming world government and New World Order that have been associated with the Syndicate (Eisenhower's "military-industrial complex" of mega-rich élitist families motivated by their own self-interest) and have seen the possibility of a different kind of New World Order: a democratic, supranational, partly-federal World State, with a world government that will have seven aims and goals to solve the world's problems: disarmament and ending war; redistributing wealth to eliminate poverty and hunger; solving environmental problems; ending disease; extending skills development; delivering world economic growth; and ending religious conflict.

Marble head of Socrates, who declared himself a "citizen of the world", see p.137 (copy of bronze head by Lysippos), in the Louvre.

Supranationalism is a tier above internationalism, where the UN operates, and above internationalism's 193 nation-states. Under a supranational, partly-federal world government all nation-states would remain the same internally and also internationally, except in the 7 areas and goals, in which each nation will give up a little sovereignty to bring huge savings from not having to spend on defence, wars and arms. Being democratic, this world government would at first be based in the UN General Assembly, and the UN Security Council would be a link between the international World Parliamentary Assembly and the supranational World Senate and World President. It would be called the United Federation of the World (UF), "United" suggesting the United Nations and United States, and "Federation" suggesting the Russian Federation. It would be a supranational body above the UN with more powers than the UN. All four multipolar powers – the US, EU, Russia and China – would participate in the UF, which would bring peace and prosperity to the world.

The tradition of world government can be traced back to Plato (whose *Republic* was based on just the city-state of Athens) and Socrates (who according to Plutarch in *De Exilio* [*On Exile*] declared "I am not an Athenian or Greek but a citizen of the world" – a supranationalist). Dante in *De Monarchia* (*On Monarchy*, sometimes translated as *On World Government*, c.1317–1318) wrote of "the whole Earth", and Kant saw the need for an international state (*civitas gentium*) and wrote of a "federation of free states" in *Perpetual Peace* (1795), similar to my United Federation of the World. After the atomic bombs of 1945 Truman called for a world government, along with Churchill, Einstein, Russell, Gandhi, J.F. Kennedy and Gorbachev to name but a few. Truman kept a few lines from Tennyson's 'Locksley Hall' (1842, written in 1837–1838) in his wallet, which include the phrase "the Federation of the world" from which I named this world government the United Federation of the World:

> For I dipt into the future, far as human eye could see,
> Saw the Vision of the world, and all the wonder that would be; …
> Till the war-drum throbbed no longer, and the battle-flags were furled
> In the Parliament of man, the Federation of the world.
> There the common sense of most shall hold a fretful realm in awe,
> And the kindly earth shall slumber, lapt in universal law.

Alfred, Lord Tennyson, lithograph, 1890.

I emphasise that I called my supranational, democratic, partly-federal world government 'the United Federation of the World', 'the UF' for short as it suggests the UN, from this passage in Tennyson's poem. Supranationalism, world government, world federalism and a World State are key traditions within international politics and statecraft.

The influences behind this political quest for the One were the figures of past civilisations who operated the rites of their state in temples, certainly until Roman times and in different states today, including America (where "In God we trust" was adopted as the official American motto in 1956 and appears on the back of all American paper currency).

I brought in the Universal State of the Earth when I chaired the constitutional convention of the World Philosophical Forum in Athens in the presence of more than 50 international philosophers in 2015,[60] and I then regarded the Russian based in Greece as well as in Russia, Igor Kondrashin, who asked me to do this, as a fellow supranationalist. I was asked to be on the Executive Board of the World Intellectual Forum, and was made Chairman of its good global governance working group on a supranational world government based on my three books *The World Government*, *World State* and *World Constitution*.

I chaired a Zoom conference with a PowerPoint presentation to India on global governance, and called for the UN to set up a working group like mine. On 8 September 2022 the UN General Assembly passed a resolution to set up a working group on global governance to prepare for the Summit of the Future in September 2024. My attempt to set up a peaceful and prosperous World State rather than progress a nationalist confrontation that could lead to a Third World War and, possibly, a nuclear catastrophe, carries the Universalist vision to its furthest extent regarding its international politics and statecraft.

Realistically, my forebears and influences are those who have called for a World State: Socrates (according to Plutarch), Plato, Dante, Kant, Tennyson, Truman, Einstein, Churchill, Eisenhower, Gandhi, Russell, J.F. Kennedy, Gorbachev. I regard Tennyson as my guide as when I spent several days sleeping in his bedroom on the Isle of Wight in 2008 and working in the study where he wrote 'Crossing the Bar', I felt his presence, at first in his study and later in his bedroom (see pp.71–72 and my *Selected Letters*, pp.462–465). And when I returned home I found

Tennyson was also in my study. It was as if Tennyson had latched on to me to bring his "Federation of the world" in 'Locksley Hall' into practice as part of the new powers I have received since my full illumination on my Mystic Way.

The World Government (2010) came out of this experience and it would be wonderful if Tennyson, whose blank verse Christopher Ricks, a world authority on Tennyson following his editing of *The Poems of Tennyson*, urged me to follow in *Overlord*, and who lived a short drive from my house in Essex at Beech Hill Park, High Beach, is the deep source that is my editor. I wake with page numbers in my mind to check from the previous day's work, and the prompt is always right, there is always a mistake on the page that 'Tennyson' is pointing out. And I have received most of my titles, including 'Traditions and Influences' in the subtitle of this work, in my sleep, which can be attributed to 'Tennyson'. It is weird and uncanny, but ever since my contact with Tennyson in 2008 I have gone forward via *Fools' Paradise* and *Fools' Gold* in a way I did not deem possible thirteen years ago.

The traditions of religion's vision of metaphysical Reality that reveals the unity of humankind I have already dealt with (pp.39–40 and 126–127), and the traditions of the social-secular relationships of sovereign nation-states have Dewey classifications 110–119 and 341 and Library of Congress classifications B, BD, BL, D, E, JA, JX, JZ and KZ.

International politics and statecraft's traditions and influences
International politics and statecraft's 6 traditions on the Tree of Tradition that influenced me include:

1. the tradition of the vision of questing for metaphysical Reality that reveals the unity of humankind in international politics and statecraft;
2. the tradition of social and secular relationship of sovereign nation-states in international politics and statecraft;
3. the tradition of supranationalism in international politics and statecraft;
4. the tradition of world government in international politics and statecraft;

5. the tradition of world federalism in international politics and statecraft; and

6. the tradition of founding a World State in international politics and statecraft.

International politics and statecraft's 7 forebears and influences on me were:

1. Socrates
2. Plato
3. Dante
4. Kant
5. Tennyson
6. Truman
7. Igor Kondrashin

7. World culture
The Secret American Destiny (2016)

Traditional-metaphysical and social-secular traditions of world culture, and their Universalist reconciliation

In *The Secret American Destiny* I wrote that there was a tradition of the vision of metaphysical Reality which passed into all religions and therefore all cultures; and also a tradition of social-secular works of art, and I referred to the chart on pp.260–261 of *The Secret American Destiny* (see Appendix 3, also pp.224–225):[61]

> For 5,000 years culture – 'the arts and other manifestations of human intellectual achievement regarded collectively; the customs, civilization, and achievements of a particular time or people' (*Concise Oxford Dictionary*) – has been dominated by two conflicting approaches.
>
> We have seen that the vision of metaphysical Reality entered each civilization and passed into its religion, that all cultures had the Fire or Light in common. I reproduce a chart which shows this process very clearly [see Appendix 3].[62] The Fire originated

in the Central Asian civilization and passed to the Indo-European Kurgan civilization and after that passed between civilizations as the arrows show, ending in a 'worldwide civilization' which will be the coming World State. The chart is subtitled 'The Fundamental Unity of World Culture' and demonstrates the underlying cultural unity the Fire or Light makes possible.

In the early civilizations, civilization's culture was unified like a tree whose branches are nourished from its religious trunk. Within all the civilizations, including the European civilization, the arts – the tree's branches – expressed the vision of metaphysical Reality that had passed into its religion. Each civilization's culture was originally a unity, and in the European civilization until the Renaissance its works of art – in philosophy, painting, music and literature – all expressed the civilization's central idea, its vision of metaphysical Reality round which the civilization had grown. This vision can be found in European thought and in the European arts: in the philosophy of Christian Platonism and Aristotelianism which looked back to Heraclitus's 'ever-living' Fire ('Fragment 30'), Plato's Fire or 'universal Light' which causes shadows to flicker on the wall of the cave, and Plotinus's 'authentic Light' which 'comes from the One and is the One'; in paintings such as Jan van Eyck's *Adoration of the Lamb*, Fra Angelico's angels in *Christ Glorified in the Court of Heaven* and Michelangelo's Sistine Chapel ceiling; in the sacred choral music of Palestrina, Thomas Tallis, William Byrd and Claudio Monteverdi and in the Hallelujah Chorus of George Frideric Handel's *Messiah*; and in the literature of Dante, and in particular in Dante's sempiternal rose in his *Paradiso*. All expressed the sublime vision of Paradise. During the Renaissance, Plato-inspired Marsilio Ficino and Sandro Botticelli shared Dante's vision. Unity of culture continued during the Elizabethan time in spite of the Reformation, and during the time of the Metaphysical poets (the stage-30 secession from the Renaissance Humanists by Cromwell's Puritans, who wanted more rather than less metaphysical vision), the time of John Milton's 'God is light,… Celestial light' in *Paradise Lost*, book 3.

Alongside the vision of metaphysical Reality which dominated the rise of each civilization co-existed a secular, social approach whose artists presented a secular, social perspective in works of art. In the European civilization the 18th-century Augustans espoused Enlightenment reason and social virtue, and condemned social vices, and the vision of metaphysical Reality took second place. Since the 18th century the metaphysical idea has weakened. This weakening was captured in works of art within philosophy, painting, music and literature: in the Vienna Circle's verification progress; in the French Impressionists and John Constable and J.M.W. Turner; in programme music that tells a social story and evokes images; and in the 18th- and 19th-century novel. In the second decade of the 21st century, works of art by Metaphysical poets are outnumbered by works of art with social themes. The rise of film has encouraged this trend: as a medium, film is better able to describe social events than inner visions. We are living in a time when the inner has given way to the outer in many areas of our lives.

I have listed (in *The New Philosophy of Universalism*)[63] 50 'isms' or doctrinal movements that arose after the weakening of Christianity [see pp.17–18, quoted there in a post-Renaissance context rather than in the context of world culture]. They represent secular, philosophical and political traditions that indicate fragmentation and loss of contact with the One, and disunity within European civilization:

humanism; scientific revolution/reductionism; mechanism; Rosicrucianism; Rationalism; Empiricism; scepticism; Atomism/Materialism; Enlightenment/deism; Idealism; Realism; liberalism; capitalism; individualism; egoism; atheism; radicalism; utilitarianism; determinism; historicism; nationalism; socialism; Marxism; anarchism/ syndicalism; Darwinism; accidentalism; nihilism; Communism; conservatism; imperialism; totalitarianism; Nazism; Fascism; Stalinism; pragmatism; progressivism; Phenomenology/Existentialism; stoicism; vitalism; intuitionism; modernism/post-modernism; secularism;

objectivism; positivism; analytic and linguistic philosophy/ logical empiricism; ethical relativism; republicanism; hedonism/Epicureanism; structuralism/post-structuralism; and holism.

These 50 'isms' give a bird's-eye view of the fragmentation and disintegration of the once-unified European and (insofar as European civilization impacted on the world as a major part of Western civilization) world culture.

In *The Secret American Destiny* I reflected on the fragmentation and underlying unity of world culture.

As regards Universalism's reconciliation of the two traditions of world culture, in *The Secret American Destiny* I wrote:[64]

In world culture's works of art, Universalism presents the secular, social perspective within the context of ordering metaphysical Reality, Being, the Light.

As all culture emerged from one point that preceded the Big Bang and from the first cell and (via life and consciousness) the first appearance of human culture, cultural Universalism perceives all cultures as one, an interconnected unity, a whole....

We have seen [p.141, and also see pp.163–164] that a civilization's culture is like a tree, and that the European civilization's culture is like a tree. World culture can also be seen as a tree. The trunk is all the higher religions, the branches all the 25 civilizations. The thrust of the sap from the trunk into the branches is metaphysical, and the ends of the branches that have turned dry and brittle are secular and are top-heavy with 50 'isms' [listed on p.142]. The metaphysical Fire or Light has risen like sap from the roots through the trunk into each branching civilization, and that is cultural Universalism's[65] context: the vision of the metaphysical Light that is behind the genesis and growth of each civilization and its culture. All the cultures of the 25 world civilizations present their distinguishing features in relation to the metaphysical Light....

Universalism's reunification of the pairs of opposites in the seven disciplines of world culture is reunifying each of the seven disciplines, as Liberty, whose raised torch proclaims the unity of humankind, can see. In all seven, the finité is expressed within the context of the ordering infinite. In each discipline Universalism deepens the partial approach by seeing it within the context of ordering metaphysical Reality that proclaims the order in the universe. In each discipline Universalism has pieced together the conflicting social and metaphysical approaches.

Universalism also pieces all the fragmented disciplines together and combines and reunifies them into one, to restore the whole universe and its order. In all seven disciplines as a whole, the secular, social approach is united with the ordering metaphysical Reality from which it has become separated....

Universalists reconcile the contradictory pairs of opposites to reveal the pre-existing unity within the whole universe, and its order. The dialectic $+A + -A = 0$ can now be seen to be: metaphysical approach + social approach = reunified world culture through a perception of the unity and order within the universe. The Universalist Revolution can now be seen to be a Metaphysical Revolution, which has produced a metaphysical science.

How I came to the two traditions of world culture, and their influences

I was brought to look at world culture as a whole by my experience of living in the Middle and Far East. In Iraq, Japan and then Libya I encountered Islamic and Buddhist cultures that were very different from the Christian culture in the West, and my visit to China deepened my awareness of world culture.

I returned from Japan via 13 countries in 1967. I was told I could either have a first-class ticket home, or I could book stop-offs on the way back. I chose the second and spent three weeks returning via the Philippines (Manila), Hong Kong, Macao, Singapore, Vietnam (Saigon, Bien Hoa), Cambodia (Angkor Wat, Phnom Penh), Thailand (Bangkok),

India (Calcutta, Delhi), Nepal (Katmandu), Turkey (Istanbul), Hungary (Budapest), Austria (Vienna) and France (Paris) through different national cultures. I was able to see similarities as well as differences. Ezra Pound in *The Cantos* saw world culture as a whole, and when I met him in 1970 I was aware of his work in reflecting world culture in images.

I began *The Secret American Destiny* on world culture on 25 April 2015 the day after a visit to the historian Asa Briggs, who was then 93, when I discussed the coming work with him. It was completed on 21 October 2015, six months later. Asa Briggs died on 15 March 2016 and was unable to read the published book, but was extremely interested in my concept of world culture.

Nicholas Hagger with Lord Asa Briggs, then aged 93, in his kitchen on 24 April 2015. On the table are *My Double Life 1: This Dark Wood*, and Briggs' *Secret Days*; also *The Secret Founding of America* and *The Secret American Dream*.

The tradition of world culture is not mentioned in the Dewey or Library of Congress classifications, but the vision of metaphysical Reality and the tradition of a social-secular art and culture are under Dewey classifications 110–119, 128 and 300–306; and Library of Congress classifications B, BD and H.

World culture's traditions and influences

World culture's 9 traditions on the Tree of Tradition which influenced me include:

1. the tradition of questing for metaphysical Reality that reveals the unity of humankind in world culture;
2. the tradition of social-secular art in world culture;
3. the tradition of civilisations' cultures;
4. the tradition of the fundamental unity of world culture;
5. the tradition of the Light in European culture;
6. the tradition of Universalist world culture;
7. the tradition of all past influences on world culture;
8. the tradition of world-wide global culture; and
9. the tradition of 50 'isms' of fragmented European culture.

World culture's forebears and influences on me were those who achieved the vision of metaphysical Reality that reveals the unity of humankind within European art and culture (see p.140) and those who influenced me within the seven disciplines (see pp.153–154, 84 influences).

In Japan I discussed world philosophy with E.W.F. Tomlin, whose *Great Philosophers of the East* and *Great Philosophers of the West* I had by my bed at Oxford. I read T.S. Eliot's *Notes Towards the Definition of Culture* (1948), which sees religion as crucial towards world culture, and T.S. Eliot is again an influence. Later I was influenced by the world-cultural perspective of Pound and Briggs. The main four forebears and influences on me, then, were:

1. Tomlin
2. Eliot
3. Pound
4. Briggs

So that now concludes my setting out of the traditions and influences that shaped my works. A Universalist writer (see list of 63 Universalist writers on pp.22–25) is at home in many disciplines and is influenced by many traditions and other writers, and this is now apparent in my case. All my influences influenced one or more of my individual works, as I have tried to show.

To be at home in many disciplines involves Universalist writers in making a choice. In Japan I was offered a Chair for Life in English Literature in 1967, and gave notice to leave as it would have confined me to one discipline whereas I knew I had to steep myself in many disciplines, like a Renaissance man. This process involved me in a lot of research over 30 years (the entire duration of my Mystic Way) and then required daily and weekly updating.

To keep abreast of the most recent developments in all disciplines I have read four newspapers on weekdays and five newspapers on Sundays and take relevant cuttings to keep my knowledge up to date. To be at home in many disciplines and remain connected to many traditions and influences takes Universalist writers and thinkers a considerable amount of time each day.

Traditions and influences within my 60 works in seven disciplines and seven genres of literature

I have set out the traditions and influences behind my 60 published works within seven disciplines and within seven genres of literature.

On p.148 is the Tree of Tradition shown on p.xxv, with seven branches and seven offshoots reflecting the seven disciplines and seven genres of literature in my works outlined in the two columns beneath:

7 disciplines	7 genres of literature
1 mysticism	(1) poems and epic poems
2 literature	(2) verse plays, masques, prose plays and films
3 philosophy and the sciences	(3) short stories, novellas, novels and satirical works
4 history	(4) diaries
5 comparative religion	(5) autobiographies and travelogues
6 international politics and statecraft	(6) letters and essays
7 world culture	(7) the fundamental theme of world literature

The same Tree of Tradition also reflects the seven disciplines' main traditions numbered 1–109 and also the seven disciplines' main influences numbered 1–84, see the two tables below:

109 main traditions within seven disciplines and seven genres of literature in my works that influenced me (with Dewey and Library of Congress classifications when they exist, absences of which show the broad-brush inadequacy of the generalising classification system in contrast to specific traditions and influences):

1. the tradition of the Mystic Way;
2. the tradition of inner illumination by the Fire or Light, the metaphysical Reality, the One;
3. the tradition of extrovertive mysticism;

4. the tradition of Viennese mysticism;

5. the tradition of Evelyn Underhill's mysticism;

6. the tradition of Pascal's Fire;

7. the tradition of St Augustine's Light Unchangeable;

8. the tradition of unitive vision, instinctively seeing the unity of the universe, at the end of the Mystic Way;

9. the tradition of the Light within 25 civilisations;

10. the tradition of the European mystics;

11. the tradition of the North-American Light;

12. the tradition of Zen Buddhist *satori* (Enlightenment);

13. the tradition of Confucian reconciliation of opposites;

14. the tradition of questing for metaphysical Reality in literature (Library of Congress PR);

15. the tradition of condemning the social follies and vices of humankind, social satires, in literature (Library of Congress PR);

16. the tradition of a man of letters in several disciplines like Swift and T.S. Eliot holding European and Western leaders to account for the damage of their policies to the cultural health of Europe and the West;

17. the tradition of mystical poems (Dewey 821);

18. the tradition of social poems (Dewey 821);

19. the tradition of narrative poems, some with glosses (Dewey 821);

20. the tradition of Modernist poems (Dewey 821);

21. the tradition of poems on decline (Dewey 821);

22. the tradition of Catullan poems, range of emotions (Dewey 821);

23. the tradition of poems on illumination and visions (Dewey 821);

24. the tradition of metaphysical poems (quest for the One);

25. the tradition of lyrical poems (Dewey 821);

26. the tradition of Nature poems (Dewey 821);

27. the tradition of Baroque poems (Dewey 821);

28. the tradition of epic poems or poetic epics (Homer, Virgil, Milton) (Dewey 821, 883);

29. the tradition of writing in trimeters, tetrameters and pentameters;
30. the tradition of writing alternately-rhymed lines in trimeters;
31. the tradition of writing in blank verse;
32. the tradition of rhymed stanzas of 4, 8 or 10 lines;
33. the tradition of writing alternately-rhymed lines in 8-line stanzas;
34. the tradition of writing rhymed sonnets from Wyatt to Wordsworth and beyond;
35. the tradition of writing classical odes (from Horace to Keats and beyond);
36. the tradition of blank verse in epic poetry;
37. the tradition of narrating warfare in epic poetry;
38. the tradition of questing for metaphysical Reality, including visiting Hell/the Underworld and Heaven in epic poetry;
39. the tradition of unrealistic verse drama on a stage without scenery;
40. the tradition of scenery in verse drama (Dewey 822);
41. the tradition of investigating world government in verse drama;
42. the tradition of masques ending in revels (Dewey 822);
43. the tradition of paranoia in prose plays;
44. the tradition of crisis and choice in films;
45. the tradition of epic founding of a new civilisation in films;
46. the tradition of questing for metaphysical Reality in short stories (Dewey 823, Library of Congress PZ);
47. the tradition of condemning follies and vices in short stories (Dewey 823, 827);
48. the tradition of questing for metaphysical Reality in novellas (Dewey 823);
49. the tradition of questing for proof of atheism in novellas (Dewey 823);
50. the tradition of forays into disciplines in novels;
51. the tradition of satirical works in prose;
52. the tradition of literary diaries;
53. the tradition of autobiographies about a quest for metaphysical Reality;

54. the tradition of writing travelogues about remote places (Dewey 955, 961);

55. the tradition of writing letters about literary works (Dewey 826);

56. the tradition of essay-writing (Dewey 824);

57. the tradition of writing Prefaces to literary and thinking works;

58. the tradition of one fundamental theme of world literature;

59. the tradition of questing for the One in world literature (Dewey 801);

60. the tradition of condemning follies and vices in world literature (Dewey 827);

61. the tradition of questing for metaphysical Reality in philosophy (Dewey 110);

62. the tradition of a social and linguistic approach in philosophy (Dewey 160);

63. the tradition of Anaximander's *to apeiron* (boundless, infinite) (Dewey 182);

64. the tradition of Socrates' dialogues (Dewey 183);

65. the tradition of Plato's *Republic* (Dewey 184);

66. the tradition of philosophers of East and West (Dewey 180, 189, 190);

67. the tradition of Existentialist thinkers (Dewey 190);

68. the tradition of French and German Existentialism (Dewey 190);

69. the tradition of writing within many disciplines (as in Universalism);

70. the tradition of an implicate order in the universe;

71. the tradition of seeking a Theory of Everything;

72. the tradition of singularity in the universe;

73. the tradition of seeing the unity of the universe and humankind (Dewey 218, 233);

74. the tradition of an anthology of essentials in Universalist philosophy;

75. the tradition of Bossuet's metaphysical view of the Light as fundamental to the rise of civilisations;

76. the tradition of the speculative history of Gibbon, Spengler and Toynbee (Dewey 901);

77. the tradition of Providential/metaphysical world history (Dewey 909, Library of Congress CB);

78. the tradition of social events in world history (Dewey 909);

79. the tradition of classical history (Dewey 930, Library of Congress DF);

80. the tradition of the founding of America (Library of Congress E);

81. the tradition of American history (Library of Congress E);

82. the tradition of the future of America (Library of Congress E);

83. the tradition of world history (Library of Congress CB);

84. the tradition of a World State (Library of Congress JC);

85. the tradition of current affairs;

86. the tradition of the Syndicate's New World Order;

87. the tradition of eyewitness history;

88. the tradition of local history;

89. the tradition of inner quest in religion (Dewey 204);

90. the tradition of outer observance in religion (Dewey 203);

91. the tradition of Methodism (Dewey 287, 280, Library of Congress BR);

92. the tradition of Anglicanism (Dewey 283, 280, Library of Congress BR):

93. the tradition of Buddhism (Dewey 294, Library of Congress BQ);

94. the tradition of the Universalist religious experience of the One;

95. the tradition of the vision of questing for metaphysical Reality that reveals the unity of humankind in international politics and statecraft;

96. the tradition of social and secular relationship of sovereign nation-states in international politics and statecraft;

97. the tradition of supranationalism in international politics and statecraft;

98. the tradition of world government in international politics and statecraft;

99. the tradition of world federalism in international politics and statecraft;

100. the tradition of founding a World State in international politics and statecraft;
101. the tradition of questing for metaphysical Reality in world culture;
102. the tradition of social-secular art in world culture;
103. the tradition of civilisations' cultures;
104. the tradition of the fundamental unity of world culture;
105. the tradition of the Light in European culture;
106. the tradition of Universalist world culture;
107. the tradition of all past influences on world culture;
108. the tradition of world-wide global culture (Dewey 305, 306); and
109. the tradition of 50 'isms' of fragmented European culture.

The above are the 109 main traditions of the seven disciplines in my work. Universalism takes *all* traditions into account, including offshoots from main branches on the Tree of Tradition, and indeed twigs.

84 main influences on my works within seven disciplines and seven genres of literature (in alphabetical order):

1.	Addison	17.	Chaucer
2.	Aeschylus	18.	Clare
3.	Anaximander	19.	Coleridge
4.	Augustine, St	20.	Dante
5.	Barrow	21.	Davenport
6.	Blackham, H.J.	22.	Donne
7.	Blake	23.	Dryden
8.	Blunden	24.	Durrell
9.	Blyth, R.H.	25.	Eliot, T.S.
10.	Bohm	26.	Euripides
11.	Briggs	27.	Fellows
12.	Brooke	28.	Gascoyne
13.	Bryan	29.	Gibbon
14.	Buchanan	30.	Hardy
15.	Camus	31.	Heath-Stubbs
16.	Catullus	32.	Hemingway

33. Hildegard of Bingen	59. Raleigh
34. Homer	60. Ricks
35. Horace	61. Riley, Margaret
36. Horton	62. Sartre
37. Housman	63. Shakespeare
38. Hughes	64. Shelley
39. Irie	65. Socrates
40. John of the Cross, St	66. Sophocles
41. Jonson	67. Spengler
42. Kant	68. Stott
43. Keats	69. Suhrawardi
44. Kelso	70. Swift
45. Kondrashin, Igor	71. Tennyson
46. Lawrence, T.E.	72. Thompson
47. Livy	73. Thucydides
48. Marlowe	74. Tomlin
49. Marvell	75. Toynbee
50. Milton	76. Truman
51. Nishiwaki, Junzaburo	77. Tuohy
52. Ovid	78. Underhill, Evelyn
53. Pascal	79. Virgil
54. Penrose	80. Whitehead
55. Plato	81. Wilson, Colin
56. Pope	82. Wordsworth
57. Pound	83. Wyatt
58. Raine, Kathleen	84. Yeats

I repeat what I said on pp.37–38: it is possible to set out a similar Tree of Tradition for any writer or thinker who has ever lived. The Tree is in fact filled with the traditions of many more disciplines – all those in the Dewey and Library of Congress classifications, and more, and many contemporary traditions that have just been founded (see 112 main academic disciplines on pp.196–198). If I were to put every tradition in all our 193 nation-states and regions in all 14 living civilisations and 11 dead civilisations, the Tree of Tradition would be submerged in tens of thousands of past and present traditions and influences.

My Tree of Tradition based on my 60 works in 109 traditions and 84 influences is a tiny version of a vast Tree of Tradition based on millions of works, traditions and influences, within which every writer and thinker perpetuates a handful – or in the case of Universalist writers and thinkers, some 109 traditions and some 84 influences.

All writers can identify the discipline or disciplines in which they write, identify the traditions that have influenced them and their influences, and arrive at their totals of traditions and influences just as I have on pp.148–154.

I am fully aware that my explanation of the Tree of Tradition so far has the elaboration of a Metaphysical conceit. In prison Shakespeare's Richard II muses, "I have been studying how I may compare/This prison where I live unto the world..../I cannot do it. Yet I'll hammer 't out." I have hammered out a comparison of the World Tree with all the traditions and influences and, with a nod to the four-centuries-old Metaphysical conceit, hope I have brought alive the traditions and influences among which we all live and which have inspired all the world's writers and thinkers throughout recorded history. As Eliot emphasised in 'Tradition and the Individual Talent' (see p.viii) the Tree of Tradition involves "the historical sense" of the "pastness of the past" and its "presence", and it is the "timeless and temporal" together that make a writer "traditional".

3

The Tree of Tradition Behind Writers and Thinkers in all Civilisations and a World State: World Culture and a Universalist New World Order

I have set out the different forms of the Tree of Tradition. And I have shown how all writers follow its traditions and influences, using my works as an example.

Universalist stages of civilisations

The Tree of Tradition includes the 25 civilisations, each going through 61 stages, which first appeared in *The Fire and the Stones* (1991) that came with a chart 7-foot-long with the civilisations listed down on the left and 61 stages across on the right (see below).

Nicholas Hagger shows Iain McNay the 7-foot-long chart of 25 civilisations each going through 61 stages while being interviewed by him on Conscious TV on 14 April 2015.

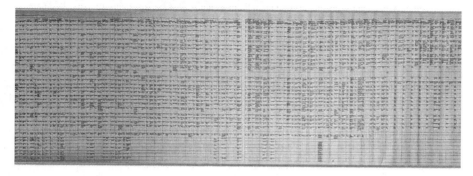

The 7-foot-long chart that accompanies *The Fire and the Stones* (1991) showing 25 civilisations rising and falling through 61 stages. The book predicted the end of Communism in the Soviet Union, and forecast the conglomerate that became the European Union.

The Tree of Tradition of all civilisations contains within its traditions the 61 stages of the 25 civilisations (see Appendix 4 on pp.226–227) and at what point civilisations adopt Universalism, seeing the unity of the universe and humankind. I now need to look at the current stages of living civilisations, and whereabouts in their life cycle they are Universalist (see below), as this gives the world a chance to draw together and for America, as the world's youngest civilisation, to play an important role.

25 Civilisations and Their Current, and Universalist, Stages

25 civilisations	Living/dead (L/D)	Which of 61 numbered stages now in	Universalism in numbered stages
1. Indo-European Kurgan	D		15, 17, 27, 29, 31, 34, 44 in each of 25 civilisations
2. Mesopotamian	D		
3. Egyptian	D		
4. Aegean-Greek	D		
5. Roman	D		
6. Anatolian	D		

25 civilisations	Living/dead (L/D)	Which of 61 numbered stages now in	Universalism in numbered stages
7. Syrian	D		
8. Israelite	D		
9. Celtic	D		
10. Iranian	D		
11. European	L	43	
12. North-American	L	15	15, 17 so far, the rest in the future
13. Byzantine-Russian	L	46	
14. German-Scandinavian	D		
15. Andean	L	46	
16. Meso-American	L	46	
17. Arab	L	46	
18. African	L	46	
19. Indian	L	46	
20. Southeast Asian	L	46	
21. Japanese	L	43	
22. Oceanian	L	43	
23. Chinese	L	43	
24. Tibetan	L	43	
25. Central Asian	L	46	

America is in stage 15, a Universalist stage. The heretical sect of stage 17 is Universalist, and the Universalist heresy of stage 27 expands in stage 29, becomes a new orthodoxy in stage 31, further expands in stage 34 and surfaces as Universalism in stage 44. (See the above table.)

In my Preface to *The Secret American Destiny* I wrote about my Law of History in a section titled 'Civilizations' Rise-and-Fall Pattern':[1]

> In my study *The Fire and the Stones*, updated as *The Light of Civilization* and *The Rise and Fall of Civilizations*, which I began in Japan, I see 25 civilizations passing through 61 stages. [See Appendix 4, pp.226–227.] Each civilization is shaped in a parabola like a rainbow: it rises through a metaphysical vision

which passes into its religion, and declines when it turns secular and loses some of the *élan* which carried it upward in its early stages. The North-American civilization is the youngest of my 25 civilizations, having been founded in 1607, and has reached stage 15, the stage the Roman Empire was in at the beginning of its expansionist phase. This North-American stage began c1913. The vision through which the civilization rose was then expressed in American ecumenical Protestantism. Europe's comparable expansion was between c.951 and 1244 and included the Crusades.

Stage 15 is soon followed by the creation of a Light-based heretical sect, after which a 'new people' graft the heresy onto the civilization's main religion and central idea. In Europe's case the new 'heresy' was the early Protestantism of the Reformation and the 'new people' were the Renaissance Humanists. The equivalent North-American heresy is a coming Universalism[2] which will draw on the Freemasonic Deistic Illuminatists I wrote about in chapters 4 and 5 of *The Secret Founding of America*, and on the more recent New Age. The 'new people' in the North-American civilization will be new Universalists who affirm a universal God drawn from all religions and perceived or experienced as Light.

If my vision of coming history is right, America's expansionist phase (which began in its stage 15) will create a democratic World State with a Universalist outlook that will include a universal God perceived as Light or Fire. This will be grafted on to Christian ecumenical Protestantism and will absorb it and offer a global religion. Just as Renaissance Humanists grafted Protestantism on to the Catholic Light, so new Universalists will graft Universalism on to the American Protestant Light.

America's stage-15 expansion

I also set out the 25 civilisations (see pp.157–158) and the dates of their expansion in stage 15 (see below):[3]

Stage-15 Expansion of 25 Civilisations

	Civilisation	Date of Expansion	Expansion
1.	Indo-European Kurgan	c.2550–2200BC	Funnel-Neck Beaker Folk
2.	Mesopotamian	c.1950–1750BC	Old Babylonian Empire
3.	Egyptian	2110–1786BC	Empire of Middle Kingdom
4.	Aegean-Greek	c.1650–1450BC	Minoan Empire on mainland Greece
5.	Roman	c.341–218BC	Roman Empire in Italy
6.	Anatolian	c.1471–1300BC	Hittite Empire in Syria/Canaan
7.	Syrian	c.1471–1360BC	Ugaritic hegemony in Canaan
8.	Israelite	c.1140–960BC	Israelite Empire to David
9.	Celtic	c.337–250BC	Celtic La Tène expansion
10.	Iranian	c.280BC–10CE	Parthian Empire
11.	European	c.951–1244	Europe's expansion into Mediterranean
12.	North-American	c.1913–c.2250?	America's world expansion
13.	Byzantine-Russian	c.677–1071	Byzantine Empire (including Balkans)
14.	Germanic-Scandinavian	c.38–170	Expansion of Germanic tribes
15.	Andean	c.350BC–300CE	Expansion of Nazca/Moche
16.	Meso-American	c.350BC–100CE	Post-Olmec expansion
17.	Arab	790–1055	Abbasid Caliphate expansion
18.	African	c.370–540	Aksum Empire
19.	Indian	c.120 or c.290–750	Gupta Empire
20.	South-East Asian	c.850–1100	7 South-East Asian Empires
21.	Japanese	c.710–1000	Imperial state ruled from Nara/Kyoto
22.	Oceanian	c.850–950	Polynesian expansion
23.	Chinese	c.354–907	Sui/Tang Empires
24.	Tibetan	c.1247–1481	Tibetan expansion
25.	Central-Asian	c.1–950	Expansion under Xiongnu (Hsiung-nu) etc

So the young North-American civilisation is in stage 15, the same stage that the Roman Empire was in after the two Punic

Wars (compare the two 20th-century World Wars), and just as the Roman Empire's Universalism brought unity to the culture of the known world during Roman times, America has already developed a Universalist outlook based on the Universalist Light that can develop a World State.

In *The Secret American Destiny* I wrote:[4]

Ever since the first English settlers left England, crossed stormy seas in fragile wooden ships, probed the shores of the River James and founded the Jamestown Settlement in 1607, migrants have crossed the Atlantic to the New World. Refugees from religious persecution and wretched living conditions in Europe have settled on America's East Coast. Towards the end of the 19th century the first sight of America that refugees had from their ship was the Statue of Liberty. To them, America was a land of promise where migrants could fulfil their dreams of a prosperous life for their families and themselves.

During the 20th century Liberty began looking outwards. The new dream was to export prosperity to the peoples of the world, the poor and huddled yearning to breathe free. During the oppressive time of Communism, Fascism and the Cold War America rolled back tyranny. And after the fall of the Soviet Union there were dreams of a new order that would transcend nation-states and bring a new era of peace to the Earth. There was a yearning for all humankind to be united under a World State, a dream rudely interrupted by regional wars in Iraq, Afghanistan, Libya and Syria. But the dream did not fade and still remains to be turned into reality.

America's vision of spiritual unity
My study of history shows that it is America's destiny to establish a political supranational World State with a democratic structure that can export the American Dream to all humankind.[5] To bring such a benevolent political unity to the peoples of the world, America must proclaim and disseminate a vision of the spiritual

161

unity of humankind and world culture that will welcome and nourish political unity.

I wrote under the heading 'Civilizations' metaphysical rise and secular fall':[6]

My study of history shows that for 5,000 years 25 civilizations have undergone a rise-and-fall pattern. They rise following experiences of the One (Reality, the metaphysical Light or Fire that is beyond the world of physics), which pass into their religion;[7] and they fall when the metaphysical vision ceases to be strong and turns secular. Civilizations have the structure of a curved rainbow which rises and falls as the metaphysical vision turns secular and social. [See Appendix 4.]

Within each of the 25 civilizations there is a pair of opposites, a thesis and antithesis, a '+A + −A': the metaphysical and the social. The +A, the civilization's metaphysical central idea, is strong during its growth; the −A, a focus on the secular and social at the expense of the civilization's original metaphysical vision, is strong during its decline and decay. When a civilization has run its course it passes into another civilization, as did the Egyptian civilization and its god Ra − Egypt passed into the new Arab civilization and worshipped Allah from 642.

All civilizations from their outset are a tension between the '+A + −A' of their metaphysical/religious vision and their secular/ social approach. Although during their growth the metaphysical vision is in the ascendancy and during their decline the secular mindset predominates, in every decade and century of a civilization's life there is an underlying tension between the two, which is reflected in the seven disciplines.

I can now sharpen the North-American and European civilisations' Universalist stages.

The United States is currently in stage 15, the stage the Roman Empire was in, and Universalism features in stage 17 (creation of a Light-based heretical sect). (Interestingly, in stage 16 there is heroic epic literature with a god of Light-led growth. My two epics *Overlord* and *Armageddon* have American heroes, Eisenhower and George W. Bush, and now is a perfect time for America to welcome epic poems.) The European civilisation is in stage 43, a Union stage, the European Union, when there is loss of national sovereignty to a secularising conglomerate. Stage 44 involves syncretism and Universalism round the Light, which is the stage the EU is in.

(The UK, wanting its sovereignty back via Brexit, is passing into stage 46, from a Union based on a considerable amount of Universalism to a federation, into a Federation of the British Isles in which England will have its own parliament. And stage 47 may have already arrived in the UK: economic decline and inflation, class conflict involving the ruling class struggling with strikes by the ruled, see Appendix 4.)

Universalism is therefore currently present in both the North-American civilisation, where it is a positive world-wide force, and in the European civilisation, where it is bringing about a more declinist syncretisation than in the younger North-American civilisation. The UK was Universalist but has returned to nationalism and is more declinist.

Also in *The Secret American Destiny* I set out the European civilisation's stage 43 and Universalism, and North-America's stage 15 and Universalism:[8]

The European civilization's stage 43 and Universalism
In the early growing period of a civilization, the metaphysical outlook exercises a unifying control of the civilization's culture. A unified culture is like a tree with sap in its branches that are all nourished by its trunk.[9] An image of the European civilization is: a tree with all the European nation-states as branches.

The European civilization had a unified culture during its growth. In the Middle Ages, the time of the Crusades, all the seven branchlike disciplines of the European culture – including European art, literature and music – were nourished by its central interconnecting metaphysical idea, the trunk of its Christian religion, and there was unity of culture and 'unity of being' (W.B. Yeats's phrase).[10] European art, sculpture, music, literature and philosophy all expressed the Christian vision of the illumined soul, or halo. The expressions of European culture reflected the examined life, progress to sainthood and contemplation of the divine in serene and ordered Gregorian chants and stone angels. The inspiration that imbued the disciplines was 'metaphysical' (in the sense of a 'Reality beyond the world of physics and Nature' and 'beyond the senses') and involved energy manifesting into the universe from beyond itself.

Despite the Reformation, unity of European culture persisted during the Elizabethan age and the time of the 17th-century Metaphysical poets. However, since the 18th century the metaphysical idea expressed through Christianity has dwindled and European culture has turned secular.

The European civilization has now reached stage 43 [as can be seen in the tables on pp.157–158 and pp.167–170]. As *The Rise and Fall of Civilizations* shows,[11] a post-imperial colonial conflict in stage 41 led to decolonization, and there is now a loss of national sovereignty to an inheriting secular conglomerate – the European Union. The conglomerate has brought in stage 44, when syncretism and universalism are prevalent as religious sects draw together with Light as a common source. Universalism earlier surfaced in stages 15, 29 and 34.[12] There is a revival of cultural purity in stage 45, which in Europe's case is likely to be a revival of the Classical/Baroque vision of stage 28.[13] (The Arab civilization's stage 45 has been heralded by IS or ISIL, the terrorist group better known in the Arab world as Daesh.) In stage 46 there will be a further attempt at counter-thrust under a foreign federalist influence as the European Union gives way to a looser, federal arrangement (just as the USSR gave way to the Russian Federation in its stage 46), and it is possible that there will be a 50-state United States of Europe ahead.[14]

The North-American civilization's stage 15 and Universalism
My study of history shows that the North-American civilization is still in stage 15, a stage all the world's civilizations have been through [as can be seen in Appendix 4 on pp.226–227, and on the table on p.160]: the expansion into empire and

Light-led renewal of growth, the stage the Roman Empire was in at its height, the ideal stage in which to create a World State. We have just seen that Europe had a unified culture in its stage 15, and we would expect the American culture to be unified, its branches energized by sap from its trunk, ecumenical Protestantism. American church attendance in 2013 was 37/39 per cent[15] (a relatively high figure typical of stage 15) against 6 per cent in Britain (a relatively low figure typical of stage 43). European church attendance is hard to measure but in 2010 49 per cent of the population in the EU states did not believe in God (again, a relatively high figure typical of stage 43).[16] America has been largely populated by migrants from Europe, beginning in a time when there was still a unified European culture and continuing today when the European culture is disunited, and although (judging from the above percentages) the metaphysical central idea of the North-American civilization is clearly stronger than its European equivalent, both a metaphysical vision and a secular/ social approach co-exist in contemporary America.

I have written elsewhere that America's recent stage-15 path was expansionist and led to superpowerdom or hyperpowerdom, and that interventionist expansion (abandoned by Obama)[17] was inspired by a Universalist Light-led renewal of growth under radical American ecumenical Protestantism that funded the World Council of Churches. African churches have been supported by donations from the church-attending 37–39 per cent of America's population.[18] In due course this ecumenical, internationalist Protestant vision can be expected to blend with the Universalist New Age vision of the metaphysical Light.[19]

The 400-year-old North-American civilization (founded in 1607 and now in stage 15) and the 1,600-year-old European civilization (founded in the 5th century after the fall of Rome and now in stage 43), which, though separate civilizations, together make up Western civilization, are at different stages in their 61-stage cycles. Other living civilizations, such as the Indian, Byzantine-Russian, Chinese, Japanese and Arab civilizations, have lived through their own stages 15 and 43 and have therefore known Universalism. There are pockets of Universalist outlook in different parts of the world, having surfaced within all the world's civilizations in those two stages. American Universalism is at present a blend of Christian and New Age, themselves a '+A + –A' or pair of opposites, and the younger American Universalism has undoubtedly influenced the drawing together of sects in older Europe. Universalism is known on both sides of the Atlantic in different historical contexts.

We can now see from the above that American civilisation has the youthful energy to bring about the United Federation (UF) of discipline 6 (international politics and statecraft), as I argued in *The Secret American Dream*. We have seen that the world culture is in conflict between metaphysical and social traditions within the seven disciplines. In *The Secret American Destiny* I wrote under the heading 'Metaphysical and social approaches in seven disciplines':[20]

> The growing North-American civilization's metaphysical outlook is signalled by the confident 'In God we trust', which the US currency proclaims. Although the North-American civilization is younger and more metaphysical than the more secular European civilization, in both civilizations both the metaphysical vision and social approach co-exist within the seven disciplines of world culture, as we have just seen.
>
> We can now see that in each of the seven disciplines the original metaphysical approach has been challenged by, and now co-exists with, a secular, social approach. In each of the seven disciplines there is a '+A + –A' or pair of opposites that make for disunity in world culture.
>
> As we look at each of the seven disciplines, our focus is on the last 4,500–5,000 years and each discipline has a strong European contribution. America has inherited each discipline and added to it during the last century or more, often with distinguished and impressive results.

So Universalism is present in stage 15 (and in its accompanying stage 17) in America's young civilisation, and in European and older civilisations it was present in stages 15, 17, 27, 29, 31, 34 and 44 (see pp.157–158). In the UF there would be 12 main regions based on the 14 living civilisations: South America, one region, includes two living civilisations (the Andean and Meso-American civilisations). Twelve of the 13 civilisation-based regions (excluding the North-American) and 13 of the 14 living civilisations (excluding the North-American) are all either within stage 43 or stage 46 (see pp.157–158 for overview). I wrote in *The Secret American Destiny* under the heading '13 regions, 14 living civilisations and the World State: Federations and World Federation':[21]

Twelve of the 13 civilization-based regions (excluding the North-American) – and 13 of the 14 living civilizations (excluding the North-American) – are all either within stage 43 or stage 46. The five stage-43 living civilizations are: the European civilization; the Japanese civilization; the Oceanian civilization; the Chinese civilization (which entered stage 43 in 1949); and the Tibetan civilization. The conglomerates or unions of all the stage-43 civilizations and their dates, which assume no World State, are:

Civilisations Losing Sovereignty to Conglomerates:

Civilisation	Loss of sovereignty to conglomerate, which acts as secularizing foreign influence	Date
1. Indo-European Kurgan/Old European	Unetice-Tumulus people's Empire in West with trade in Cornwall, Ireland, Central Europe and the Baltic	c.1550–1400BC
2. Mesopotamian	Cyrus's Achaemenian Persian Empire which was united with Babylonia into a conglomerate	c.539–331BC

Civilisation	Loss of sovereignty to conglomerate, which acts as secularizing foreign influence	Date
3. Egyptian	Saite dynasty's Assyrian-backed conglomerate under the Assyrian vassal prince Psamtik I of Sais, who took the Assyrian name Nabushezibanni in 663BC	c.664–525BC
4. Aegean-Greek	Persian-backed Peloponnesian League controlled by the Persian Great King; Athens revived again from c.378BC but was checked by the Persian Artaxerxes III Ochus and lost a Second Athenian Empire while the rest of Greece was a Persian-controlled conglomerate	c.404–337BC
5. Roman	Empire of the German chieftan Odoacer, who deposed the last Roman Emperor in the West in 476 and established a Kingdom of Italy; Visigothic Kingdom in Spain and France; Vandal Kingdom in North Africa, Sicily, Sardinia and Corsica; after 488, rule of the Ostrogoths who invaded Italy, besieged Ravenna and overthrew Odoacer	c.476–540
6. Anatolian	Cyrus's Achaemenian Persian Empire	c.546–334BC
7. Syrian	Cyrus's Achaemenian Persian Empire (language spoken, Imperial Aramaic)	c.538–333BC
8. Israelite	Cyrus's Achaemenian Persian Empire	c.538–333BC
9. Celtic	Secular internationalist Saxon rule spreading from East Britain to West Britain	c.540–687

Civilisation	Loss of sovereignty to conglomerate, which acts as secularizing foreign influence	Date
10. Iranian	Arab Caliphate in Iran	c.642–821
11. European	European Union with its own legal personality after the Lisbon Treaty, developing into a United States of Europe eventually comprising 50 states[22]	From 1992 (EU)/2009 (EU after Lisbon Treaty)–c.2150?: conglomerate created when an expanded, economically integrated European Community led via a European Union to a USA-influenced politically unified United States of Western, Central and Eastern Europe
12. North-American	—	
13. Byzantine-Russian	Conglomerate of USSR based on an internationalist foreign Marxian ideology	c.1918–1991
14. Germanic-Scandinavian	Reunification of the Franks under Mayors of the Palace, beginning with Pepin II and Charles Martel	c.687–843
15. Andean	Internationalist Spanish colonial Empire	c.1572–1810
16. Meso-American	Internationalist Spanish colonial Empire	c.1542–1810
17. Arab	Arab world passed into internationalist European colonial Empires which secularized Islam in North Africa and the Middle East	c.1881–1980 (Semi-colonial occupation in Iraq and Afghanistan 2001–2006)
18. African	Internationalist European colonial Empires which secularized African religion following scramble for Africa	c.1914–1980
19. India	Internationalist British Empire (British Raj), unification of Indian states into one India	c.1818–1947

Civilisation	Loss of sovereignty to conglomerate, which acts as secularizing foreign influence	Date
20. South-East-Asian	European colonization and Empires in South-East Asia (by British, French and Dutch)	c.1876–1947
21. Japanese	American occupation of Japan under General MacArthur in 1945–1951, then unified conglomerate of 47 prefectures or provinces	c.1945–c.2050?
22. Oceanian	Western (European and North-American) colonization and Empire in Oceania	c.1900–2007 (Federation of Oceania began in 2007. Some islands still under Western rule)
23. Chinese	Conglomerate of People's Republic of China based on an internationalist foreign Marxian ideology, devised by a German Jew in European London	c.1949–c.2050?
24. Tibetan	European Internationalist Chinese occupation which has secularized Tibetan religion	c.1951–c.2050?
25. Central-Asian	Chinese Manchu occupation of Mongolia (conquest completed in 1759)	c.1644–1911

If the five stage-43 living civilizations pass into a World State, their conglomerates or unions will be superseded by the World State and will pass into the World Federation.

The eight stage-46 living civilizations are: the Byzantine-Russian civilization (which passed into stage 46, the Russian Federation, in 1991); the Andean and Meso-American civilizations; the Arab civilization; the African civilization (which entered stage 46 with the advent of the African Union); the Indian civilization (a federation since 1947); the South-East-Asian civilization; and the Central-Asian civilization. The stage-46 federations of all the 13 living civilizations (excluding the stage-15 North-American civilization) and their dates, which assume no

World State – i.e. projected dates for the federations of the eight currently in stage 46 and for the eventual federations of the five still in stage 43 – are:

Living Civilisations Passing into Federations

Civilisation	Date	Stage 46: Foreign Federalist Influence
11. European	c.2150–2250?	Federation of European nation-states?
13. Byzantine-Russian	c.1991–2100?	Federalist post-Communist Russia linked to coming United States of Europe
15. Andean	c.1810–2050?	Pan-American federalism in Latin America under US (now through the 1948 Organization of American States, the 2005 Free Trade Area of the Americas, FTAA, of 34 nation-states including the US, and the 2008 Union of South American Nations)
16. Meso-American	c.1810–2050?	Pan-American federalism in Latin America under US (now through the 1948 Organization of American States, the 2005 Free Trade Area of the Americas, FTAA, of 34 nation-states including the US, and the 2008 Union of South American Nations)
17. Arab	c.1980–2100?	Coming Federation of Arab and Islamic states through the 1945 Arab League (which in 2004 proposed an Arab Union that is still being discussed)?
18. African	c.1980–2100?	Coming Federation of African states (starting with OAU 1963–2002 and based on the African Union, AU, of 54 states founded in 2001)?
19. Indian	c.1947–2050?	Independent federal India under West?
20. South-East-Asian	c.1950–2050?	Coming Federation of South-East-Asian states based on the 1967 Association of South-East Asian Nations (ASEAN) (eventually Pacific Community)?
21. Japanese	c.2050–2150?	Coming Federation of Japanese Pacific territories
22. Oceanian	c.2007–2100?	Federation of Oceania began in 2007
23. Chinese	c.2050–2150?	Federalist post-Communist China linked to coming Federation of South-East-Asian states?

Civilisation	Date	Stage 46: Foreign Federalist Influence
24. Tibetan	c.2050–2150?	Coming Federation of South-East-Asian states (eventually Asia-Pacific Community)?
25. Central-Asian	c.1911–2050?	Federalism under Russia and China, and coming Federation of Arab and Islamic states?

If the eight stage-46 living civilizations pass into a World State, these federations will be superseded by the World State and will pass into the World Federation.

As the North-American civilization is in stage 15 [see table on pp.157–158], in the same stage that the Roman civilization was in before 218BC when it expanded its Republican Empire in Carthage, Macedonia, Greece and Spain as a result of the Punic Wars – and before its expansion during Caesar's campaigns into Gaul, Britain, Dacia, Armenia, Assyria and Mesopotamia – it can harness all the stage-46 federations and can organize the stage-43 unions into entering an American-initiated World State or World Federation for the 13 living civilizations other than the North-American civilization. As the only superpower, the North-American civilization would preside over the World Federation just as the Roman civilization presided over the world state of its day, the Roman Empire. However the North-American civilization would preside in a non-imperial way, over a Federation as a system of interconnected federations.

From the dates it looks as if three of the stage-43 living civilizations, the Japanese, Chinese and Tibetan civilizations, will enter federalism c.2050, which could also be when the World State comes into being. The European civilization looks as if it will enter federalism later, c.2150. It looks as if five of the stage-46 civilizations, the Andean, Meso-American, Indian, South-East-Asian and Central-Asian civilizations, will end their federalism c.2050 and then undergo foreign occupation, while the Arab, Byzantine-Russian and African civilizations will end their federalism in 2100 and then undergo foreign occupation.

If the World State or World Federation is formed over a period of time, then the living civilizations we have just looked at can be expected to enter in batches by consent, like nation-states entering the EU; some c.2050, and some c.2100. It is possible to see how a World State could take shape by studying the living civilizations' patterns of union (stage 43), federation (stage 46) and foreign occupation (stage 49).

The World State or World Federation would be *partly* federal in limiting itself to seven supranational goals [see p.135]: bringing peace and disarmament between nation-states, sharing resources and energy, solving environmental problems such as global warming, ending disease, ending famine, solving the world's financial crisis and redistributing wealth to eliminate poverty. It would be partly federal in loosely allowing nation-states and civilizations to continue at local regional level outside these seven policy areas.

So America is well-placed to organise a one-world movement with American Universalism, in which there will be a one-world mysticism, one-world literature, one-world philosophy and sciences, one-world history, one-world comparative religion, one-world international politics and statecraft, and one-world culture. The size of America's coming expansion can be seen from the table on p.160.

We are now back to the United Federation, the UF, which I have dealt with in *World State* (see p.135).

The Tree of Tradition as World State

The Tree of Tradition as World Tree in its two forms of the Tree of Knowledge that reaches down into the Underworld and up into Heaven, as does the Norse Yggdrasil, and the Tree of Life that connects all forms of creation, contains all traditions within its branches, including the stages which 14 living civilisations have reached.

As we have seen (see p.160) we are living in a time when the North-American civilisation is in stage 15 with an expansionist Universalism and when, of the other 13 living civilisations, 5 (the European, Japanese, Oceanian, Chinese after 1949 and Tibetan civilisations) are in stage 43 (unions with a united Universalist outlook) and 8 (the Byzantine-Russian after 1991, Andean, Meso-American, Arab, African, Indian, South-East Asian, and Central Asian civilisations) are in stage 46 (federations with a federal Universalist outlook).

By following these 14 living civilisations (see the long chart that accompanies *The Fire and the Stones*, pp.156–157, and Appendix 4, pp.226–227), writers and thinkers can arrive at a true understanding of where the current morass of civilisations has reached, and how open they are, or will soon be, to be in a federation that can take a lead from a civilisation that is in its outward-looking world-wide Universalist stage 15, as is the United States.

The Tree of Tradition as World Tree works at all levels. Besides reflecting the traditions and influences in writers' and thinkers' works, and the traditions and influences of their civilisation (in my case, the European civilisation), the World Tree connects writers and thinkers to both the Underworld and Heaven (visits to both of which feature in my two epic poems *Overlord* and *Armageddon*), and this combines the metaphysical and the social-secular, and it also connects all civilisations in its crown and shows in its one crown how all the branches of the past 11 civilisations and the present living 14 civilisations can unite in a partly-federal democratic supranational World State. The branches of each nation-state have not changed and are individual, but they all have a place in the one crown of the Tree of Tradition as World Tree when it is viewed from a distance.

The supranational level

As can be seen from the chart on p.175, which first appeared in my book *The World Government* (2010), there are three levels in international affairs: (1) the level of nation-states – these would carry on internally without change; (2) the international level, the level of the UN – international relationships would continue but would be linked via the

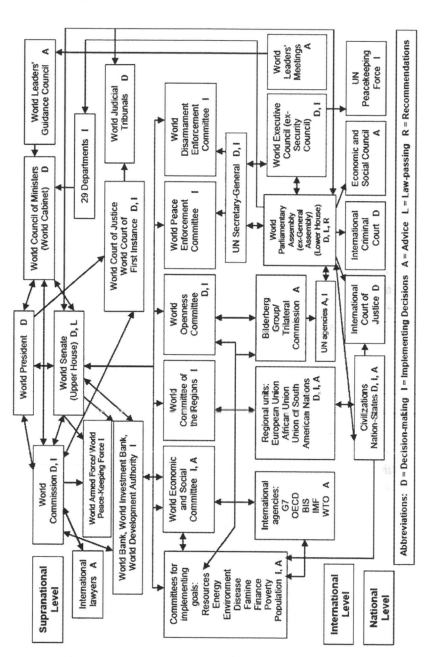

Diagram/Flow Chart of the Supranational Authority: The Structure of the World State

Abbreviations: D = Decision-making   I = Implementing Decisions   A = Advice   L = Law-passing   R = Recommendations

UN Secretary-General to a third level that is at present missing; and (3) the supranational level, which would have legal powers beyond those of the UN at the international level to solve the world's problems: disarmament and ending war; redistributing wealth to eliminate poverty and hunger; solving environmental problems; ending disease; skills development; delivering world economic growth; and ending religious conflict.

In *The Secret American Destiny* I wrote under the heading 'Liberty's Supranational Destiny':[23]

'Destiny' has featured in American expansion ever since 'manifest destiny' surfaced in 1845: the idea that the United States had a special divinely-ordained, predetermined and providential destiny to lead the world, that the ideals of liberty in the Declaration of Independence placed it above all other nations. The political Universalism of an American-led World State may seem divinely-ordained but it can be freely chosen. As Obama said at the end of his Prague speech on April 5, 2009, 'Human destiny will be what we make of it.' America's Universalist destiny is what America makes of it.

The present structure of global governance is inter-national, based on the relations *between* nations. It is not supranational. The UN, World Bank, IMF and G20 will need to be fundamentally reformed to accommodate the World Commission, World Senate and World Parliamentary Assembly. The US President would have to go before the UN General Assembly and make the case for a World Constitutional Convention to bring in the supranational structure of a democratized World State – similar to what the Lisbon Treaty did for the then 27 (now 28) members of the supranational European Union. The World State would live by the rule of law, which Eisenhower called for. The rule of law which a World State would introduce has been called for by Einstein, Russell, Truman, Eisenhower, Churchill, Gandhi, and Pope John Paul II.

The religious Universalism that would accompany the political Universalism of a World State would also be supranational (and 'suprareligional'), and would focus on the common Light, which can be found in the Christian Light of the World and transfiguration, the Islamic lamp-like Light of Allah, Buddhist enlightenment (Mahayana *sunyata*, Zen *satori*), Hindu Yogic *samadhi*, and the Taoist Void of *Tao*. It would also take note of Freemasonry's syncretistic roots in the early Egyptian, Canaanite and Israelite religions.

The supranational World State would transcend and transform civilizations. For 5,000 years history has been a story of inter-national rising-and-falling civilizations, and Universalist history has focused on the vision of the metaphysical Light that has passed into the religion of each inter-national civilization at a very early stage. Huntington wrote of the 'clash of civilizations' – between the Arab and North-American civilizations – at the inter-national level. The history of civilizations would continue at the inter-national level within the 13 civilization-based regions, but the World State would transcend it even though it is within a stage in each civilization's development, be above it: supranational and above civilizations.

This was how Fukuyama envisaged the 'end state' of political development, a permanent liberal democracy, the 'end of history' in Hegel's sense of 'end-state'. Fukuyama should have seen this liberal democracy as a temporary stage, perhaps lasting 230 years [c.2020–c.2250, within the North-American civilization's stage 15, see p.160]. America, the most powerful living civilization and the only living civilization in its inter-national stage 15, the stage in which worldwide empires are founded, would be breaking the mould and doing something utterly and fundamentally new by founding a supranational *Pax Americana*, a *Pax Universalis* that would legally resolve all inter-national level conflicts at the supranational level.

A Universalist New World Order

I have devoted a quartet of books to the coming New World Order, the most recent of which are *The Fall of the West* and *The Golden Phoenix*. As I write, the Russia-Ukraine war makes a peace-bringing New World

Order seem a long way away, and world culture is split between democratic and authoritarian outlooks: the democratic West (the US, the UK and the EU) and the authoritarian East (Russia and China).

But following America's withdrawal from Iraq, Afghanistan and "pivoting to the East" to cope with expanding China's trade surplus and Belt-and-Road Initiative in 140 countries, we are now living in a multipolar world with four superpowers: the US, the EU, Russia and China. There have been massive demonstrations in China calling for President Xi to stand down, suggesting that the Chinese people would happily amalgamate in a Universalist New World Order. And there has been a development in Russia suggesting that President Putin might do the same.

In *The Golden Phoenix*[24] I tell how on 9 October 2022 I responded to a request for an interview on my books that was accompanied by written questions. I understood the interview for Den-TV, an analytical internet channel, would be streamed to India, and found I was talking to Anton Serov, a Russian. I asked him where our interview would be viewed. He said, "Throughout Russia". Thinking it might be a follow-on from my visit to Russia in 2019, when I gave a lecture calling for a World State two miles from the Kremlin to a large audience containing a number in military uniform and met three of Putin's assistants and signed my books *World State* and *World Constitution* to Putin, I stayed in the interview and talked for two hours on Russian culture (Dostoevsky and Solzhenitsyn) and the need for Russia to escape from the war in Ukraine into a multipolar New World Order that would include the US, EU, Russia and China as peaceful partners to bring prosperity to the world.

At the end I was asked, "What message have you for the Russian people?" I said, "Beneath all conflicts is unity, all opposites are reconciled in an underlying harmony." (I was thinking of the algebraic formula $+A + -A = 0$ that reconciles all opposites in a unity and features in all my works.) I said that in the future Russia could join a redesigned multipolar New World Order in which it would be equal alongside the US, EU and China. That would be a fresh start.

On 24 October Putin spoke to Club Valdai, a Russian think-tank, for three hours on Russian culture. He mentioned Dostoevsky and Solzhenitsyn at some length, and echoed my multipolar New World Order several times. It looked as if Putin had watched the interview, as a journalist, Geoff Ward, concluded. He interviewed me as an accidental go-between and sent copies of his online articles in Medium.com to President Biden and the UN Secretary-General Antonio Guterres as proof of a seeming willingness on Putin's part for Russia to take part in a war-ending multipolar New World Order.

I received two video links with Russian talk-overs from Anton Serov covering approximately 1 hour 47 minutes on 29 December 2022. On 24 February 2023 (the first anniversary of the start of Russia's war with Ukraine) I received a third video introduced by the Russian author and analyst Dmitry Peretolchin containing an interview on my literary works, including my meeting with Ezra Pound in 1970, for just over 17 minutes on a video that had already been viewed by 56,000.

On 2 March 2023 I received from Anton Serov the first two links in one new link, without the Russian talk-overs. In the accompanying email he sent me an explanation of Den-TV's project. It began by referring to the rebellious, "liberal" spirit of the Bolotnaya-Square protests in Moscow in 2012, and spoke of Den-TV "patriots" who feel that "Russia should be huge, uniting in itself great spaces" (presumably including Crimea and Ukraine) with a vision of the future as interacting with other nations, building "a single imperial project" in "a spirit of love and harmony", remaining a religious country, "the Third Rome of the Orthodox", revealing "God" in "its historical work" (i.e. empire building).

As I said to the Russian people, beneath all conflicts is unity, all opposites (+A + −A) are resolved in underlying reconciliation (= 0). These conflicting parts of the world are like conflicting branches on the Tree of Tradition, which has lived through countless wars, including 162 the UN was unable to resolve from 1945 to 2017, and 40 wars still being fought at the present time.[25] A unification of world culture at its democratic and authoritarian levels, and at the metaphysical and social-secular levels, can happen, and there can be a New World Order in which all nation-states live in harmony beneath a partly-federal World State dedicated to solving the world's problems in seven areas, with seven goals. World culture can become one-world world culture, with a New World Order levelling down the West and levelling up the East.[26]

The traditions and influences are already within the Tree of Tradition that can make this happen. It may look like a gnarled 500-year-old – perhaps 1,500-year-old – angel oak that is ancient and no longer a growing tree, but its crown is still teeming with life and new buds, and its traditions include those I have followed and their Universalism, which I leave as one of my legacies.

The Tree of Tradition as World Tree's united crown stands as the way forward for all in our uncertain and chaotic world. It represents the way forward to a Golden Age of peace and prosperity. As the Tree of Tradition of all civilisations it includes in its crown the thinking of all humankind during the 5,000 years of recorded history along with the most recent thinking, including my own. It includes all 25 civilisations and their progress and achievements, their inventions and governmental policies and fresh vision and new ways of reorganising the world for those in the rising generation who are ready to take up the challenge.

Enough has been said to indicate that the Tree of Tradition as World Tree, the Tree of all civilisations and world history as well as all traditions and influences, is also a World State waiting to be brought into existence. Universalists everywhere, have courage. Identify the traditions and influences that most deserve to be followed, and bring in a new World State for all humankind that expresses the burgeoning leafy crown of the Tree of Tradition in its form of World Tree. Follow my leadership and petition the American President and the UN General Assembly.

Nicholas Hagger's crest and coat of arms awarded by the College of Arms. The Patent is dated 22 May 2019, his 80th birthday. The crest shows a stag with two seven-branched antlers and one hoof on a roundel in Libyan colours with a spying eye near four acorns, against a seven-banded rainbow. The coat of arms shows the three lions from the Hagar 1605 coat of arms brandishing quills, and two oak trees with endless knots, representing time and infinity/eternity. The two oak trees also represent the Tree of Tradition and the Tree of Imagination. The spying eye near Libyan colours is also the eye of a poet's observation and mystic's unitive vision. The motto has the globe of the earth and the sun at each end, suggesting Nicholas Hagger's Universalist perspective. (See pp.794–797, 809, 814–815 and 833 of *Selected Letters* for fuller explanation.)

Timeline

List of dates and key events referred to in *The Tree of Tradition*

Indo-European religions	World Tree, with roots in the underworld and branches in the sky, connects underworld, earth and heavens.
c.2300BC	*The Epic of Gilgamesh* on cuneiform tablets on the quest of Gilgamesh.
c.575BC flourished	Anaximander of Miletus sees the earth as hanging in space and the universe surrounded by '*to apeiron*' (the moving boundless/infinite).
c.399BC	Socrates drinks hemlock and is put to death.
c.375BC	Plato's *Republic*.
c.400	St Augustine's *Confessions* includes his account of the Light.
c.600–700	The Tree of Tradition on Johns Island (or John's Island), off South Carolina, may have begun to grow.
1175	Hildegard of Bingen's account of the Light in a letter to Guibert of Gembloux.
c.1270	Old Norse Yggdrasil, an ash tree with roots in the underworld, land of the giants and home of the gods, in *The Poetic Edda*.
1613–1619	Renaissance disciplines on the Quadrangle doorways at Oxford's Bodleian Library.
1617	Robert Fludd draws the *sefirot* Tree of Life with inverted roots in the sky.
1647	Preface to the French translation of Descartes' Tree of Knowledge or Philosophy, seeing philosophy as a tree whose roots are metaphysics, trunk physics and branches the sciences.
23 Nov 1654	Pascal experiences full illumination.
1876	Dewey Decimal Classification published in the US.
1897	Library of Congress Classification published in the US.
1919, 1944	T.S. Eliot writes 'Tradition and the Individual Talent'; and 'The Man of Letters and the Future of Europe'.
Mar 1957	NH called to be a poet and sips from Horace's spring.

Jan 1962	NH visits a descendant of the Tree of Knowledge of Good and Evil in Gourna, Iraq, in the Garden of Eden near the junction of the Tigris and Euphrates rivers.
20 Jul 1964 – 6 Dec 1993	NH's 29-year-long Mystic Way (see p.45).
Jan 1965 – Jun 1966	NH writes 'The Silence' on his centre-shift and its metaphysical consequences.
Oct 1965	NH's centre-shift from rational, social ego to deep centre in Japan.
5 Oct 1965	NH is given the Confucian algebraic formula $+A + -A = 0$, which sums up the wisdom of the East, by Junzaburo Nishiwaki in Tokyo.
16 Jul 1970	NH visits Ezra Pound in Rapallo.
10 Sep 1971	NH experiences full illumination.
Mar 1979	NH gets to grips with the Kabbalah's Tree of Life in Ammerdown, Somerset.
24, 31 Dec 1979	NH writes first draft of 'The Tree of Imagination', mentioning the Tree of Tradition.
3 May 1993	NH has a vision and glimpses two new finished works, *Overlord* and *Classical Odes*, and writes them during the next 12 years.
20–25 Jul 2008	NH stays in Tennyson's Farringford on the Isle of Wight.
5 Sep 2019	NH talks to Charles Walker MP of "the oak tree of tradition", the Tree of Tradition of English Literature and political parties.
14 Aug 2022	NH receives a title *Traditions and Influences* in sleep.
11 Oct 2022	Title changed to *The Tree of Tradition*.
18 Oct 2022 – 12 Apr 2023	NH writes *The Tree of Tradition*.

Appendices

Appendix 1

'The Tree of Imagination'

Poem and notes taken from Nicholas Hagger,
Collected Poems 1958–2005

I

Walk through these snowy courts to garden gates
Where Milton's ancient mulberry tree withstands,
Climb a staircase where a Professor waits
Among variant readings, and shake hands
And feel this balding scholar's warm vigour
And exactness. He has no pedestals.
In the Buttery there is a rigour
As he talks of the Metaphysicals.

He now helps keep the Tree of Tradition
That only precise understanding sees.   10
Its leaves have fed each true reputation
In the long line of rhymers' pedigrees.
The timeless whole appears from the outside
As different branches which have borne each name,
Yet each green difference that each Age has tried
Is an illusion: all leaves are the same.

To some keepers, each bough has been begun
For some poet to use, scholar to stir:
The branch of verbal wit sprang up for Donne
And his school, its ambiguous leaves were   20
Budded by linguistic philosophy,
Then Empson, and now this learned domed head
Which hatched me on veined puns, then offered me
The mystic branch of English verse instead.

Young poets feed on leaves of this mulberry Tree,
Amid blackberry-like images, and spin
One thousand-yard-long thread from what they see,
Cocoon a vision from the world, shut in –
Surround – beauty with work it leaves behind
When, three-day-old moths, they lay eggs, starve and die.　　30
True poets, like silkworms, gnaw truths and wind
Fine thread which others weave and sell, or buy.

He snicks out energies, he quotes tersely,
But he assumes that, as language is grown
By "social interaction" in a nursery,
Symbols have meaning where custom has blown
"Separate" forests into "sacred" trees,
As if the Tree of Life were banned, a trend
Set by unclean men and so taboo. Now freeze:
"For verbal atheists, death is the end."　　40

II

The Tree of Tradition merely reflects
A more unseen one which hangs from the sky:
The Tree of Imagination projects
All things, and then reclaims them when they die.
Silkworms on Tradition's toothed leaves sometimes see
Visions of each infused branch, trunk and root
And send their souls into this more real Tree
In the form of hawks which bring back imaged fruit.

As four worlds channel sap and make seed sprout,
Ideas pour from light through their meanings' root　　50
Into a formless matrix, and squeeze out
Each limb and branch, return to their source as fruit.
Symbols express in language, ramify
Spiritual truths in their material green.
An inverted Tree with roots in the sky
Pours the invisible into what is seen

And ripens symbols of a layered One,
Manifesting the eternal; and blind-
-ly hangs images like oranges from a dark sun
That have not yet formed in nature or mind,   60
Which can be reached and seized by a tranquil
Hawk-like soul which ascends up through green leaves
And flies between two worlds with a crammed bill,
Brings Ideas down to meanings sense perceives.

As visualising can warm hands and feet,
Cure migraines and tensions, act on dense mind;
As imaged light raises a body's heat
And sends photons to a crown that was blind;
So images burst round a poet's head,
Windfalls from a leafy beyond that heal   70
A sick society, which has been fed
Poisoned perspective, with a divine meal.

Four worlds touch in beauty, which consciousness
Reflects. When a wind ripples the surface of crowned
Wisdom, ruffles reflected upperness
To ground, imagination is earthbound,
Hawk sleeps in worm. Doubts prune language, screening
Symbols are mere analogies that blend,
As if fruit just harmonised trees. Meaning
From upper worlds is lopped. Death is the end.   80

III

Two Trees branch Idea into mental forms,
Are seen by poets who spin a cocoon,
Shut out the world's winds, interfering storms,
Open crowns to a dark influx and moon.
One Tree is seen by daylit consciousness,
To closed crowns symbols are fancies that please,
As if fruit decorated leafy dress
Like coloured globes hung on dark Christmas trees.

Symbols, that are sown beyond, from within
Manifest into language, whose form fits,   90
And picture layered Reality, *Yin-*
Yang that hints at one in many small bits.
Ask "What Reality does it describe?"
And if "Only social" say "Ah!" and grin:
"Man lives in a universe, not a tribe
Whose eye imprisons like a body's skin."

Heaven opens to crown knowledge. Artists
Who hawk into its leaves know what was known to Donne,
That a rising chain of being untwists
Worlds tangled in one moment; have rewon   100
A metaphysic; and, when they disclose
The lost vision of golden fruit, thus catch
Truth, reroot the symbol, and must oppose
The world of silkworm-keepers whose puns hatch.

Now dine with dons, and take the coffee black
In a snoozy common room aglare with snow.
Whisper on silence, then trudge slowly back
To the staircase. Under Milton's window
The scholar's life is like a clock that stopped,
But warm judgement, precise stoic despair   110
Keeps an actual Tree and so cannot opt
For the high symbols on a trunk of air.
                    24, 31 December 1979; revised 26–27 April 1980

Notes from *Collected Poems*, pp.442, 450–452:

From notes to *The Fire-Flower*

Between Christmas 1979 and February 1980 in six creative weeks I wrote 'The Tree of Imagination', 'Firethorn', 'A Temple-Dancer's Temple-Sleep', 'A Metaphysical's Light-Mandala' and 'The Fire-Flower' while living at 46 Ritherdon Road in Wandsworth.

From notes to 'The Tree of Imagination'

'The Tree of Imagination' was first written on 24 and 31 December 1979 and subsequently revised. The poem is about the contrast between the academic scholars' social and sceptical view of the poetic tradition, and the true poet's imaginative vision of poetic symbols and of metaphysical Reality. (The Tree of Tradition stands in the physical world, the Tree of Imagination is in the metaphysical world.) The central image of silkworm, chrysalis and moth suggests the three ages of the poet: the visionary, the writer of poetry, and the mature poet whose work is behind him.

The Professor, Christopher Ricks, my tutor when I read English Literature at Oxford, is one of the most brilliant Professors of English Literature to have emerged since the war. Until the late 1980s at Christ's College, Cambridge, and more recently at Boston University, he has carried on Empson's "verbal" approach to literature, and his reinterpretations have transformed our understanding of some classical texts (for example, of Middleton's *The Changeling*). Though he is a true Augustan at heart, and takes a social view of poetry (see his *Keats and Embarrassment* and *Eliot and Prejudice*, for example), I have a great respect for, and indebtedness to, the originality and sharpness of his mind.

I met Empson when Ricks invited him to chat with some of his pupils, and in the 1960s I taught at the Japanese university where Empson taught from 1931 to 1934. The Japanese Professor who looked after me was a pupil of Empson's.

2.	"Milton's ancient mulberry tree". There is a mulberry tree at Christ's College, Cambridge which Milton (a pupil there) knew. "Withstands", "resists" modern materialism and therefore "endures".
18.	"Stir", i.e. stir to life.
23.	"Veined". Besides suggesting the veins which carry blood to the heart and the ribs of a leaf, "vein" of course has a geological meaning: "fissure in rock filled with deposited matter".
25–32.	The poet as silkworm. The true poet feeds on the hallucinogenic mulberry Tree of Tradition which is only known to those who

have "precise understanding", and protects his vision from the world in a cocoon of verse (i.e. "work"). It is a fact that a silkworm's cocoon is made of one often unbroken thread of silk some 1,000 yards long. It is also a fact that a hatched silk moth does not feed much or fly, and that its life-span is a mere three days or so. This corresponds to the post-chrysalis phase of a poet when he "lays eggs", i.e. hands on the seeds of his work, imparts a knowledge of what he has learned to his successors, and prepares to die. The poets provide the raw material, the silk, which critics weave into saleable dresses in their critical and educational works, and profit from; hence their interest in guarding the Tree of Tradition.

29. "Beauty". Again, the Kabbalistic Self, the fifth sefira. Also, in line 73.

30. "Three-day-old moths", i.e. mature, fully grown.

33. "Snicks out energies", "snicks energies into being so that they express themselves in form".

34. "As", "just as".

37. "'Sacred' trees". See the anthropologist Mary Douglas, 'Social and Religious Symbolism of the Lele' (in *Implicit Meanings*), which argues that religious symbolism derives its meaning from everyday social practices, that consecration is connected with prohibition (cf the basic feeling of taboo). Thus, the rain forest's being regarded as "the place of God" is associated with the fact that humans are separated from it, e.g. menstruating women are excluded from it.

40. Ricks told me, "I am an Empsonian atheist, I believe that if I walk under a bus this afternoon, death is the end."

42–48. See note to line 111.

49. "Four worlds", cf the note to line 33 of 'Clouded-Ground Pond', on the four worlds of the Kabbalah. "Matrix", "womb, mould in which type is cast or shaped" (*Concise Oxford Dictionary*).

55. The Tree of Life or cosmic tree (cf 38) is an aspect of the inverted Tree. In the Kabbalah the invisible is shown as an upside-down Tree, its roots in the heavens, manifesting through its

branches into visible form as from the quantum vacuum. Each fruit is therefore a symbol of Eternity.

59.   "Images", cf the introductory note to 'An Aesthete's "Golden" Artefacts'. An "image" is an external or pictorial form perceived by the heart, whereas a symbol has a spiritual layer perceived by the soul. "Image" is used in this poem (e.g. in lines 48 and 69 as well as here) in place of "symbol" as it is the pictorial form of the symbol that is being stressed. "Dark sun", dark because spiritual.

63.   "Hawk". Compare the note on the gull in lines 38–9 of 'Sea-Fire' for the association of Horus the hawk flying to Ra. The hawk is the part of the soul which bears the main soul and flies between physical and spiritual worlds.

65.   That visualising or active imaging can warm hands and cure migraine, and warm feet and cure hypertension, has been established by the work of Dr Elmer and Alyce Green of the Menninger Foundation. In the same way the passive reception of images rather than their active generation, has a healing effect. "Visualising". Visualising in images has the power to change body temperature and health, and a poet's images therefore have a healing effect on the reader's mind and on "a sick society" with a "poisoned perspective".

66.   "Body" is "dense mind" according to the spiritual view.

67.   That actively imaging light increases photons in the body has been established by a Romanian team.

68.   "Crown", the crown chakra of Hinduism, and also *Keter*, the topmost sefira in the Kabbalah. (Cf lines 74–5.)

72–80. The social, sceptical view blocks out the metaphysical vision.

73–74. "Four worlds... which consciousness/Reflects". When consciousness does reflect the four worlds, it becomes fully aware, its horizons are fully extended.

77.   "Worm", silkworm. "Screening", "separate without completely cutting off" (*Concise Oxford Dictionary*), i.e. symbols which act as a screen that separates from Reality without completely cutting it off.

78.	"Blend", "form harmonious compound" (in this case of language and ideas).
79.	"Harmonised", "bring into harmony", i.e. decorated.
86.	"Fancies". Fancy is decorative imagery which plays on a social vision, whereas imagination enters spiritual or divine Reality. Mulberries are decorative, optional fruits rather than a staple diet. See the 'Preface on the New Baroque Consciousness' for the distinction between timebound fancy and eternal imagination.
89–96.	Symbols and language are layered and are capable of metaphysical and not merely social meanings.
89.	"Sown beyond". Symbols come from an eternal, transpersonal, spiritual source, the repository of all Ideas, the *unus mundus*, and enter form as language.
89–96.	These lines insist that man lives in a universe before he lives in a society.
97.	"Heaven opens to crown knowledge". Crown and Knowledge are the *sefirot* in the Kabbalah which go straight up to the divine world from Beauty of Self. The idea expressed is that the upper part of the Tree of Imagination is Heaven. The meanings of "to crown knowledge" therefore include "to the knowledge or *gnosis* of the crown *chakra* or centre", the Kabbalistic *sefira Keter* (p.451, *Collected Poems*).
99.	"Chain of being". The Elizabethan idea of a great chain of being which is found in many of Shakespeare's plays (e.g. *Julius Caesar*) and in Marvell came from the worlds of the Kabbalah. It included all creation, and therefore all the four worlds of the Kabbalah, which are "tangled in one moment". Here, the *sefirot* Beauty, Knowledge and Crown (psychological, spiritual and divine worlds).
100–104.	The metaphysical vision is opposed by academics who have a sceptical, social view.
104.	"The word", i.e. influenced by anthropologists who see symbols in terms of customs.

110–112. Concern with the "actual" social tradition precludes opening oneself to the symbols of the beyond, which are glimpsed in the metaphysical vision.

111. "Ungolden Tree". To scholars, the fruit of the Tree of Tradition is decorative rather than edible. Only the true poets who feed on the Tree of Tradition can see and taste the nourishing Heavenly symbols of the Tree of Imagination. The "golden fruit" of line 102 makes the soul gold.

From notes to 'Firethorn'

34–35. "Four clouded worlds, down/Which fire descends." See the note to line 33 of 'Clouded-Ground Pond', on the four worlds of the Kabbalah. Light zigzags down the Kabbalistic Tree of Life to the lower *sefirot*, but the mystic sees straight up from Beauty through Knowledge to Crown (line 36); cf the note to line 99 of 'The Tree of Imagination'.

From notes to 'A Temple-Dancer's Temple-Sleep'

5. "Images". See the note on line 59 of 'The Tree of Imagination'. In this poem, the "images" of past lives are "images" when their pictorial side is being stressed, but they are later found to be "symbols" with spiritual layers and are eventually understood as such (lines 69–72).

Appendix 2

Academic Disciplines and Fields, and Classifications

Universalists have seven main disciplines (see pp.21–22).

Academic disciplines are areas of study taught and researched at institutions in higher education (universities and colleges). These include traditional disciplines taught for centuries, and recent disciplines reflecting new industries and professions.

Academic disciplines can also be seen as fields of study and branches of knowledge. There are no formal criteria for defining disciplines or fields, and disciplines vary between universities and their programs. Many disciplines are offshoots in sub-branches known as subdisciplines.

Below is a list of 112 main academic disciplines:[1]

Accounting

Aerospace Engineering

Agriculture

Anthropology

Applied Arts

Applied Mathematics

Applied Science

Archaeology

Architecture

Astrobiology

Astrophysics

Behavioural Science

Biochemistry

Bioethics

Biology

Biophysics

Biotechnology

Botany

Business Law

Business/Commerce

Chemical Engineering

Chemistry

Civil Engineering

Communication

Computer Science

Culinary Arts

Cultural Studies

Dance

Data Science

Design

Divinity

Early Childhood

Education

Earth Science

Economics

Education

Electrical Engineering

Engineering

Environmental Studies

Ethics

Fashion

Film

Finance

Fine Arts

Forensic Science

Forestry

Geography

Geometry

Health Sciences

Health Technology

History

Hospitality
  Management

Human Geography

Humanities

Industrial Engineering

Information Science

Information Technology

Journalism

Kinesiology

Landscape Architecture

Languages

Law

Library Science

Linguistics

Literature

Logic

Management

Marine Biology

Marketing

Materials Science/
  Engineering

Mathematics

Mechanical Engineering

Media Studies

Medicine

Museology

Music

Neuroscience

Numerical Analysis

Nursing

Organisational Studies

Pathology

Performing Arts

Pharmaceutical Sciences

Philosophy

Physical Fitness

Physics

Physiology

Physiotherapy

Planetary Science

Political Science

Project Management

Psychology

Public Administration

Public Policy	Systems Science/Engineering
Rehabilitation Science	Theatre
Risk Management and Insurance	Theology
Robotics	Urban and Regional Planning
	User Experience Design
Science	
Social Science	Veterinary Medicine
Social Work	Visual Arts
Sociology	
Space Science	Wildlife Management
Sports Science	
Statistics	Zoology

An idea of the quantity of academic disciplines and fields can be formed by looking at lists online: a list of 1,986 academic disciplines[2] and a list of 2,428 academic fields.[3]

The Tree of Tradition includes all the disciplines and subdisciplines in existence.

Library classifications have endeavoured to cope with the ever-increasing number of academic disciplines and fields. The two main classifications are the Dewey Decimal Classification system first drawn up in 1876, and the Library of Congress Classification system first drawn up in 1897. Both have had to adapt to the increased knowledge since the 19th century (including the invention of the car and aeroplane, and the advent of nuclear energy).

These two classification systems are presented below:

1,000 Dewey Decimal Classifications
(F. on p.xxv)

000 *Computer science, information and general works*
001 Knowledge
002 The book
003 Systems
004 Data processing and computer science

005 Computer programming, programs and data

006 Special computer methods

007 [Unassigned]

008 [Unassigned]

009 [Unassigned]

010 Bibliography

011 Bibliographies

012 Bibliographies of individuals

013 [Unassigned]

014 Of anonymous and pseudonymous works

015 Bibliographies of works from specific places

016 Bibliographies of works on specific subjects

017 General subject catalogues

018 Catalogues arranged by author, date, etc.

019 Dictionary catalogues

020 Library and information sciences

021 Library relationships

022 Administration of physical plant

023 Personnel management

024 [Unassigned]

025 Library operations

026 Libraries for specific subjects

027 General libraries

028 Reading and use of other information media

029 [Unassigned]

030 General encyclopaedic works

031 Encyclopaedias in American English

032 Encyclopaedias in English

033 In other Germanic languages

034 Encyclopaedias in French, Occitan and Catalan

035 In Italian, Romanian and related languages

036 Encyclopaedias in Spanish and Portuguese

037 Encyclopaedias in Slavic languages

038 Encyclopaedias in Scandinavian languages

039 Encyclopaedias in other languages

040–049 [Unassigned]

050 General serial publications

051 Serials in American English

052 Serials in English

053 Serials in other Germanic languages

054 Serials in French, Occitan and Catalan

055 In Italian, Romanian and related languages

056 Serials in Spanish and Portuguese

057 Serials in Slavic languages

058 Serials in Scandinavian languages

059 Serials in other languages

060 General organisations and museum science
061 Organisations in North America
062 Organisations in British Isles; in England
063 Organisations in central Europe; in Germany
064 Organisations in France and Monaco
065 Organisations in Italy and adjacent islands
066 In Iberian Peninsula and adjacent islands
067 Organisations in Eastern Europe; in Russia
068 Organisations in other geographic areas
069 Museum science

070 News media, journalism and publishing
071 Newspapers in North America
072 Newspapers in British Isles; in England
073 Newspapers in central Europe; in Germany
074 Newspapers in France and Monaco
075 Newspapers in Italy and adjacent islands
076 In Iberian Peninsula and adjacent islands
077 Newspapers in Eastern Europe; in Russia
078 Newspapers in Scandinavia

079 Newspapers in other geographic areas

080 General collections
081 Collections in American English
082 Collections in English
083 Collections in other Germanic languages
084 Collections in French, Occitan and Catalan
085 In Italian, Romanian and related languages
086 Collections in Spanish and Portuguese
087 Collections in Slavic languages
088 Collections in Scandinavian languages
089 Collections in other languages

090 Manuscripts and rare books
091 Manuscripts
092 Block books
093 Incunabula
094 Printed books
095 Books notable for bindings
096 Books notable for illustrations
097 Books notable for ownership or origin
098 Prohibited works, forgeries and hoaxes
099 Books notable for format

100 *Philosophy and psychology*
101 Theory of philosophy
102 Miscellany
103 Dictionaries and encyclopaedias

104 [Unassigned]

105 Serial publications

106 Organisations and management

107 Education, research and related topics

108 Kinds of persons treatment

109 Historical and collected persons treatment

110 Metaphysics

111 Ontology

112 [Unassigned]

113 Cosmology

114 Space

115 Time

116 Change

117 Structure

118 Force and energy

119 Number and quantity

120 Epistemology, causation and humankind

121 Epistemology

122 Causation

123 Determinism and indeterminism

124 Teleology

125 [Unassigned]

126 The self

127 The unconscious and the subconscious

128 Humankind

129 Origin and destiny of individual souls

130 Parapsychology and occultism

131 Parapsychological and occult methods

132 [Unassigned]

133 Specific topics in parapsychology and occultism

134 [Unassigned]

135 Dreams and mysteries

136 [Unassigned]

137 Divinatory graphology

138 Physiognomy

139 Phrenology

140 Specific philosophical schools

141 Idealism and related systems

142 Critical philosophy

143 Bergsonism and intuitionism

144 Humanism and related systems

145 Sensationalism

146 Naturalism and related systems

147 Pantheism and related systems

148 Eclecticism, liberalism and traditionalism

149 Other philosophical systems

150 Psychology

151 [Unassigned]

152 Perception, movement, emotions and drives

153 Mental processes and intelligence

154 Subconscious and altered states

155 Differential and developmental psychology

156 Comparative psychology

157 [Unassigned]

158 Applied psychology

159 [Unassigned]

160 Logic

161 Induction

162 Deduction

163 [Unassigned]

164 [Unassigned]

165 Fallacies and sources of error

166 Syllogisms

167 Hypotheses

168 Argument and persuasion

169 Analogy

170 Ethics

171 Ethical systems

172 Political ethics

173 Ethics of family relationships

174 Occupational ethics

175 Ethics of recreation and leisure

176 Ethics of sex and reproduction

177 Ethics of social relations

178 Ethics of consumption

179 Other ethical norms

180 Ancient, medieval and eastern philosophy

181 Eastern philosophy

182 Pre-Socratic Greek philosophies

183 Socratic and related philosophies

184 Platonic philosophy

185 Aristotelian philosophy

186 Sceptic and Neoplatonic philosophies

187 Epicurean philosophy

188 Stoic philosophy

189 Medieval western philosophy

190 Modern western philosophy

191 Philosophy of United States and Canada

192 Philosophy of British Isles

193 Philosophy of Germany and Austria

194 Philosophy of France

195 Philosophy of Italy

196 Philosophy of Spain and Portugal

197 Philosophy of former Soviet Union

198 Philosophy of Scandinavia

199 Philosophy in other geographic areas

200 Religion

201 Religious mythology and social theology

202 Doctrines

203 Public worship and other practices

204 Religious experience, life and practice

205 Religious ethics

206 Leaders and organisation

207 Missions and religious education

208 Sources

209 Sects and reform movements

210 Philosophy and theory of religion

211 Concepts of God

212 Existence, knowability and
    attributes of God

213 Creation

214 Theodicy

215 Science and religion

216 [Unassigned]

217 [Unassigned]

218 Humankind

219 [Unassigned]

220 Bible

221 Old Testament (Tanakh)

222 Historical books of Old
    Testament

223 Poetic books of Old Testament

224 Prophetic books of Old
    Testament

225 New Testament

226 Gospels and Acts

227 Epistles

228 Revelation (Apocalypse)

229 Apocrypha and pseudepigrapha

230 Christianity and Christian
    theology

231 God

232 Jesus Christ and his family

233 Humankind

234 Salvation and grace

235 Spiritual beings

236 Eschatology

237 [Unassigned]

238 Creeds and catechisms

239 Apologetics and
    polemics

240 Christian moral and devotional
    theology

241 Christian ethics

242 Devotional literature

243 Evangelistic writings for
    individuals

244 [Unassigned]

245 [Unassigned]

246 Use of art in Christianity

247 Church furnishings and articles

248 Christian experience, practice
    and life

249 Christian observances in
    family life

250 Christian orders and
    local church

251 Preaching

252 Texts of sermons

253 Pastoral office and work

254 Parish administration

255 Religious congregations and
    orders

256 [Unassigned]

257 [Unassigned]

258 [Unassigned]

259 Pastoral care of families and
    kinds of persons

260 Social and ecclesiastical theology

261 Social theology

262 Ecclesiology

263 Days, times and places of
    observance

264 Public worship

265 Sacraments, other rites and acts

266 Missions

267 Associations for religious work

268 Religious education

269 Spiritual renewal

270 History of Christianity and Christian church

271 Religious orders in church history

272 Persecutions in church history

273 Doctrinal controversies and heresies

274 History of Christianity in Europe

275 History of Christianity in Asia

276 History of Christianity in Africa

277 History of Christianity in North America

278 History of Christianity in South America

279 History of Christianity in other areas

280 Christian denominations and sects

281 Early church and Eastern churches

282 Roman Catholic Church

283 Anglican churches

284 Protestants of Continental origin

285 Presbyterian, Reformed and Congregational

286 Baptist, Disciples of Christ and Adventist

287 Methodist and related churches

288 [Unassigned]

289 Other denominations and sects

290 Other religions

291 [Unassigned]

292 Greek and Roman religion

293 Germanic religion

294 Religions of Indic origin

295 Zoroastrianism

296 Judaism

297 Islam, Babism and Bahai Faith

298 (Optional number)

299 Religions not provided for elsewhere

300 *Social sciences*

301 Sociology and anthropology

302 Social interaction

303 Social processes

304 Factors affecting social behaviour

305 Social groups

306 Culture and institutions

307 Communities

308 [Unassigned]

309 [Unassigned]

310 Collections of general statistics

311 [Unassigned]

312 [Unassigned]

313 [Unassigned]

314 General statistics of Europe

315 General statistics of Asia

316 General statistics of Africa

317 General statistics of North America

318 General statistics of South America

319 General statistics of other areas

320 Political science

321 Systems of governments and states

322 Relation of state to organized groups

323 Civil and political rights

324 The political process

325 International migration and colonisation

326 Slavery and emancipation

327 International relations

328 The legislative process

329 [Unassigned]

330 Economics

331 Labour economics

332 Financial economics

333 Economics of land and energy

334 Cooperatives

335 Socialism and related systems

336 Public finance

337 International economics

338 Production

339 Macroeconomics and related topics

340 Law

341 Law of nations

342 Constitutional and administrative law

343 Military, tax, trade and industrial law

344 Labour, social, education and cultural law

345 Criminal law

346 Private law

347 Civil procedure and courts

348 Laws, regulations and cases

349 Law of specific jurisdictions and areas

350 Public administration and military science

351 Public administration

352 General considerations of public administration

353 Specific fields of public administration

354 Administration of economy and environment

355 Military science

356 Infantry forces and warfare

357 Mounted forces and warfare

358 Air and other specialized forces

359 Sea forces and warfare

360 Social problems and services; associations

361 Social problems and social welfare in general

362 Social welfare problems and services

363 Other social problems and services

364 Criminology

365 Penal and related institutions

366 Associations

367 General clubs

368 Insurance

369 Miscellaneous kinds of associations

370 Education

371 Schools and their activities; special education

372 Elementary education

373 Secondary education

374 Adult education

375 Curricula

376 [Unassigned]

377 [Unassigned]

378 Higher education

379 Public policy issues in education

380 Commerce, communications and transportation

381 Commerce

382 International commerce

383 Postal communication

384 Communications; telecommunication

385 Railroad transportation

386 Inland waterway and ferry transportation

387 Water, air and space transportation

388 Transportation; ground transportation

389 Metrology and standardisation

390 Customs, etiquette and folklore

391 Costume and personal appearance

392 Customs of life cycle and domestic life

393 Death customs

394 General customs

395 Etiquette (Manners)

396 [Unassigned]

397 [Unassigned]

398 Folklore

399 Customs of war and diplomacy

400 *Language*

401 Philosophy and theory

402 Miscellany

403 Dictionaries and encyclopaedias

404 Special topics

405 Serial publications

406 Organisations and management

407 Education, research and related topics

408 Kinds of persons treatment

409 Geographic and persons treatment

410 Linguistics

411 Writing systems

412 Etymology

413 Dictionaries

414 Phonology and phonetics

415 Grammar

416 [Unassigned]

417 Dialectology and historical linguistics

418 Standard usage and applied linguistics

419 Sign languages

420 English and Old English
421 English writing system and phonology
422 English etymology
423 English dictionaries
424 [Unassigned]
425 English grammar
426 [Unassigned]
427 English language variations
428 Standard English usage
429 Old English (Anglo-Saxon)

430 Germanic languages; German
431 German writing systems and phonology
432 German etymology
433 German dictionaries
434 [Unassigned]
435 German grammar
436 [Unassigned]
437 German language variations
438 Standard German usage
439 Other Germanic languages

440 Romance languages; French
441 French writing systems and phonology
442 French etymology
443 French dictionaries
444 [Unassigned]
445 French grammar
446 [Unassigned]
447 French language variations
448 Standard French usage

449 Occitan and Catalan

450 Italian, Romanian and related languages
451 Italian writing systems and phonology
452 Italian etymology
453 Italian dictionaries
454 [Unassigned]
455 Italian grammar
456 [Unassigned]
457 Italian language variations
458 Standard Italian usage
459 Romanian and related languages

460 Spanish and Portuguese languages
461 Spanish writing systems and phonology
462 Spanish etymology
463 Spanish dictionaries
464 [Unassigned]
465 Spanish grammar
466 [Unassigned]
467 Spanish language variations
468 Standard Spanish usage
469 Portuguese

470 Italic languages; Latin
471 Classical Latin writing and phonology
472 Classical Latin etymology
473 Classical Latin dictionaries
474 [Unassigned]
475 Classical Latin grammar
476 [Unassigned]

477 Old, postclassical and Vulgar Latin

478 Classical Latin usage

479 Other Italic languages

480 Hellenic languages; classical Greek

481 Classical Greek writing and phonology

482 Classical Greek etymology

483 Classical Greek dictionaries

484 [Unassigned]

485 Classical Greek grammar

486 [Unassigned]

487 Preclassical and postclassical Greek

488 Classical Greek usage

489 Other Hellenic languages

490 Other languages

491 East Indo-European and Celtic languages

492 Afro-Asiatic languages; Semitic languages

493 Non-Semitic Afro-Asiatic languages

494 Altaic, Uralic, Hyperborean and Dravidian

495 Languages of East and Southeast Asia

496 African languages

497 North American native languages

498 South American native languages

499 Austronesian and other languages

500 *Natural sciences and mathematics*

501 Philosophy and theory

502 Miscellany

503 Dictionaries and encyclopaedias

504 [Unassigned]

505 Serial publications

506 Organisations and management

507 Education, research and related topics

508 Natural history

509 Historical, geographic and persons treatment

510 Mathematics

511 General principles of mathematics

512 Algebra

513 Arithmetic

514 Topology

515 Analysis

516 Geometry

517 [Unassigned]

518 Numerical analysis

519 Probabilities and applied mathematics

520 Astronomy and allied sciences

521 Celestial mechanics

522 Techniques, equipment and materials

523 Specific celestial bodies and phenomena

524 [Unassigned]

525 Earth (Astronomical geography)

526 Mathematical geography

527 Celestial navigation

528 Ephemerides

529 Chronology

530 Physics

531 Classical mechanics; solid mechanics

532 Fluid mechanics; liquid mechanics

533 Gas mechanics

534 Sound and related vibrations

535 Light and infrared and ultraviolet phenomena

536 Heat

537 Electricity and electronics

538 Magnetism

539 Modern physics

540 Chemistry and allied sciences

541 Physical chemistry

542 Techniques, equipment and materials

543 Analytical chemistry

544 [Unassigned]

545 [Unassigned]

546 Inorganic chemistry

547 Organic chemistry

548 Crystallography

549 Mineralogy

550 Earth sciences

551 Geology, hydrology and meteorology

552 Petrology

553 Economic geology

554 Earth sciences of Europe

555 Earth sciences of Asia

556 Earth sciences of Africa

557 Earth sciences of North America

558 Earth sciences of South America

559 Earth sciences of other areas

560 Palaeontology; paleozoology

561 Paleobotany; fossil microorganisms

562 Fossil invertebrates

563 Fossil marine and seashore invertebrates

564 Fossil mollusca and molluscoidea

565 Fossil arthropods

566 Fossil chordates

567 Fossil cold-blooded vertebrates; fossil fishes

568 Fossil birds

569 Fossil mammals

570 Life sciences; biology

571 Physiology and related subjects

572 Biochemistry

573 Specific physiological systems in animals

574 [Unassigned]

575 Specific parts of and systems in plants

576 Genetics and evolution

577 Ecology

578 Natural history of organisms

579 Microorganisms, fungi and algae

580 Plants (Botany)

581 Specific topics in natural history

582 Plants noted for characteristics and flowers

583 Dicotyledons

584 Monocotyledons

585 Gymnosperms; conifers

586 Seedless plants

587 Vascular seedless plants

588 Bryophytes

589 [Unassigned]

590 Animals (Zoology)

591 Specific topics in natural history

592 Invertebrates

593 Marine and seashore invertebrates

594 Mollusca and molluscoidea

595 Arthropods

596 Chordates

597 Cold-blooded vertebrates; fishes

598 Birds

599 Mammals

600 *Technology*

601 Philosophy and theory

602 Miscellany

603 Dictionaries and encyclopaedias

604 Special topics

605 Serial publications

606 Organisations

607 Education, research and related topics

608 Inventions and patents

609 Historical, geographic and persons treatment

610 Medicine and health

611 Human anatomy, cytology and histology

612 Human physiology

613 Personal health and safety

614 Incidence and prevention of disease

615 Pharmacology and therapeutics

616 Diseases

617 Surgery and related medical specialties

618 Gynaecology, obstetrics, paediatrics and geriatrics

619 [Unassigned]

620 Engineering and allied operations

621 Applied physics

622 Mining and related operations

623 Military and nautical engineering

624 Civil engineering

625 Engineering of railroads and roads

626 [Unassigned]

627 Hydraulic engineering

628 Sanitary and municipal engineering

629 Other branches of engineering

630 Agriculture and related technologies

631 Techniques, equipment and materials

632 Plant injuries, diseases and pests

633 Field and plantation crops

634 Orchards, fruits and forestry

635 Garden crops (Horticulture)

636 Animal husbandry

637 Processing dairy and related products

638 Insect culture

639 Hunting, fishing and conservation

640 Home and family management

641 Food and drink

642 Meals and table service

643 Housing and household equipment

644 Household utilities

645 Household furnishings

646 Sewing, clothing and personal living

647 Management of public households

648 Housekeeping

649 Child rearing and home care of persons

650 Management and auxiliary services

651 Office services

652 Processes of written communication

653 Shorthand

654 [Unassigned]

655 [Unassigned]

656 [Unassigned]

657 Accounting

658 General management

659 Advertising and public relations

660 Chemical engineering

661 Industrial chemicals

662 Explosives, fuels and related products

663 Beverage technology

664 Food technology

665 Industrial oils, fats, waxes and gases

666 Ceramic and allied technologies

667 Cleaning, colour and coating technologies

668 Technology of other organic products

669 Metallurgy

670 Manufacturing

671 Metalworking and primary metal products

672 Iron, steel and other iron alloys

673 Nonferrous metals

674 Lumber processing, wood products and cork

675 Leather and fur processing

676 Pulp and paper technology

677 Textiles

678 Elastomers and elastomer products

679 Other products of specific materials

680 Manufacture for specific uses

681 Precision instruments and other devices

682 Small forge work (Blacksmithing)

683 Hardware and household appliances

684 Furnishings and home workshops

685 Leather, fur goods and related products

686 Printing and related activities

687 Clothing and accessories

688 Other final products and packaging

689 [Unassigned]

690 Buildings

691 Building materials

692 Auxiliary construction practices

693 Specific materials and purposes

694 Wood construction and carpentry

695 Roof covering

696 Utilities

697 Heating, ventilating and air-conditioning

698 Detail finishing

699 [Unassigned]

700 *The arts; fine and decorative arts*

701 Philosophy of fine and decorative arts

702 Miscellany of fine and decorative arts

703 Dictionaries of fine and decorative arts

704 Special topics in fine and decorative arts

705 Serial publications of fine and decorative arts

706 Organisations and management

707 Education, research and related topics

708 Galleries, museums and private collections

709 Historical, geographic and persons treatment

710 Civic and landscape art

711 Area planning

712 Landscape architecture

713 Landscape architecture of trafficways

714 Water features

715 Woody plants

716 Herbaceous plants

717 Structures in landscape architecture

718 Landscape design of cemeteries

719 Natural landscapes

720 Architecture

721 Architectural structure

722 Architecture to c.300

723 Architecture from c.300 to 1399

724 Architecture from 1400

725 Public structures

726 Buildings for religious purposes

727 Buildings for education and research

728 Residential and related buildings

729 Design and decoration

730 Plastic arts; sculpture

731 Processes, forms and subjects of sculpture

732 Sculpture to c.500

733 Greek, Etruscan and Roman sculpture

734 Sculpture from c.500 to 1399

735 Sculpture from 1400

736 Carving and carvings

737 Numismatics and sigillography

738 Ceramic arts

739 Art metalwork

740 Drawing and decorative arts

741 Drawing and drawings

742 Perspective

743 Drawing and drawings by subject

744 [Unassigned]

745 Decorative arts

746 Textile arts

747 Interior decoration

748 Glass

749 Furniture and accessories

750 Painting and paintings

751 Techniques, equipment, materials and forms

752 Colour

753 Symbolism, allegory, mythology and legend

754 Genre paintings

755 Religion

756 [Unassigned]

757 Human figures

758 Other subjects

759 Historical, geographic and persons treatment

760 Graphic arts; printmaking and prints

761 Relief processes (Block printing)

762 [Unassigned]

763 Lithographic processes

764 Chromolithography and serigraphy

765 Metal engraving

766 Mezzotinting, aquatinting and related processes

767 Etching and drypoint

768 [Unassigned]

769 Prints

770 Photography, photographs and computer art

771 Techniques, equipment and materials

772 Metallic salt processes

773 Pigment processes of printing

774 Holography

775 Digital photography

776 Computer art (Digital art)

777 [Unassigned]

778 Fields and kinds of photography

779 Photographs

780 Music

781 General principles and musical forms

782 Vocal music

783 Music for single voices; the voice

784 Instruments and instrumental ensembles

785 Ensembles with one instrument per part

786 Keyboard and other instruments

787 Stringed instruments

788 Wind instruments

789 (Optional number)

790 Recreational and performing arts

791 Public performances

792 Stage presentations

793 Indoor games and amusements

794 Indoor games of skill

795 Games of chance

796 Athletic and outdoor sports and games

797 Aquatic and air sports

798 Equestrian sports and animal racing

799 Fishing, hunting and shooting

800 *Literature and rhetoric*

801 Philosophy and theory

802 Miscellany

803 Dictionaries and encyclopaedias

804 [Unassigned]

805 Serial publications

806 Organisations and management

807 Education, research and related topics

808 Rhetoric and collections of literature

809 History, description and criticism

810 American literature in English

811 American poetry in English

812 American drama in English

813 American fiction in English

814 American essays in English

815 American speeches in English

816 American letters in English

817 American humour and satire in English

818 American miscellaneous writings

819 (Optional number)

820 English and Old English literatures

821 English poetry

822 English drama

823 English fiction

824 English essays

825 English speeches

826 English letters

827 English humour and satire

828 English miscellaneous writings

829 Old English (Anglo-Saxon)

830 Literatures of Germanic languages

831 German poetry

832 German drama

833 German fiction

834 German essays

835 German speeches

836 German letters

837 German humour and satire

838 German miscellaneous writings

839 Other Germanic literatures

840 Literatures of Romance languages

841 French poetry

842 French drama

843 French fiction

844 French essays

845 French speeches

846 French letters

847 French humour and satire

848 French miscellaneous writings

849 Occitan and Catalan literatures

850 Italian, Romanian and related literatures

851 Italian poetry

852 Italian drama

853 Italian fiction

854 Italian essays

855 Italian speeches

856 Italian letters

857 Italian humour and satire

858 Italian miscellaneous writings

859 Romanian and related literatures

860 Spanish and Portuguese literatures

861 Spanish poetry

862 Spanish drama

863 Spanish fiction

864 Spanish essays

865 Spanish speeches

866 Spanish letters

867 Spanish humour and satire

868 Spanish miscellaneous writings

869 Portuguese literature

870 Italic literatures; Latin literature

871 Latin poetry

872 Latin dramatic poetry and drama

873 Latin epic poetry and fiction

874 Latin lyric poetry

875 Latin speeches

876 Latin letters

877 Latin humour and satire

878 Latin miscellaneous writings

879 Literatures of other Italic languages

880 Hellenic literatures; classical Greek

881 Classical Greek poetry

882 Classical Greek dramatic poetry and drama

883 Classical Greek epic poetry and fiction

884 Classical Greek lyric poetry

885 Classical Greek speeches

886 Classical Greek letters

887 Classical Greek humour and satire

888 Classical Greek miscellaneous writings

889 Modern Greek literature

890 Literatures of other languages

891 East Indo-European and Celtic literatures

892 Afro-Asiatic literatures; Semitic literatures

893 Non-Semitic Afro-Asiatic literatures

894 Altaic, Uralic, Hyperborean and Dravidian

895 Literatures of East and Southeast Asia

896 African literatures

897 North-American native literatures

898 South-American native literatures

899 Austronesian and other literatures

900 *History and geography*

901 Philosophy and theory

902 Miscellany

903 Dictionaries and encyclopaedias

904 Collected accounts of events

905 Serial publications

906 Organisations and management

907 Education, research and related topics

908 Kinds of persons treatment

909 World history

910 Geography and travel

911 Historical geography

912 Atlases, maps, charts and plans

913 Geography of and travel in ancient world

914 Geography of and travel in Europe

915 Geography of and travel in Asia

916 Geography of and travel in Africa

917 Geography of and travel in North America

918 Geography of and travel in South America

919 Geography of and travel in other areas

920 Biography, genealogy and insignia

921 (Optional number)

922 (Optional number)

923 (Optional number)

924 (Optional number)

925 (Optional number)

926 (Optional number)

927 (Optional number)

928 (Optional number)

929 Genealogy, names and insignia

930 History of ancient world to c.499

931 China to 420

932 Egypt to 640

933 Palestine to 70

934 India to 647

935 Mesopotamia and Iranian Plateau to 637

936 Europe north and west of Italy to c.499

937 Italy and adjacent territories to 476

938 Greece to 323

939 Other parts of ancient world to c.640

940 History of Europe

941	British Isles	969	South Indian Ocean islands
942	England and Wales		
943	Central Europe; Germany	970	History of North America
944	France and Monaco	971	Canada
945	Italian Peninsula and adjacent islands	972	Middle America; Mexico
		973	United States
946	Iberian Peninsula and adjacent islands	974	North-eastern United States
		975	South-eastern United States
947	Eastern Europe; Russia	976	South central United States
948	Scandinavia	977	North central United States
949	Other parts of Europe	978	Western United States
		979	Great Basin and Pacific Slope region
950	History of Asia; Far East		
951	China and adjacent areas		
952	Japan	980	History of South America
953	Arabian Peninsula and adjacent areas	981	Brazil
		982	Argentina
954	South Asia; India	983	Chile
955	Iran	984	Bolivia
956	Middle East (Near East)	985	Peru
957	Siberia (Asiatic Russia)	986	Colombia and Ecuador
958	Central Asia	987	Venezuela
959	Southeast Asia	988	Guiana
		989	Paraguay and Uruguay
960	History of Africa		
961	Tunisia and Libya	990	History of other areas
962	Egypt and Sudan	991	[Unassigned]
963	Ethiopia and Eritrea	992	[Unassigned]
964	Northwest African coast and offshore islands	993	New Zealand
		994	Australia
965	Algeria	995	Melanesia; New Guinea
966	West Africa and offshore islands	996	Other parts of Pacific; Polynesia
967	Central Africa and offshore islands	997	Atlantic Ocean islands
		998	Arctic islands and Antarctica
968	Southern Africa; Republic of South Africa	999	Extra-terrestrial worlds

228 Library of Congress Classifications
(G. on p.xxv)

A	*General Works*	BT	Christianity: Doctrinal theology
AC	Collections, Series, Collected Works	BV	Christianity: Practical theology
AE	Encyclopaedias	BX	Christian denominations
AG	Dictionaries and other general reference works	*C*	*Auxiliary Sciences of History*
AI	Indexes	C	General, Auxiliary Sciences of History
AM	Museums, Collectors and collecting	CB	History of civilisation
AN	Newspapers	CC	Archaeology
AP	Periodicals	CD	Diplomatics, Archives, Seals
AS	Academies and societies, and learned societies	CE	Technical chronology, Calendar
AY	Yearbooks, Almanacs, Directories	CJ	Numismatics
		CN	Inscriptions, Epigraphy
AZ	History of scholarship and learning, the humanities	CR	Heraldry
		CS	Genealogy
		CT	Biography

B	*Philosophy, Psychology, Religion*	*D*	*History: General and Old World, World History and History of Europe, Asia, Africa, Australia, New Zealand, etc.*
B	Philosophy (General)		
BC	Logic		
BD	Speculative philosophy		
BF	Psychology, Parapsychology, Occultism	D	History, General
		DA	Great Britain
BH	Aesthetics	DAW	Central Europe
BJ	Ethics, Social usages, Etiquette	DB	Austria, Liechtenstein, Hungary, Czechoslovakia
BL	Religions, Mythology, Rationalism		
		DC	France, Andorra, Monaco
BM	Judaism	DD	Germany
BP	Islam, Bahaism, Theosophy, etc.	DE	Mediterranean region – Classical
BQ	Buddhism		
BR	Christianity	DF	Greece, Greco-Roman World
BS	The Bible	DG	Italy, Malta

DH	Low Countries: Benelux Countries	GV	Recreation, Sports, Games, Leisure
DJ	Netherlands (Holland)		
DJK	Eastern Europe (General)	*H*	*Social Sciences*
DK	Russia, Soviet Union, Former Soviet Republics, Poland	H	Social Sciences (General)
		HA	Statistics
DL	Northern Europe, Scandinavia	HB	Economics, Economic theory, Demography
DP	Spain, Portugal		
DQ	Switzerland	HC	Economic history and conditions
DR	Balkan Peninsula, Turkey		
DS	Asia	HD	Land use, Agriculture, Industry, Labour
DT	Africa		
DU	Oceania, Australia, New Zealand (South Seas)	HE	Transportation and communications
DX	Gypsies, Romanies	HF	Commerce
		HG	Finance
E–F	*History: Western Hemisphere*	HJ	Public Finance
E	America	HM	Sociology (General)
F	US local history, Canada, Latin America	HN	Social history and conditions, Social problems, Social reform
G	*Geography, Anthropology, Recreation*	HQ	Family, Marriage, Women and Sexuality
G	Geography (General), Atlases, Maps	HS	Societies: secret, benevolent, Clubs
GA	Mathematical geography, Cartography	HT	Communities, Classes, Races
		HV	Social pathology, Social Service, Social and public welfare, Criminology
GB	Physical geography		
GC	Oceanography		
GE	Environmental Sciences	HX	Socialism, Communism, Anarchism
GF	Human ecology, Anthropogeography		
GN	Anthropology	*J*	*Political Science*
GR	Folklore	J	General legislative and executive papers
GT	Manners and customs (General)		
		JA	Political science (General)

JC	Political theory, the state	KB	Religious law in general, Comparative religious law, Jurisprudence
JF	Constitutional history – General, Political institutions and public administration	KBM	Jewish law
JJ	Political institutions and public administration (North America)	KBP	Islamic law
		KBR	History of canon law
		KBS	Canon law of Eastern churches
JK	Constitutional history/ Political institutions and public administration (United States)	KBT	Canon law of Eastern Rite Churches in Communion with the Holy See of Rome
JL	Constitutional history/ Political institutions and public administration (Canada, Latin America, etc.)	KBU	Law of the Roman Catholic Church, The Holy See
		KD/	
		KDK	United Kingdom and Ireland
		KDZ	America, North America, OAS
JN	Constitutional history/ Political institutions and public administration (Europe)	KE	Canada
		KF	United States
JQ	Constitutional history/ Political institutions and public administration (Asia, Africa, Australia, Oceania, Pacific area, etc.)	KG	Latin America, Mexico and Central America, West Indies, Caribbean area
		KH	South America
		KJ–	
JS	Local government, Municipal government	KKZ	Europe
		KL–	
JV	Colonies and colonisation, Emigration and immigration, International migration	KWX	Asia and Eurasia, Africa, Pacific Area and Antarctica
		KU/	
JX	International law, International relations, see JZ and KZ (obsolete)	KUQ	Law of Australia and New Zealand
		KZ	Law of nations
JZ	International relations		
		L	*Education*
K	*Law*	L	Education (General)
K	Law in general, Comparative and uniform law, Jurisprudence	LA	History of Education
		LB	Theory and practice of education

LC   Special aspects of education
LD   Individual Institutions –
      United States
LE   Individual Institutions – Other
      Americas (except United States)
LF   Individual Institutions – Europe
LG   Individual Institutions –
      Asia, Africa, Oceania, Indian
      Ocean Islands, Australia, New
      Zealand, Pacific islands
LH   College publications, school
      magazines and papers
LJ   Student fraternities and
      sororities/societies, United
      States
LT   Textbooks

M   *Music*
M   General
ML   Literature of Music
MT   Music Instruction and study

N   *Fine Arts*
N   Visual arts (General)
NA   Architecture
NB   Sculpture
NC   Drawing, Design, Illustration
ND   Painting
NE   Print media
NK   Decorative arts, applied arts
NX   Arts in general

P   *Language and Literature*
P   Philology and linguistics
PA   Classical languages and
      literature/Greek language and

      literature and Latin language
      and literature
PB   Modern languages, Celtic
      languages and literature
PC   Romance languages
PD   Germanic languages,
      Scandinavian languages
PE   English languages
PF   West Germanic languages,
      Dutch, German
PG   Slavic, Baltic, Armenian
      languages and literature
PH   Finno-Ugrian languages and
      literature/Uralic languages,
      Basque languages
PJ   Oriental languages and
      literature
PK   Indo-Iranian languages and
      literature
PL   East Asian languages and
      literatures/languages and
      literature of Eastern Asia,
      Africa, Oceania
PM   American Indian languages,
      Artificial languages,
      Hyperborean, Native
      American
PN   Literature, General literary
      history and collections,
      Performing arts
PQ   Romance literatures/French
      literature, Italian literature,
      Spanish literature, Portuguese
      literature
PR   English literature
PS   American literature

PT	Germanic literature/Dutch literature, Flemish literature since 1830, Afrikaans literature, Scandinavian literature, Old Norse literature: Old Icelandic and Old Norwegian, Modern Icelandic literature, Faroese literature, Danish literature, Norwegian literature, Swedish literature	RJ	Paediatrics
		RK	Dentistry
		RL	Dermatology
		RM	Therapeutics, Pharmacology
		RS	Pharmacy and *materia medica*
		RT	Nursing
		RV	Botanic, Thomsonian, and eclectic medicine
		RX	Homeopathy
PZ	Fiction and juvenile belle lettres	RZ	Other systems of medicine
		S	*Agriculture*
		S	Agriculture (General)
Q	*Science*	SB	Plant culture, Horticulture, Plant propagation, Plant breeding
Q	Science (General)		
QA	Mathematics	SD	Forestry, Arboriculture, Silviculture
QB	Astronomy		
QC	Physics	SF	Animal culture, Animal husbandry, Animal science
QD	Chemistry		
QE	Geology	SH	Aquaculture, Fisheries, Angling
QH	Natural history, Biology		
QK	Botany	SK	Hunting
QL	Zoology		
QM	Human Anatomy		
QP	Physiology	*T*	*Technology*
QR	Microbiology	T	Technology (General)
		TA	Engineering – General and civil engineering
R	*Medicine*		
R	Medicine (General)	TC	Hydraulic engineering, Ocean engineering
RA	Public aspects of medicine		
RB	Pathology	TD	Environmental technology, Sanitary engineering
RC	Internal medicine		
RD	Surgery	TE	Highway engineering, Roads and pavements
RE	Ophthalmology		
RF	Otorhinolaryngology	TF	Railroad engineering and operation
RG	Gynaecology and Obstetrics		

TG   Bridges: bridge construction

TH   Building construction

TH   Mechanical engineering and machinery

TK   Electrical engineering, Electronics, Nuclear engineering

TL   Motor vehicles, Aeronautics, Astronautics

TN   Mining engineering, Metallurgy

TP   Chemical technology

TR   Photography

TS   Manufacturing engineering, Mass production

TT   Handicrafts, Arts and crafts

TX   Home economics

U   *Military Science*

U   Military Science (General)

UA   Armies: Organisation, distribution, military situation

UB   Military administration

UC   Military maintenance and transportation

UD   Infantry

UE   Cavalry, armoured cavalry

UF   Artillery

UG   Military engineering, Air forces, Air warfare

UH   Other military services

V   *Naval Sciences*

V   Naval science (General)

VA   Navies: Organisation, distribution, naval situation

VB   Naval administration

VC   Naval maintenance

VD   Naval seamen

VE   Marines

VF   Naval ordnance

VG   Minor services of navies

VK   Navigation, Merchant Marine

VM   Naval architecture, Shipbuilding, Marine engineering

Z   *Bibliography: Library Science*

Z   Books (General), Writing, Palaeography, Book industries and trade, Libraries, Library Science, Bibliography

25 Civilizations and Cultures: From One to One,

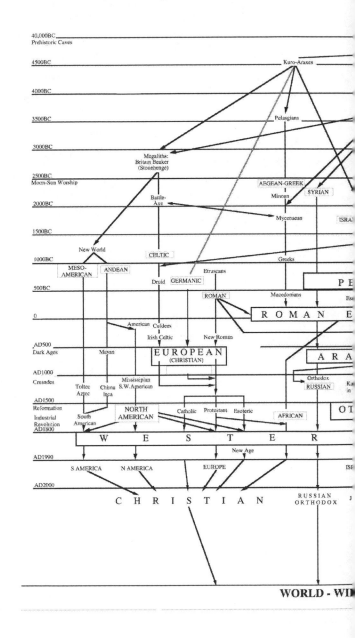

the Fundamental Unity of World Culture

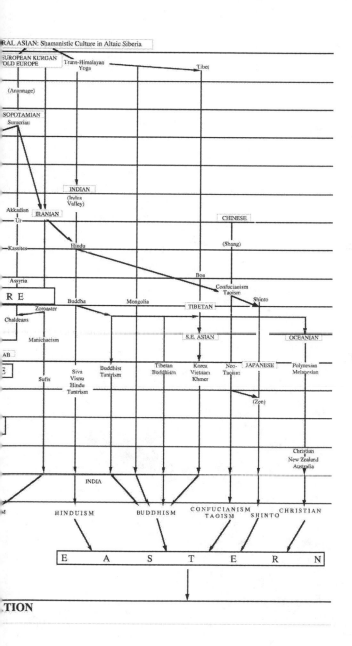

CRAL ASIAN: Shamanistic Culture in Altaic Siberia

EUROPEAN KURGAN
OLD EUROPE

Trans-Himalayan
Yoga

Tibet

(Anunnage)

SOPOTAMIAN
Sumerian

INDIAN
(Indus
Valley)

Akkadian
Ur   IRANIAN

CHINESE

Kassites   Hindu

(Shang)

Assyria

Bon

Confucianism
Taoism

R E   Buddha   Mongolia   Shinto

Zoroaster   TIBETAN

Chaldeans

Manichaeism   S.E. ASIAN   OCEANIAN

AB

Sufis   Siva   Buddhist   Tibetan   Korea   Neo-   JAPANESE   Polynesian
          Visnu   Tantrism   Buddhism Vietnam Taoism   Melanesian
          Hindu   Khmer
          Tantrism
                                                  (Zen)

Christian
New Zealand
Australia

INDIA

HINDUISM   BUDDHISM   CONFUCIANISM   CHRISTIAN
                                    TAOISM   SHINTO

E   A   S   T   E   R   N

TION

Appendix 4

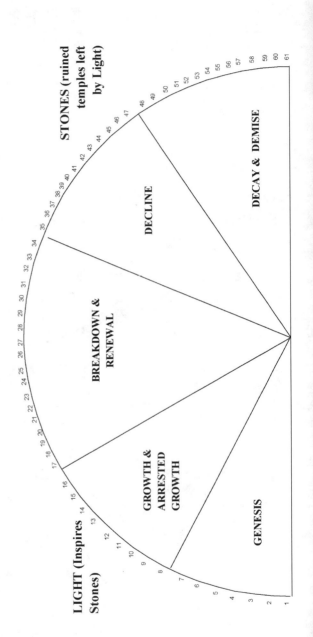

CHART 1: THE RAINBOW-LIKE PARABOLA
61 STAGES IN A CIVILIZATION'S LIFE CYCLE

LIGHT (Inspires Stones)

STONES (ruined temples left by Light)

GENESIS

GROWTH & ARRESTED GROWTH

BREAKDOWN & RENEWAL

DECLINE

DECAY & DEMISE

1. Light originates in earlier civilisation
2. Light migrates to new culture
3. Light absorbs new culture
4. Light creates new religion through religious unification
5. Light precedes genesis
6. Light creates Central Idea amid 16 alternatives
7. Light attracts, converts & unifies peoples round Central Idea
8. Light strong during growth
9. Light inspires stones
10. Doctrinal controversy round Light
11. Political unification
12. Schism between supporters of rival gods
13. Foreign military blow
14. Arrest in growth of secularized civilisation (50 years)
15. Counterthrust: expansion into Empire, Light-led renewal of growth
16. Heroic epic literature with god of Light-led growth
17. Creation of Light-based heretical sect
18. Persecution of heretical sect
19. Decline of religion as a result of heretical sect & foreign influence
20. Mystics resist decline
21. Foreign military blow
22. Breakdown of civilisation (100 years)
23. Secularization in response to foreign threat
24. Revival of past culture of another civilisation
25. Civil War: Rulers v heretical New People
26. New People in limelight
27. Heresy grafted on to Central Idea as new religious focus
28. New people's heretical renewal of Light and Central Idea
29. Geographical expansion of New People
30. Secession from New People's God
31. New People persecute seceders and become New Orthodoxy
32. Scientific materialism weakens religion
33. Artistic reaction
34. Further expansion into Empire over-extends civilisation
35. Light weakens as energy is dispersed abroad
36. Light disappears from official religion
37. Breakdown of certainties after military event
38. Central Idea/Religion weaken, Arts become secular
39. Rationalism & scepticism weaken religion
40. Industrial decline as civilisation over-extends itself
41. Colonial conflict ending in decolonisation & occupation
42. Proletarianisation & egalitarianism
43. Loss of national sovereignty to secularizing conglomerate
44. Syncretism & Universalism round Light
45. Revival of lost past of civilisation
46. Counterthrust under foreign federal influence
47. Economic decline & inflation, class conflict
48. Light ceases to be publicly recognised by religion
49. Invaders undermine Lightless religion
50. Foreign invaders destroy Stones
51. Loss of Central Idea as peoples secede to foreign invaders' culture
52. Final independent phase
53. Further occupation by foreign power
54. Contemplative mystics turn from decaying religion to foreign cults
55. Civilisation resists occupier
56. Occupier persecutes defectors from its cults
57. Coteries continue Light & Central Idea in mysteries
58. Further occupation
59. Occupier's religion suppresses & kills Lightless religion
60. Sudden final conquest or religionless civilisation
61. Demise of civilisation which now passes into a successor civilisation

Appendix 5

The Tree of European Civilisation Geschichtsbaum Europa

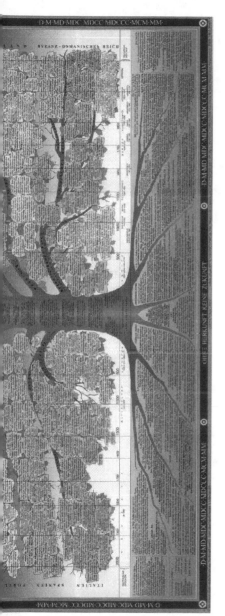

The Tree of Tradition of all civilisations, showing their traditions and influences, presented as the Tree of European civilisation, Geschichtsbaum Europa, with its eventual 50 branches (see pp.21–22 and 157).

Notes and References to Sources

Preface: The Tree of Tradition as World Tree in all Civilisations, and a Universalist World State

1. The Tree whose Traditions and Influences Have Shaped the Works of Writers and Thinkers in all Civilisations
    1. Nicholas Hagger, *Collected Poems*, p.450.
    2. Hagger, *The New Philosophy of Universalism*, p.35.
    3. Hagger, *The New Philosophy of Universalism*, p.290.
    4. Hagger, *The Fire and the Stones*; Hagger, *The Rise and Fall of Civilizations*.
    5. Hagger, *The New Philosophy of Universalism*, pp.338–339.
    6. Hagger, *Selected Letters*, pp.841–843.
    7. For example, Nicholas Hagger's contribution to *Spiritual Awakenings: Scientists and Academics Describe Their Experiences* (ed. by Marjorie Woollacott and David Lorimer).
    8. Samuel Taylor Coleridge, *Biographia Literaria*, ch.XIII, p.356, published 1854, original from the University of Michigan, digitized 23 November 2005, http://books.google.co.uk/books?id=5xg5G-4ai3oC&pg=PA356 &dq=esemplastic+power+of+the+imagination.
    9. Hagger, *The New Philosophy of Universalism*, pp.339–340.
    10. T.S. Eliot, *Selected Prose*, p.23.
    11. T.S. Eliot, *Selected Prose*, p.25.
    12. T.S. Eliot, 'The Man of Letters and the Future of Europe', 1944.
    13. T.S. Eliot, *Selected Prose*, p.27.
    14. Hagger, *A New Philosophy of Literature*, pp.312–313.
    15. Hagger, *The Secret American Destiny*, pp.2–40.
    16. See https://www.masterclass.com/articles/what-are-the-different-genres-of-literature-a-guide-to-14-literary-genres.
    17. See https://www.servicescape.com/blog/144-genres-and-subgenres-for-fiction-writing.
    18. See https://www.studiobinder.com/blog/movie-genres-list/.

2. The Tree of Tradition as World Tree: Traditions and Influences in a Universalist Writer's and Thinker's 60 Works
    1. Hagger, *The Rise and Fall of Civilizations*, pp.xi–xii.

2. Hagger, *The Secret American Destiny*, pp.30–31.

3. Hagger, *The Secret American Destiny*, p.7.

4. Hagger, *The Secret American Destiny*, pp.7–8, 12, 13.

5. Evelyn Underhill, *Mysticism*, pp.75–82.

6. Hagger, *My Double Life 2: A Rainbow over the Hills*, pp.776–780.

7. Hagger, *My Double Life 1: This Dark Wood*, pp.53, 60–61, 92–93, 110–111.

8. William Wordsworth, 'Lines composed a few miles above Tintern Abbey', lines 100–102.

9. Hagger, *The Secret American Destiny*, pp.150–151.

10. Hagger, *My Double Life 2: A Rainbow over the Hills*, p.912.

11. See 'Mystic Way behind Works' in Hagger, *My Double Life 2: A Rainbow over the Hills*, p.912.

12. Hagger, *My Double Life 1: This Dark Wood*, Episode 14: Illumination and Nationalism, pp.364–407.

13. Pascal's 'Fire' parchment: facsimile in Abbé Bremond's *Sentiment Religieux en France*, iv, 368; quoted in Dom Cuthbert Butler, *Western Mysticism*, p.74.

14. Hagger, *The Secret American Destiny*, p.12.

15. Hagger, *The Light of Civilization*, pp.7–10.

16. St Augustine, *Confessions*, 7.10.

17. Hildegard von Bingen quoted in John Ferguson, *An Illustrated Encyclopaedia of Mysticism and the Mystery Religions*, p.77.

18. Hagger, *The Secret American Destiny*, pp.11–12; also, *The Universe and the Light*, p.8; and *The Light of Civilization*, pp.498–499.

19. Hagger, *The Secret American Destiny*, p.9; also *The Light of Civilization*, pp.29–355.

20. Hagger, *The Light of Civilization*, pp.113–227; also *The Secret American Destiny*, pp.9–10.

21. Hagger, *The Light of Civilization*, pp.228–234; also *The Secret American Destiny*, p.10.

22. Hagger, *The Light of Civilization*, pp.359–494; also *The Secret American Destiny*, p.11.

23. Hagger, *The Promised Land*, pp.209–215.

24. Hagger, *The Secret American Destiny*, pp.14–15.

25. Hagger, *The Secret American Destiny*, pp.14–18.

26. Hagger, *The Secret American Destiny*, pp.18–19.

27. Hagger, *The Secret American Destiny*, p.19.

28. Hagger, *The Secret American Destiny*, pp.151–152, 154.

29. For further details, see Hagger, *My Double Life 1: This Dark Wood*, pp.73–74.

30. Hagger, *The Secret American Destiny*, p.18.

31. Hagger, *The Secret American Destiny*, p.19.

32. Hagger, *The Secret American Destiny*, pp.19–21.

33. Hagger, *My Double Life 1: This Dark Wood*, p.166; Hagger: 'The Contemporary Literary Scene in England: The Missing Dimension', *The Rising Generation*, 1 July 1964.

34. Hagger, *My Double Life 2: A Rainbow over the Hills*, p.330.

35. *Selected Poems* draws on Hagger's *Collected Poems, Classical Odes*, two poetic epics *Armageddon* and *Overlord*, and *Collected Verse Plays*; and *Selected Stories* draws on the 1,001 short stories of *Collected Stories*.

36. Hagger, *The Secret American Destiny*, pp.21–23.

37. Hagger, *The New Philosophy of Universalism*, pp.11–22, 23–54, which cite all sources reflected in this section.

38. Aristotle, *Metaphysics IV*, 1–2/1003a.

39. Hagger, *The Secret American Destiny*, pp.155–156.

40. Hagger, *The Secret American Destiny*, pp.24–48.

41. Hagger, *The Fire and the Stones*, pp.350–353; *The Light of Civilization*, pp.502–506.

42. Hagger, *The Light of Civilization*, pp.525–529, 'Toynbee's Choice of Civilizations'.

43. Hagger, *The Secret American Destiny*, p.28.

44. Hagger, *The Rise and Fall of Civilizations*, pp.11–56.

45. Hagger, *The Light of Civilization*, p.506.

46. Hagger, *The Secret American Destiny*, pp.161–163.

47. Hagger, *The Secret American Destiny*, pp.29–31.

48. Hagger, *The Universe and the Light*, pp.139–161; *The Rise and Fall of Civilizations*, pp.11–34.

49. Hagger, *The Universe and the Light*, pp.140–161.

50. Hagger, *The Universe and the Light*, p.140.

51. Hagger, *The Light of Civilization*, pp.523–525.

52. Hagger, *The Fire and the Stones*, pp.317–324; *The Light of Civilization*, pp.216–218.

53. Hagger, *The Fire and the Stones*, pp.743–753; *The Rise and Fall of Civilizations*, pp.412–428.

54. Hagger, *The Secret American Destiny*, pp.164–165.

55. Hagger, *The New Philosophy of Universalism*, pp.357–360.

56. Hagger, *The Secret American Destiny*, pp.32–36.

57. Hagger, *The World Government*, pp.122–158.

58. Hagger, *The Secret American Destiny*, pp.166–168.

59. Hagger, *The New Philosophy of Universalism*, pp.355–357.

60. Hagger, *Peace for our Time*, pp.34–51.

61. Hagger, *The Secret American Destiny*, pp.36–38.

62. Hagger, *The Light of Civilization*, pp.534–535.

63. Hagger, *The New Philosophy of Universalism*, pp.339–340.

64. Hagger, *The Secret American Destiny*, pp.168–169, 176–177.

65. Hagger, *The New Philosophy of Universalism*, pp.337–344.

3. **The Tree of Tradition Behind Writers and Thinkers in all Civilisations and a World State: World Culture and a Universalist New World Order**

1. Hagger, *The Secret American Destiny*, pp.xvii–xxiii.

2. Hagger, *The Rise and Fall of Civilizations*, pp.131–132.

3. Hagger, *The Secret American Destiny*, pp.227–228.

4. Hagger, *The Secret American Destiny*, pp.2–3.

5. Hagger, *The Secret American Destiny*, pp.224–225.

6. Hagger, *The Secret American Destiny*, pp.3–4.

7. Hagger, *The Fire and the Stones*, pp.378–414; *The Rise and Fall of Civilizations*, pp.11–64.

8. Hagger, *The Secret American Destiny*, pp.4–7.

9. T.S. Eliot, *Notes Towards the Definition of Culture*, p.26; Hagger, *The One and the Many*, p.105.

10. W.B. Yeats, *The Autobiography of William Butler Yeats*, p.128.

11. Hagger, *The Rise and Fall of Civilizations*, pp.244–290.

12. Hagger, *The Rise and Fall of Civilizations*, p.274.

13. Hagger, *The Rise and Fall of Civilizations*, pp.188–278.

14. Hagger, *The Rise and Fall of Civilizations*, p.285, predicted a 48-state Europe; Hagger, *The Dream of Europa*, which predicts a 50-state Europe.

15. Pew Research Center 2014 found 37 per cent; Gallup 2013 found 39 per cent.

16. See http://ec.europa.eu/public_opinion/archives/ebs/ebs_341_en.pdf.

17. Hagger, *The Secret American Dream*, p.221.

18. Hagger, *The Rise and Fall of Civilizations*, pp.116–117. For Nicholas Hagger's article in *The Times* on the World Council of Churches' funding of the African liberation movements, 'The war against racialism', 3 October 1970, see *My Double Life 1: This Dark Wood*, pp.522–527.

19. Hagger, *The Rise and Fall of Civilizations*, pp.510–512.

20. Hagger, *The Secret American Destiny*, p.7.

21. Hagger, *The Secret American Destiny*, pp.235–242.

22. Hagger, *The Dream of Europa*.

23. Hagger, *The Secret American Destiny*, pp.247–248.

24. Hagger, *The Golden Phoenix*, pp.158–159.

25. Hagger, *World State*, pp.268–281, 288–293.

26. Hagger, *The Fall of the West*, chs.2 and 8.

Appendices

1. See https://simplicable.com/en/academic-disciplines.

2. See https://en.wikipedia.org/wiki/Outline_of_academic_disciplines.

3. See https://en.wikipedia.org/wiki/List_of_academic_fields.

Bibliography

Aristotle, *Metaphysics*, books I–IX, trans. Hugh Tredennick, Harvard University Press, Cambridge, Massachusetts, 1933/2003.

Augustine, St, *Confessions*, trans. R.S. Pine-Coffin, Penguin, London, 1961.

Butler, Dom Cuthbert, *Western Mysticism*, Arrow Books, London, 1922 and 1960.

Coleridge, Samuel Taylor, *Biographia Literaria*, published 1854, original from the University of Michigan, digitized 23 November 2005.

Eliot, T.S., *Notes Towards the Definition of Culture*, Faber and Faber, 1948.

Eliot, T.S., *Selected Prose*, ed. by John Haywood, Penguin Books, 1953.

Eliot, T.S., 'The Man of Letters and the Future of Europe', *The Norseman* (July–August 1944) and reprinted in the *The Sewanee Review*, Volume 53, 1945.

Ferguson, John, *An Illustrated Encyclopaedia of Mysticism and the Mystery Religions*, Thames & Hudson, London, 1976.

Hagger, Nicholas, *A New Philosophy of Literature*, O-Books, 2012.

Hagger, Nicholas, *Armageddon*, O-Books, 2010.

Hagger, Nicholas, *Classical Odes*, O-Books, 2006.

Hagger, Nicholas, *Collected Poems 1958–2005*, O-Books, 2006.

Hagger, Nicholas, *Collected Stories*, O-Books, 2007.

Hagger, Nicholas, *Collected Verse Plays*, O-Books, 2007.

Hagger, Nicholas, *My Double Life 1: This Dark Wood*, O-Books, 2015.

Hagger, Nicholas, *My Double Life 2: A Rainbow over the Hills*, O-Books, 2015.

Hagger, Nicholas, *Overlord*, O-Books, 2006.

Hagger, Nicholas, *Peace for our Time*, O-Books, 2018.

Hagger, Nicholas, *Selected Letters*, O-Books, 2021.

Hagger, Nicholas, *Selected Poems*, O-Books, 2015.

Hagger, Nicholas, *Selected Stories*, O-Books, 2015.

Hagger, Nicholas, 'The Contemporary Literary Scene in England: The Missing Dimension', *The Rising Generation*, 1 July 1964.

Hagger, Nicholas, *The Dream of Europa*, O-Books, 2015.

Hagger, Nicholas, *The Fall of the West*, O-Books, 2022.

Hagger, Nicholas, *The Fire and the Stones*, Element, 1991.

Hagger, Nicholas, *The Golden Phoenix*, O-Books, 2023.

Hagger, Nicholas, *The Light of Civilization*, O-Books, 2006.

Hagger, Nicholas, *The New Philosophy of Universalism*, O-Books, 2009.

Hagger, Nicholas, *The One and the Many*, Element, 1999.

Hagger, Nicholas, *The Promised Land*, O-Books, 2023.

Hagger, Nicholas, *The Rise and Fall of Civilizations*, O-Books, 2008.

Hagger, Nicholas, *The Secret American Destiny*, Watkins, 2016.

Hagger, Nicholas, *The Secret American Dream*, Watkins, 2011.

Hagger, Nicholas, *The Universe and the Light*, Element, 1993.

Hagger, Nicholas, *The World Government*, O-Books, 2010.

Hagger, Nicholas, *World Constitution*, O-Books, 2018.

Hagger, Nicholas, *World State*, O-Books, 2018.

Spiritual Awakenings: Scientists and Academics Describe Their Experiences (ed. by Marjorie Woollacott and David Lorimer), AAPS (The Academy of the Advancement of Postmaterialist Sciences) Press, 2022.

Underhill, Evelyn, *Mysticism*, Methuen, London, 1911 and 1960.

Yeats, W.B., *The Autobiography of William Butler Yeats*, Collier Books, New York, 1965.

Indexes

Index of Traditions

109 main traditions within 7 disciplines in NH's works
(see pp.148–153)

Index of Influences

84 main influences within 7 disciplines on NH's works (see pp.153–154)

245

Main Index

Liberalis is a Latin word which evokes ideas of freedom, liberality, generosity of spirit, dignity, honour, books, the liberal arts education tradition and the work of the Greek grammarian and storyteller Antoninus Liberalis. We seek to combine all these inter-linked aspects in the books we publish.

We bring classical ways of thinking and learning in touch with traditional storytelling and the latest thinking in terms of educational research and pedagogy in an approach that combines the best of the old with the best of the new.

As classical education publishers, our books are designed to appeal to readers across the globe who are interested in expanding their minds in the quest of knowledge. We cater for primary, secondary and higher education markets, homeschoolers, parents and members of the general public who have a love of ongoing learning.

If you have a proposal that you think would be of interest to Liberalis, submit your inquiry in the first instance via the website: www.liberalisbooks.com.